Prince of Edisto

General Micah Jenkins
From a painting in the lobby of Jenkins Hall, The Citadel.

Photograph by Penny Swisher

Prince of Edisto

Brigadier General Micah Jenkins, CSA

By
James K. Swisher

WHITE MANE BOOKS
SHIPPENSBURG, PENNSYLVANIA

This White Mane Books publication
was printed by
Beidel Printing House, Inc.
63 West Burd Street
Shippensburg, PA 17257-0708 USA

The acid-free paper used in this book meets the guidelines for permanence and durability of the Committee on Production Guidelines for Book Longevity of the Council on Library Resources.

First Printing by
Rockbridge Publishing Company
Berryville, Virginia

ISBN 1-57249-304-6 (formerly ISBN 1-883522-10-2)

For a complete list of available publications
please write
White Mane Books
Division of White Mane Publishing Company, Inc.
P.O. Box 708
Shippensburg, PA 17257-0708 USA

Library of Congress Cataloging-in-Publication Data

Swisher, James K., 1939-
    Prince of Edisto : brigadier general Micah Jenkins, CSA / by James K. Swisher.-- 2nd
rev., updated ed.
        p. cm.
    Includes bibliographical references (p.) and index.
    ISBN 1-57249-304-6 (alk. paper)
        1. Jenkins, Micah, 1835-1864. 2. Generals--Confederate States of America--Biography.
3. Confederate States of America. Army--Biography. 4. Confederate States of America.
Army. Palmetto Sharpshooters--History. 5. Confederate States of America. Army. South
Carolina Infantry Regiment, 5th--History. 6. Edisto Island (S.C.)--Biography. I. Title.

E467.1.J4 S95 2002
973.7'3'092--dc21
[B]
                                                                2002028050

PRINTED IN THE UNITED STATES OF AMERICA

*This endeavor is dedicated to memorialize
the unforgettable character of*

MRS. CAROLINE JAMISON JENKINS

*Widowed at 26, responsible for four sons from age seven months
to seven years, she gracefully embodied the courage, persistence, and equanimity of Southern womanhood in that generation so altered by warfare and death. She succumbed at 63
and was interred alongside Micah in Magnolia Cemetery,
Charleston, South Carolina, still loyal to the husband she so
loved and the cause for which he died.*

Contents

vii

Maps

Preface

The American Civil War is a much written about and widely discussed period of our national heritage. Published manuscripts, articles, and materials abound, and many have enjoyed several renaissances since the war's 1865 conclusion. The initial popularity of such writings was often based on the memoirs and reminiscences of those who participated in the catastrophic events and survived to retell those memories to others. The biographical writings of ranking officers who experienced noteworthy service were highly valued and prized as authoritative sources. These popularized articles published in *Battles and Leaders* and the *Southern Historical Association Papers* gained widespread fame and acclaim. Memoirs of individuals of reputation such as Ulysses S. Grant, John B. Hood, John B. Gordon, Jubal A. Early, Daniel H. Hill, and others were instantly successful. As time passed and controversies developed, these veterans, like most authors, tended to overlook their personal errors, glorify their successes, and in some instances belittle the actions of others—particularly when desirous of blaming another for inadequacies in one's sphere of influence or control.

The sum of such writing popularized the living and overlooked those who did not survive, a serious offense when one considers the fact that the Army of Northern Virginia suffered a 37 percent casualty rate among its general officers from the Wilderness to Appomattox. As manpower became scant and supplies and equipment more scarce, officers became more inclined to "lead from in front," seeking to infuse courage into their decreasing followers. In an army well known for such exposed leadership, this practice merely amplified the casualty lists.

Many truly outstanding—some would argue the best—regimental, brigade, and divisional leaders in Southern armies died on the field of battle in the concluding year of the war. A number of these men have become shadowy, dim pictures staring at us from books or albums. Such men as the mustache-wearing Major General Robert Emmett Rodes, perhaps the best divisional commander in the Army of Northern Virginia, remains an underappreciated and largely unknown participant in numerous, very significant, battles and events. Rodes left few letters or reports; and most personal traces have since disappeared. We have little material to gain insight into what must have been a truly interesting personality.

Micah Jenkins shares similarities with Rodes. His personality, character, and achievements are largely unknown even in his native South Carolina, except by Civil War historians and aficionados, but he left a wealth of letters, materials, and reports written in his own hand. These papers, combined with the descriptions of others, give us a detailed, accurate picture of Jenkins's persona—a capable, intelligent, and attractive young man whose leadership in the early years of the war was almost brilliant. Ambitious and desirous of recognition but disappointed by a dearth of opportunity, he struggled through periods of controversy and was fatally struck by friendly fire at age 29 while leading his brigade in the Wilderness. From a family accustomed to every comfort and advantage, he was, above all, a brave, naïve, restless, and ambitious Christian gentleman.

Acknowledgments

I would like to gratefully acknowledge the courteous and capable staffs of the various document repositories, libraries, and museums that have assisted in the gathering of material for this project. Of special merit was the assistance of John M. Bingham of the South Carolina Confederate Relic Room and Museum in Columbia, South Carolina, who graciously spent a full day arranging display materials so that photographs could be taken of many of the outstanding exhibits available in that collection.

Kirsten Fischer, reference intern at the William Perkins Library, Duke University, provided access to the papers of Mrs. Caroline Jenkins. This collection contains a wealth of information on Micah Jenkins, including more than 50 letters from Brigadier General Jenkins to his wife, written over the four-year period while he was stationed in Virginia and Tennessee.

Patrick McCawley, archivist at the South Carolina Department of Archives and History, forwarded a collection of the papers of John Jenkins Jr., brother of Micah Jenkins. This collection includes a voluminous exchange of letters between the brothers as well as copies of most of General Jenkins's battle reports. Many of these reports were previously unpublished, even in official records.

Eleanor M. Richardson, reference librarian at the South Caroliniana Library at the University of South Carolina, provided further papers of John Jenkins and the Jenkins family as well as unpublished material from theses written at the university.

The South Carolina Historical Society on Meeting Street in Charleston, South Carolina, was extremely generous in opening their files on the Jenkins family. Louise Pettus, a local historian of Rock Hill, South Carolina, provided several of her fine local history articles, which were originally written for newspaper publication. *Sandlapper* magazine was helpful in solving a search for articles published by its predecessor. An interview with Mr. and Mrs. Harry Hutson, descendants of General Jenkins, was invaluable.

Additionally, the staffs of the Charleston Library, Jones Memorial Library, and The Citadel Library were of significant assistance. The use of the Rare Books Room at The Citadel was certainly appreciated. Jim Castanes provided meticulous assistance and patience in dealing with the enclosed maps.

Finally, I especially appreciate the assistance of two special individuals: Mr. David Rutledge of Greenville, South Carolina, and my wife, Penny. Mr. Rutledge's knowledge and respect for his ancestors were only exceeded by his generosity in allowing me to use selections from his extensive collection of family photographs; and Penny provided sustaining encouragement, traveled the back roads with me in search of information, took most of the modern photographs, and endured the emotional roller coaster of a first-time writer attempting to complete a coherent manuscript.

Prologue

When the glaciers retreated thousands of years ago, a vast system of rivers developed, draining the eastern slopes of the Appalachian Mountains. These streams formed in the mountain heights and sometimes rushed, but more often meandered their way to the Atlantic. Whatever their pace, they were laden with topsoil, mud, and rock from the upcountry slopes and highlands. As the rivers slowed their journey in the flatter lowlands, this rich debris settled on the coastal plains of Virginia, the Carolinas, and Georgia. The lightest of these deposits formed sand bars along the coast. In South Carolina and Georgia these sediments formed on the reefs until a chain of costal sea islands was born.

Only a few feet above sea level, these islands developed in a manner unlike the remainder of the southeastern United States. Warmed by close proximity of the Gulf Stream and accompanied by abundant rainfall, these offshore islands became lush green oases washed by the Atlantic. Not quite tropical in climate, they nonetheless developed junglelike foliage during their lengthy growing season. Giant live oak trees festooned with gray Spanish moss proliferated. Towering pines and distinctive palmettos multiplied, and lush vegetation spread unchecked under the trees. By the ocean, sea oaks danced on the sand dunes in the warm gulf breezes.

In 1562 a small group of Frenchmen explored the Port Royal area.[1] They erected a fort that they called Charlesfort and attempted to plant sustaining crops. Their stay was brief, for after several years, hungry and near mutiny, the survivors departed. Four years later, a more organized Spanish force advanced up the coast from Florida and constructed Fort St. Felipe near the crumbling French fort on St. Elena Island, now called Parris Island.[2] Accompanied by their ever-present priests, they cleared and planted fields, erected a mission, and set about converting the Indians to Christianity. The small colony prospered until 1587 when English raiders captured and sacked St. Augustine, the Spanish capital of Florida. Flanked and overextended, the St. Elena Spanish settlers reluctantly abandoned their colony.[3] The islands remained free of Europeans for the next 83 years, except for the occasional transient stops of freebooters and pirates of various nationalities. In 1670 Sir Anthony Ashley Cooper established a colony of followers at Albemarle Point near present-day Charleston.[4] With the protection of growing cities at Charleston and Beauford, the sea islands were soon rapidly populated with Englishmen of wealth and influence.

Increasingly restless Europeans quickly noticed this beautiful land, sparsely populated by peaceful native Edistoes. Sometime after 1670 English settlers began to appear along the coast in significant numbers. The 17th century witnessed tremendous economic changes in the world, nowhere more so than in the jewel of Great Britain's Caribbean possession, Barbados. An increased demand for sugar required more efficient production methods, which included consolidation of plantations and large increases in manpower, in turn producing a decrease in the number of landowners on Barbados. Between 1643 and 1663 the number of plantation owners fell from 8,300 to about 760.[5] This unusual upheaval produced a class of wealthy Englishmen accustomed to farming near tidal water, but lacking the necessary land. The sea islands of the

American coast lured these planters with their ready avail-ability of property with deep, rich topsoil; access to creeks and rivers for transportation; and bountiful quantities of fish, oys-ters, crabs, and shrimp. This influx of unlanded English set-tlers with Barbadian backgrounds initiated permanent occupation of the sea islands.

Early awards of land were based on English land grants systems. Large blocks of acreage, sometimes thousands of acres, were granted to a proprietor who, in turn, distributed plots to individuals of his acquaintance. The usual allotment of 75 acres was granted to each individual applicant, with an additional 50 acres awarded for each slave or indentured ser-vant.[6] This was extremely advantageous for the wealthy and influential Barbadians who, although without land, possessed ample slaves to gain large estates on the mainland. An owner of 15 slaves with some influence at court could easily attain an eight- to nine-hundred, acre plantation.

Initially, many of these affluent immigrants attempted to establish rice plantations. While successful throughout much of the mainland low country, such attempts were not so prof-itable on the sea islands, though estates such as Jehosee on Little Edisto provided a pointed exception. Lack of an unlim-ited pure water supply, together with the close proximity of the ocean, presented an insurmountable problem. Storms on the Atlantic occurred frequently, creating tidal surges that overflowed the control gates that regulated water levels in the rice fields. Such a flood of salt water could ruin a year's crop and injure the fields for a decade. Indigo production gradu-ally replaced rice as the principal island crop. The British bounty on indigo created a protected market for the islanders, and they flourished until the American Revolution destroyed their monopoly. The process of turning indigo leaves into little cakes of blue dye by cooking them in large wood-fired vats was labor intensive, evil smelling, and extremely hot, difficult work in the humid island climate. Large numbers of slaves

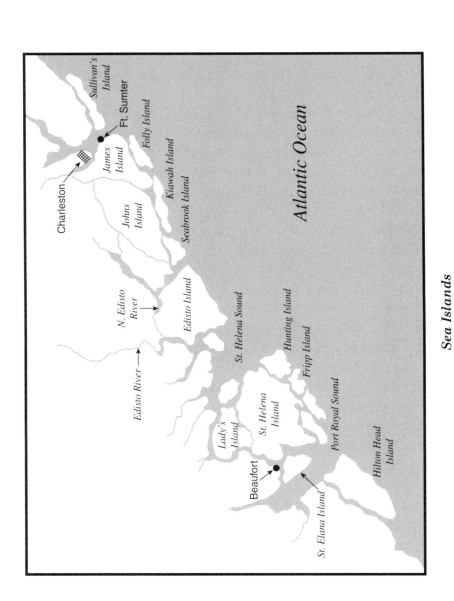

Sea Islands
Charleston to Beaufort, South Carolina

were imported to work the indigo fields. The years 1763–1775
saw the peak of indigo production, with many planters dou-
bling their net worth every four or five years.[7]

In the 1790s, however, life on the sea islands changed
dramatically. A form of long-staple cotton, introduced to the
planters in 1788, was soon discovered to be exceedingly adapt-
able to the soil and climate afforded by the islands. Thus these
fortunate cotton planters introduced another golden age of
prosperity to the sea islands. The original cottonseeds were
shipped from India via Barbados, but each planter quickly and
secretly developed and protected his own seed. So valuable
was the product that English and French mills, bidding
through Charleston cotton factors, usually purchased Edisto
Island cotton before it was even sown. Despite the toils of planting, the profits were so great that soon the islands appeared
almost covered with the small white cotton balls. Edisto Island was the virtual center of growth, seemingly the site where
conditions were perfect for growing the long-staple crop. Cul-
tivation was difficult and required extensive labor. After preparing the plant beds, the actual sowing began in late March
or early April. A driller with a long stick proceeded down the
rows and created holes, followed by a sewer, who dropped seeds
in the holes; a coverer then closed the holes. With distinctive
long-handled hoes developed specifically for cotton production,
each field was hoed five or six times per season to prevent
weeds. In late summer the pickers would begin their backbreaking labor. A good picker could gather 35 to 50 pounds
per day.[8] Yet when picking was finished, the task was only
half complete. The cotton was then ginned. Unlike Eli
Whitney's steam-driven machine designed for short staple
cotton, the roller gins were operated by foot power, one man
to a gin. The operator stood on his one leg and pedaled with
the other, pumping a crank similar to a sewing machine.
When tired, he switched legs. Expert ginners could change
feet so rapidly the machines never slowed their pace. Some

plantations had 30 or 40 ginners aligned in a row, competing for the rank of top ginner.⁹ These roller gins, designed to remove the sticky seeds of long-staple cotton, were of English manufacture and were usually purchased through the firm of Bailey-Libby in Charleston.¹⁰ Long-staple bales weighed about 350 pounds, while short-staple cotton was usually baled into 600-pound lots. As late as 1861, three bales of long-staple cotton stored on Brown's Wharf in Charleston were insured by the Home Insurance Company for $1,050 or about one dollar per pound. Short-staple cotton was then selling for 15 cents a pound. The island plantations that raised long-stable cotton did not need to be so expansive as other cotton estates. They were usually three hundred acres or less, whereas short-staple cotton plantations further inland often exceeded two thousand acres.¹¹

This was fortunate, since marshy ground on the islands precluded much of the acreage from cotton production. Cotton yield per acre was so high that a planter could recoup his original investment in land and slaves in about three years.¹² The crop was, however, unusually hard on the soil, encouraging planters to develop elaborate methods of rotating and fertilizing their fields. One of the more successful methods was the utilization of marsh mud, dug and spread by hand, which tended to restore nutrients to the soil.¹³ The workday was dictated by the tides. At low tide the slaves went into the tidal creeks with long-handled pitchforks to dig out the swamp mud; during high tide they hauled the mixture by wagon and spread it on the fields.

Tremendous wealth flowed into the hands of a few island planters from the small white bales they shipped to Charleston each fall. A society or culture developed on the sea islands which was unlike most ever witnessed before or since on this continent. The 50 square miles of Edisto Island, the largest of the sea islands, was populated by 5,000 inhabitants of whom 4,600 were slaves.¹⁴ Four hundred members of the plantation gentry controlled every aspect of life in the small kingdom. The homes first built on the islands were certainly not elaborate in style, but as money poured in, these original buildings were lavishly expanded or rebuilt. Most were located on tidal creeks or inlets, for these watercourses furnished the only available roadways. The domiciles were of no single architectural style, many being colorfully constructed of native materials including the concretelike tabby, a material that consisted of lime from burnt oyster shells mixed with crushed shells and water. Barbados-style porches and large windows were employed to take advantage of any available breezes. Other homes copied English manor houses, as even those residents who recently arrived from Barbados were not long removed from England. All manor homes were soon furnished with expensive luxury imports. Furniture, drapes, rugs, china, and glassware were of the finest European manufacture. Gardens, fishponds, gazebos, and orchards were added, often with imported, exotic fruit trees. Each estate maintained a large fishpond where fresh seafood was stored for immediate use.

Contact with outsiders was minimal—most often with Europeans via Charleston. The society was, in a word, insular. The islanders sat on the coast of America, but they faced east toward Europe. They associated only with other islanders and select Charlestonians, and families expected their sons and daughters to marry within the island society. Eventually, they developed their own standards of education, amusement, conduct, and even religion. They were hospitable, charming, kind, benevolent, and always deferential to women. Strangers, visiting among the estates, were treated royally. Yet the islanders' highly individualistic lifestyle included an exaggerated sense of personal honor and family pride which could be dangerous to the unwary. The sands of Edingsville Beach were famed for the spilt blood of duelers, and the church cemeteries contained many who rashly violated the islander's code.

At first the planter barons sent their sons to England or Scotland for education after extensive preparation by private

Tidal marshes on Edisto Island are cut with creeks and tidal inlets. During low tide, mud was dug from these inlets to fertilize the cotton fields.

Photograph by Penny Swisher

Back roads on Edisto Island are identical to roadways of the past. With a sand base they are difficult to traverse during periods of heavy rain. The live oak trees festooned with Spanish moss are typical of the lush vegetation on the Sea Islands.

Photograph by Penny Swisher

tutors. Later some American schools such as Princeton or the University of Virginia became favored. Amusements were local, such as feasting, dancing, hunting, fishing, and horse racing. Meals were elaborate and included numerous courses of seasonal seafoods and meats. Almost all of the planters imported blooded horse stock, and large sums of money exchanged hands in flat or straight-line racing on the few decent island roads. Gambling and cockfighting were also popular. The consumption of alcohol was high, but public drunkenness almost nonexistent. Men were expected to "handle their liquor." Religion was equally important, and most islanders were members of either the Episcopal or Presbyterian Church. Since no laboring class existed on the islands, other denominations such as Methodists or Baptists would find their beginnings in the trading centers of Charleston and Beaufort. Many planters constructed chapels on their estates, and ministers were employed to conduct Sunday afternoon services for the slaves, as well as the planter's entire family.

The quality of life was extremely fortunate for those privileged few, and personal dangers were minimal. After the pirates were suppressed, the only threats to islanders were the "fevers" and rattlesnakes. Each island family had its share of young children who fell victim to both. Likewise, as the rivers and the sea were depended upon for almost all communication and transportation, it was imperative that all learn to sail, yet the unforeseeable tides and currents also claimed their quota of young lives. Developed in such isolated splendor, the society promoted a strong spirit of independence and brooked little interference from outsiders. The islanders' unusually strong support of the American Revolution typified their attitude. Economically, an alliance with the British would have proven beneficial to most cotton and indigo planters, but their strong feelings of independence overcame their pursuit of economic benefits.

This tremendous wealth and power, coupled with near isolation, produced men who were barons on their own estates, whose every word was law, and who, despite their veneer of charm and hospitality, would have been more at home in the crude courts of medieval kings than the halls of 18th-century legislators. It was from such baronies and such a lifestyle that Micah Jenkins and others like him rode forth to fight in the year of 1861.

Chapter 1

A Soldier Develops

Micah Jenkins was born on the first day of December 1835 into one of the most prestigious, powerful, and affluent families residing on Edisto Island, South Carolina. He was the third surviving son of Captain John Jenkins and Elizabeth Gimball Clark Jenkins's six children. The Jenkins family first appeared in America when three brothers, Richard, Joseph, and John, emigrated from Glamorganshire in Wales. Richard, an ancestor of future Confederate Cavalry Brigadier General Albert Gallatin Jenkins, eventually settled in Pennsylvania while the two remaining brothers established themselves on St. Helena Island, South Carolina, across the wide tidal river from the growing town of Beaufort. The brothers prospered, establishing cotton plantations on Hilton Head and Ladies Islands and constructing a beautiful manor house at Lands End on St. Helena.[1] The Lands End manor became noteworthy for its expansive gardens and large, comprehensive library of rare, expensive books.

The Jenkinses' Hilton Head holdings, though profitable and fertile, did not contain a residence. As was the custom, quarters were erected to house the labor force and overseers during the planting season while the property owners enjoyed their manor homes near Beaufort, visiting their fields daily via boat. Soon the descendants of these brothers developed

1

plantations on a number of the islands scattered up the coast between Hilton Head and Charleston. John Jenkins Sr., a descendant of Joseph, married Elizabeth Adams and grew wealthy from the production of his inherited Ladies Island estate. His eldest son, Richard, was married twice: first to Abigail Townsend and secondly to Martha Rippon.[2] Richard had large families by each wife, but it remained for a son of his and Martha's, Joseph, to establish permanent Jenkins residence at the family holdings on Edisto Island.

Captain Joseph Jenkins and his wife, Elizabeth Evans, initially settled on Edisto at Mount Field Plantation near seaside. Joseph was a handsome, distinguished gentleman of more than six feet, four inches.[3] He was active in militia affairs, as were most of the Jenkins men. At 17 Joseph served as a lieutenant of St. Helena Volunteers and then joined the Continental Army line.[4] He was appointed a captain in the 20th Regiment, South Carolina Militia, following the conflict. For many years Joseph represented Edisto in the South Carolina General Assembly and was widely acclaimed as an eloquent and forceful speaker.

In 1791 Joseph Jenkins purchased Brick House Plantation inland on Russell Creek, "because he was tired of pirates worrying him from the inlet."[5] Paul Hamilton, whose grandson was a governor of South Carolina and had served as secretary of the navy under President James Madison, originally erected Brick House Manor before 1720, making the manor house one of the first brick homes constructed in America.[6] Small Dutch bricks made in Boston were used in construction, and timbering was entirely of cypress. While all inside woodwork and trim was of aged cedar, the house contained very ornate plastered corners and trim of Italian design.[7] European architects and workmen were probably employed, but with extensive slave assistance. Mounds around the present ruins suggest that a number of support buildings, including kitchens, storage buildings, and servant quarters,

Ruins of Brick House Manor, the Jenkinses' ancestral home from 1791. Erected in 1720 with three-foot-thick walls of bricks cast in Boston and shipped south as ballast.

Photograph by Penny Swisher

once surrounded the principal structure. The basic design of the edifice was rectangular with tremendous freestanding fireplaces providing heat for each room. Captain Jenkins's plantation rapidly became famous for the lavish hospitality offered to visitors.

Captain Jenkins amassed great wealth from the sale of cotton produced at Brick House and his other plantations. His family lived in elegance on the estate and at their residence in downtown Charleston, as well as enjoying a summer home on Edingsville Beach.[8] Joseph and Elizabeth reared a large family with a number of sons, the most prominent of whom were Joseph Evans Jenkins and John Jenkins. Upon their marriages, Joseph bestowed an Edisto Island plantation on each.

Joseph Evans Jenkins, the eldest son, was a tall figure of integrity and energy. He attended South Carolina College and was commissioned a captain during the War of 1812. To his regret, he did not see action.[9] His later title of colonel was due his rank in the state militia. Colonel Jenkins married Ann Jenkins Fripp, his cousin, and they enjoyed a large family with six sons, all over six feet tall.[10] He represented the parish in the state senate for many years and was a delegate to the Secessionist Convention. At that heated convocation in Columbia, it was said that after much debate, Colonel Jenkins rose and stated: "Gentlemen, if South Carolina does not secede from the Union, Edisto Island will."[11]

Captain John Jenkins was also a large man standing six feet, two inches. He likewise served in the state assembly and was a well-read legislator, although not a gifted orator. Captain John, despite his aristocratic upbringing, was widely known as a friend to all people. He was a proponent of the aristocracy of merit and virtue and he installed those values in his sons.[12] Some of the most aristocratic islanders wondered at his policy of entertaining his overseers on festive occasions. He married Elizabeth Gimball Clark in January of 1824 on Edisto Island.[13] Their union was blessed with six children, of whom Micah was the youngest surviving son. The exact origin of the name Micah is unknown but was used extensively in the family for several hundred years, as were the given names John and Joseph. Micah's brothers were John and Edward; his three sisters Elizabeth, Abigail, and Lydia. All three girls married brothers of a French Huguenot planter family titled LaRoche.

The wealth and power of the extended family allowed John and Elizabeth to rear their children in a life of unimagined luxury. Micah and his siblings from birth were surrounded by servants assigned to provide only to their needs, accompanied by an army of additional vassals who tended the household. The sheltered lives of the children were dominated by the presence of their mother in their early years, but as the boys grew older, their father and several older servants became more influential. With this guidance, the young men developed their horsemanship on the blooded stock of Brick House Plantation. Micah learned to shoot while pursuing the plentiful game of the nearby islands. He learned to sail while fishing and crabbing the creeks, tidal marshes, and ocean reaches. While in residence in Charleston, the young lords received instruction in dancing and swordsmanship. The family employed private tutors who instructed the young gentlemen in the classics during the winter months. Micah was exposed to the harsh, tyrannical nature of tutors who used the rattan stick as common practice, a punishment that was rather difficult for the lordly young gentlemen to abide. One contemporary of Micah's spoke of his taking one cut of the rattan, in terms implying that he had received capital punishment:

> When that one cut came down we thought there was a red-hot poker in our hand. I feel the tingle to this day. Too proud to cry out, we hopped first on one foot, then the other, rubbing our maimed hand and blowing on it in the vain attempt to ease the pain.[14]

A story told of young Micah Jenkins demonstrates the development of his early character and the guiding influence of his mother. At about age 12 he impaled a large fishhook in his wrist. The surgeon, as he readied to remove the barb, prepared to administer whiskey, then the accepted anesthetic. The boy firmly refused to take the whiskey, stating he had promised his mother never to take a drink of intoxicating liquor. So Micah submitted to the surgeon's blade without chloroform or drugs, although his strong determination could not prevent him from fainting under the pain.[15]

Micah developed a strong sense of family pride early in his life and carefully avoided actions that might dishonor the family. He listened to stories of the activities of his military-minded

Jenkins ancestors, and it seemed almost natural that the intense, dark-haired youth would attend a school with a military background.

On the first day of January in 1851, 15-year-old Micah Jenkins enrolled at the South Carolina Military Academy in Charleston, South Carolina. Each political district was allowed to send only a certain number of free cadets to the school; so Micah, from the Colleton District, was classified as a pay cadet due the affluent status of his family. The fee was two hundred dollars per year, payable in four installments.[16]

The South Carolina Military Academy was only nine years old in 1851 but had already established a glowing reputation among the military-oriented planter class as a source of an excellent education opportunity for their sons. Civilian colleges in the mid-1800s were often undisciplined, maintaining a wild, chaotic atmosphere that was in sharp contrast to the stern regimentation of the military academy.

In 1842 the South Carolina legislature approved the establishment of two state military schools, one located on the grounds of the arsenal in Columbia and the other on the site of the Revolutionary War "hornwork" fortifications in Charleston.[17] As early as 1783, Charleston had set aside a plot of land bounded by Hutson, Meeting, King, and Boundary (later changed to Calhoun) Streets as a base for a powder magazine to be guarded by a force of 150 militiamen. This 12-acre plot was also used as a tobacco inspection station and also sometimes as a jail. Several famous pirates were incarcerated at the magazine while awaiting the hangman's noose on battery point. The guard detail, in addition to protecting the magazine, was charged with maintaining order in the city. One of the most famous instances of guard police action was their substantial role in subduing the slave rebellion of Denmark Vesey in 1822.[18]

The original building for the military college in Charleston was a plain, two-story, brick structure crowned by a wooden

The "old" Citadel building on Marion Square in Charleston, South Carolina. The structure is now used as administrative offices by the city.

Photograph by Penny Swisher

parapet and covered with tabby. This initial structure was soon increased to three levels, then four, and wings were added on either end for staff accommodations.

Original admission requirements for the military schools were quite simple. Candidates had to be able to read and write, to be of proper age and height, and to be of good moral character. Once admitted, no distinction was to be made among the cadets except for those determined by merit.[19] Both the Arsenal and the South Carolina Military Academy provided a broad and practical education for the young men of South Carolina, but their purposes were also military; therefore, the curriculum of both schools was modeled on that of the United States Military Academy at West Point, New York. As the legislature became increasingly concerned as to the state's ability to offer a proper defense, a highly specific course of study was developed and instituted as follows:

4th Class—Mathematics, Geography, English, State History, and School of the Duties of the Private.

3rd Class—Algebra, Geometry, English, French, American History, and School of the Company and Duties of the
Corporal.

2nd Class—Trigonometry, French, Rhetoric, Philosophy,
Modern History, and School of Artillery Drill and Duties
of the Sergeant.

1st Class—Civil and Military Engineering, Science, Law,
and Evolutions of the Line and Duties of Commissioned
Officers.[20]

Charlestonians soon began to refer to the fortresslike
building as "The Citadel," thus coining its now official name.
By 1845 The Citadel was prospering, but its sister school, the
Arsenal in Columbia, was experiencing great difficulty. Several attempts were made to merge the two academies, all of
which were easily defeated in the legislature since both geographic areas desired to retain their academy. In 1850 the
Solons voted to restrict admission to instate residents.

The services provided to Confederate armies by the military academies of South Carolina and Virginia, in particular,
are a remarkable record in themselves. Of 224 living graduates of The Citadel in 1861, 193 served in Confederate armies,
including 4 brigadier generals, 17 colonels, and 142 other commissioned officers.[21] Graduates of these state schools provided
a cadre that served as the backbone of numerous regiments in
the Confederate army.

The freshman or 4th class of 1851 was made up of 68
young cadets. From the very onset Micah Jenkins demonstrated a competitive nature and strong desire to excel. John
P. Thomas, then a senior and assistant instructor in English,
remembered their initial meeting:

It was, as I remember, the day he enrolled that he stated to
me, as we stood together near the sally port of The Citadel,

that he intended to be first in his class. This he stated not arrogantly but resolutely.[22]

Jenkins soon immersed himself in the rigors of military life. How different from the lifestyle to which he was accustomed on Edisto where servants brought his water, brushed his shoes, and saddled his horse. Here he must provide for the care of his own needs.[23] His day began at 6:00 a.m. and was regulated in detail by the bugle calls. Meals, classes, drill, and even study periods were strictly scheduled and demanded punctual attendance. Infractions of discipline were sternly punished without recourse to appeal. Guard duty and weekly dress parades demanded spotless appearances, and inspections were demanding and strict. Emphasis was placed on the development of strong moral character, self-confidence, and responsible conduct. Micah seemed to thrive in the stressful atmosphere. He developed the habit of studying until midnight and commented to his brother that he had learned to enjoy studying. His expectations were high, as was his level of effort.

In the spring of 1853 an incident occurred which caused Cadet Jenkins to consider leaving The Citadel. A typical skirmish between young men of the town and cadets became a minor scandal. The cadets, including Micah, were confined to the campus and awarded a significant number of demerits. While Micah disagreed with the administration's decision, he was willing to accept an unfair judgment if the demerits were removed. He felt that the number of demerits was so large that he could not hope to be ranked first in his class on a soldierly basis before his matriculation.[24] After much review the punishments were relaxed and the demerits rescinded. How far he might have gone toward withdrawal had the punishment stood unrelieved is unknown.

Young Jenkins's pursuit of perfection extended from his academic and military endeavors to his personal life. He was

constantly searching for means of self-improvement. Asbury
Coward, a classmate and later business partner, described one
of Micah's attempts to develop self-discipline:

> During the first two years of his cadet life he had fallen
> into the senseless habit of freely using profane expres-
> sions in his conversations. A companion, not free himself
> from the same habit, undertook to lecture him on the habit,
> and the result was a banter from Jenkins that both should
> drop the habit from that moment, with the understand-
> ing that the first to lapse should turn his back and let the
> other strike him with utmost force between the shoulders.
> In less than five minutes Jenkins incurred the penalty.
> The blow given with vigor and received with good faith,
> and for both of them the habit was broken for life. From
> that day on, no one heard a profane expression fall from
> his lips; from that day, with him began in earnest the dis-
> cipline of self-control.[25]

As Micah matured and grew, he was still not immune to
the extreme pride and sensitivity of character of those persons accustomed to wealth and privilege. He was quick to take
exception to those he felt had wronged him or those around
him; in fact, he displayed the courage to challenge those situ-
ations directly. Dr. William Hume, professor of experimental
science, was well known among the cadets for conducting rough
oral recitations. While Micah was always meticulously prepared for Hume's questioning, he became embroiled in an incident involving another student. Cadet Holmes, a fellow Edisto
Islander, was not well prepared on a particular day. Hume's
questioning of Holmes was relentless, and Micah, attempting to reduce his classmate's embarrassment, began to prompt
Holmes in a low voice. When Hume realized the situation, he
verbally attacked Micah, threatening to send him from his
section room. Micah did not reply, but after class was dismissed he returned to the room and confronted Hume. While

admitting his error in assisting Holmes, Jenkins admonished Hume for the manner in which he had been addressed. He demanded that Hume treat him in a more gentlemanly manner.[26] While Micah stopped short of issuing a challenge, in light of his background, there is little doubt that he would have considered such an action proper. Those born to privilege would not easily submit to humiliation, no matter how slight.

In January of 1854 Jenkins returned to The Citadel as a first classman or senior. The academy's academic year corresponded precisely to the calendar year. The initial term of each school year began about January 1 and continued until late April. A military exercise traditionally followed, and the cadets were then released for a summer leave. They returned in mid-August for the second term, which progressed until early December. Commencement was held prior to Christmas. Upon his return, Micah was pleased to learn he had been commissioned a second lieutenant in the corps of cadets by superintendent F. W. Capers.[27] In addition, he was assigned the position of assistant professor in the department of belles-lettres. This assignment, while an honor, also entailed a heavy responsibility in that he was expected to assist and evaluate all written compositions of a number of first-year students. This mundane and irksome assignment proved quite advantageous, however, when in subsequent years Micah undertook a career in teaching.

The Citadel faculty considered the military aspects of the school's program equally important as the academic program; the institution was expected to provide a trained officer corps for the state militia. During the summer of 1854 an ambitious military exercise was scheduled, whereto the entire cadet corps was dispatched on a march through the Carolina upcountry.[28] The goal would be twofold, a vigorous and demanding military exercise for the young students and exposure of the sharply dressed cadets in the upcountry towns and villages.

The hope was that this exposure might increase the number of student applications from that underrepresented area.

The corps and faculty traveled by train to the state capital in Columbia where the Arsenal cadets joined their ranks. After several days of organization, the march began. The cadets struggled in full military gear through stifling summer heat, maintaining a pace of 17 miles per day. Feet and legs suffered and soon each cadet had a full set of blisters, yet compensatory rewards were available. Each night the entourage camped near one of the upcountry towns or villages, and each small community attempted to outperform the previous site in providing a memorable reception for the travelers. Hospitable citizens, especially young ladies, served a welcome feast each night, and numerous parties and dances were scheduled to coincide with the arrival of the cadets.[29] As tired as they must have been, no records exist of refusal to fully participate in these festivities. In late May the cadets returned to Columbia, entraining for Charleston and summer leave.

Micah enjoyed the exercise and the opportunity to interact with the college staff, who marched alongside. For perhaps the first time he began to consider his future. Lieutenant Stevens, who had complimented him on his efforts as an assistant professor, urged him to consider a career in education. Stevens felt that Micah, in consultation with several other cadets, should consider establishing a military preparatory school in the upcountry. Professor Charles Tew, another advisor, was concerned over the large number of Citadel students who left school before graduation due to what he felt was improper preparation for the academic course of study. Micah and other low-country cadets performed well, but they had been well prepared by learned private tutors. Others, particularly upcountry young men, did not enjoy this advantage and were forced to compete in the stern academic program with only rudimentary preparatory schooling. Sixty-eight cadets entered Micah's class in 1851, yet only 13 graduated. Tew and Stevens were convinced that a proper preparatory school in the upcountry could correct this inequity. Who better to initiate this endeavor than some of the best graduates of The Citadel? Micah, flattered by their interest, began to consider the possibilities.

Upon completion of the military exercise, Micah composed a lengthy, patriotic anniversary address for the Calliopean Society. Cadets were permitted to join one of two literary organizations. The Calliopeans were primarily low-country cadets, while the rival Polytechnic Society comprised mostly young men from the upcountry. Micah delivered his address on July 28, 1854, resulting in high praise for both composition and delivery.[30]

After a summer vacation on Edisto and the Edingsville beaches, Micah returned to the academy in mid-August to complete his final term. A severe yellow fever outbreak in Charleston caused the administration to suspend school and send the senior cadets to the Arsenal in Columbia to complete their studies. In early November the first classmen returned to campus to prepare for final examinations and on November 24, the streets of Charleston rang with the boots of the gray-clad cadets as they marched down Meeting Street and filed into Hiberian Hall. At promptly 10:30 a.m., the 13 members of the class of 1854 were presented their diplomas and commissions in the state militia. Cadet Micah Jenkins presented the valedictory address and was recognized for ranking first in his class in both scholarship and soldiership.[31] Jenkins had attained those goals he stated four years earlier and he wrote his brother, John, with some satisfaction: "At commencement my prospect of doing you all credit is promising."[32]

Jenkins developed many qualities that would prove valuable in future life while a cadet. He learned to rely on his own resources, he matured, gained self-confidence, and developed leadership skills. He also learned the value and importance of maximum effort or plain hard work to attain the absolute best from one's abilities. Other innate qualities were also revealed, at least one of which would cause him great duress. He was competitive and intensely ambitious, both for self-fulfillment and for the approval of his family. The fires within absolutely drove him to seek and achieve distinction in whatever he undertook.

Hiberian Hall on Meeting Street, Charleston, South Carolina. Used as an assembly hall, the Citadel graduation was held in the structure during Micah Jenkins's tenure.

Photograph by Penny Swisher

Chapter 2

Education Is Surely an Honorable Profession

Upon graduation from The Citadel, Micah Jenkins and several associates determined to establish a military school in the South Carolina upcountry whereupon they could prepare young men for enrollment at the two state military academies; a suggestion of two of their teachers, Lieutenant Stevens and Professor Tew. As the project matured, most of the involved cadets became disinterested and deferred until only two, Jenkins and his good friend, Asbury Coward, remained.[1] This deflection placed a large fiscal responsibility on the two 19 year olds, and they approached their respective families for not only approval but needed capital resources.

The Jenkins family was easily capable of financing the venture, but did not solidly support the idea. In 1850s Carolina society, sons of the planter class were expected to become soldiers, enter the learned professions of law or medicine, or continue the tradition of managing the family estates. Education as a profession or career was not considered becoming to their status. The eldest Jenkins brother, John, had attended Princeton University for one year and upon the illness of his father, returned home to assume responsibility for the family estates.[2] Edward, the middle brother, a graduate of South Carolina College and Charleston Medical College, was at that moment in Paris studying surgery and children's diseases.[3]

The family preferred that young Micah seek a career in military service or perhaps pursue the study of law. Micah personally favored a military future, but the prospects of a Citadel graduate being offered a United States Army commission were dim unless war were to occur and the state militia be activated. Edward wrote to Micah in June of 1854 encouraging his consideration of the legal profession by stating, "to an energetic man it would open a vast field, much preferable to any other profession."[4] He advised his brother that if education were still to be his determined field, then he should consider joining him in Europe and preparing himself at one of the famed universities. A degree in the classics would possibly secure for Micah a prestigious position at a college or university.

Jenkins's strong family allegiance presented him with a distasteful quandary. He sincerely desired to pursue a career in education, yet he did not wish to discomfort his family. He eventually compromised with brother John and arranged to enroll in the study of law on a part-time basis with William Wilson, a Yorkville attorney,[5] while continuing to establish the military school. Under these provisions John reluctantly agreed to provide the capital funds meeting Micah's share of the academy expenses.[6] Micah's commitment to the pursuit of law was certainly suspect, for as soon as the academy began to flourish, he discontinued his studies. Given his penchant for performing tasks at the highest possible level of excellence, his motives are indeed dubious.

Asbury Coward and Micah Jenkins became good friends while cadets at The Citadel, and their relationship continued to grow and endure. Coward was, like Jenkins, a product of the low-country planter class, born at Hyde Park Plantation on the south side of the Cooper River in 1835.[7] Also similar to Jenkins, he had brief aspirations concerning a legal career and even planned to enroll in study under the same attorney.

Both young men, however, preferred hunting, fishing, and horsemanship to the indoor life of a lawyer.[8]

In early December 1854, they committed themselves to found an academy in the upcountry community of Yorkville, South Carolina, a village with a population of about one thousand persons that already boasted one educational institution, a flourishing Presbyterian Female College. The two young men began their work with optimism and vigor despite the gloomy forecast of others. Brother John was still not convinced, and he wrote Micah a letter expressing doubts that such a school could prosper in a thinly settled and remote district.[9] He also had concerns that the age of the two principals, each barely 20, was a detrimental factor to immediate success. Since both were still considered minors under South Carolina law, John doubted that Carolinians would entrust their sons to such youthful instructors.

Despite these misgivings, Jenkins and Coward proceeded to purchase a plot near Yorkville consisting of 10 acres of land and boasting several substantial wooden buildings. Cost of the purchase was equally shared between the young men. They drew up a formal agreement of duties that equally divided all tasks, expenses, and profits. In all business matters Asbury Coward was to act as senior partner, whereas, in organization, regulation, and discipline of students, Micah Jenkins was to be regarded as senior.[10]

The existing frame buildings were hastily renovated to serve as lecture halls, and in January 1855, Kings Mountain Military Academy officially opened with an enrollment of 12 students.[11] The initial curriculum provided for a five-year program including mathematics through trigonometry, Latin, French, German, grammar, chemistry, astronomy, geology, physiology, history, English literature, and philosophy.[12] Young men continued to appear on a daily basis and by March 1855 the number of enrollees had increased to 43. Jenkins and Coward desired to initiate construction of an official academy building at

once but determined that they could not commit themselves
to this undertaking until they had 53 boarders, the number
deemed necessary to place the enterprise on a profitable basis. Until that time the students would be spread throughout
the town, boarding at the local hotel and in private homes. By
the conclusion of the first term 49 students were present as
number 50 "got scared and ran off."[13] After a two-month summer vacation the second term began with renewed enthusi-
asm which was seriously dampened by a fire that completely
destroyed the old frame lecture halls. All activities with the
exception of daily drill had to be relocated. The Rose Hotel
was contracted to provide meals for students, and classroom
spaces were devised on the upper floors of local stores or
warehouses.[14]

The support and interest of the citizens of Yorkville were
critical at this juncture and were abundantly provided. Without this generous assistance the fledgling school would surely
have failed. Enrollment continued to increase, and finally
Coward and Jenkins decided to take a risk.[15] An Irish-born
brick mason, Richard Hare of Hare and Bransford in Yorkville,
was employed to lay the foundations in May 1856 for a large
brick building designed to house all facets of cadet life at the
academy.[16]

Jenkins, while excited about this early success, was concerned that the school's development would be compromised
if the building were not rapidly completed. Although the
citizens of Yorkville graciously assisted the school in its moment of peril, these scattered accommodations were both
unsatisfactory and inconvenient. A large building that could
centralize all activities on a single site would provide rooms
for an increased number of boarders, decrease outside in-
fluences and, thereby, create a decidedly more military atmosphere. The stern discipline, rigid course of study, and
behavior of the cadets sharply contrasted with most educational institutions of the period, and favorable comments

were continually received from parents, citizens, and newspapers throughout the state.

During the second term an event occurred which greatly enhanced the academy's prestige and reputation. The cadet corps of The Citadel was scheduled to participate in the 75th anniversary celebration of the revolutionary Battle of Kings Mountain. The cadets were to travel to Yorkville by train, march to the battlefield, and encamp for a three-day period, celebrating the battle on October 4, 1855.[17] This revolutionary clash, fought on South Carolina soil, was a great source of pride to many natives of the state. Jenkins, through his Citadel contacts, convinced the college authorities to permit his young cadets to accompany the Citadel cadets, participating in both the march and the encampment. The orations from several major political figures drew huge crowds and the Citadel and Kings Mountain cadets performed drill exercises and displays each day. Public recognition and acclaim for the young cadets spread widely and the infant Kings Mountain Academy benefited greatly from its association with the prestigious Citadel cadet corps.

With high anticipation of the completion of the main building, the academy's second year began on the first Monday in January 1856. Cato A. Seabrook of Edisto Island, an 1851 graduate of South Carolina College, was added to the previous two-man faculty as instructor of Greek and Latin.[18] By February 74 scholars were present, although surprisingly few were from York County. Jenkins was convinced that religious bias lay in that fact since Yorkville contained four churches: three Presbyterian and one Methodist.[19] Coward and Jenkins were among the few Episcopalians in the area. Jenkins complained in a letter to his brother that "a decided sectarian spirit, the different denominations of Presbyterians being all violently opposed to the Episcopal Church, has been brought to bear against us, but as this is so absurd, so unjust, I hope it will die away if it really exists."[20]

While support of the school in times of distress had been high and probably reflected the populace's true feeling, the ferocity of their Presbyterian ministers prevented these local citizens from enrolling their sons. Of course, Jenkins's rather hasty condemnation of the local populace demonstrated his equally partisan viewpoint in this religious matter. It is ironic that he wrote thus to his brother, John, who would one day convert to Presbyterianism. Micah could perhaps not imagine that he would soon marry in a Presbyterian Church, although remaining an Episcopalian.

Initial payments were due the builders in May, and Jenkins appealed to John for his portion of the payment.[21] Since Micah was still legally a minor, John handled his property and legal matters. Few planters could raise large cash sums, but John was able to forward a draft for $2,000, which Jenkins paid as his share, leaving his outstanding debt at $3,500. In April the cornerstone was laid with much pomp and ceremony. As the observance concluded, the young ladies of the female college presented Jenkins and Coward with a beautiful school flag. The banner was adorned on one side by a view of the mountains with the motto "Kings Mountain: Our Country— Her Rights and Her Honor" and on the reverse by the arms of the state with the motto "South Carolina—Her Past and Her Future."[22] The two educators gratefully accepted the flag and Jenkins's acceptance speech was said to be chivalrous and inspiring. The banner with its mottos represented well the current attitude of most South Carolinians of that date. They believed strongly in the right of state self-determination in all matters, and more and more frequently their beliefs were at odds with those of their Northern sisters.

In August, South Carolina Governor, J. H. Adams, promoted Jenkins to the rank of major in the state militia, and Coward was advanced to the rank of captain. A few days later, in compliance with such a promotion, Jenkins swore before a local magistrate to be faithful and bear true allegiance to the state of South Carolina.[23]

The main building was not quite ready when the second term began, but by October 4, 1856, Jenkins reported that the school numbered 90 cadets and all were in their barracks.[24] The new structure was considered a model of tasteful institutional architecture, being three stories tall and containing 26 rooms. On the first floor were four large, well-lighted recitation rooms and four smaller study rooms. On the upper two floors were 18 barracks-type rooms complete with fireplaces and ventilation. At each end of the main building were two-story, eight-room, double-piazza wings, built to house the academy's principals and teachers. The main building and wings were of brick with wooden railings and shutters. A large wooden attachment to the rear housed kitchen facilities and another addition contained sewage and washing accommodations of the latest design.[25]

With the campus complete, the academy expanded rapidly. As the school's reputation grew, the sons of prominent families began applying in large numbers. Two additional faculty members were employed for the third academic year: Evander McIver Law, professor of belles-lettres, and H. T. Abbott, assistant professor in mathematics.[26] Tuition was set at $200 per year for two five-month semesters. The school was now considered among the state's best and in May of 1857 the local newspaper stated: "no other school suits so well the Southern youth...the various extravagances and excesses which characterized the civilian schools, lax discipline and insubordination were absent. Instead young men were trained in promptness, temperance, punctuality, and obedience while still receiving an excellent academic background."[27]

As the academy became more renowned, so too did the reputations of Major Jenkins and Captain Coward, despite their youth. The initial graduates were so well respected that admission was offered to them as second-year cadets at The

Citadel. The local populace, particularly the young female academy students, eagerly anticipated the weekly dress parades and occasional military balls. By the 1858 school year, 125 cadets were enrolled and a band of black musicians, including Micah's valet, employed to liven military exercises. On March 27 a fire occurred in the wooden kitchen annex that consumed it entirely and threatened the main structure.[28] However, a speedy response by the cadets and the citizen firemen of Yorkville contained the blaze and minimized the damage. Again, the Rose Hotel was pressed into service as a dining facility.

The annual Kings Mountain Celebration became a school tradition. Each year the cadets marched to the battlefield and encamped for several days. Drill exhibitions and political orations keynoted the occasion. In 1858 Dr. William Gilmore Simms, a famed historian, novelist, and poet, delivered an address in which he fancifully compared the Battle of Kings Mountain to the Spartan defense of Thermopalae.[29] This exercise became a physical and military test for the young cadets prior to their departure for their two-month summer furlough.

Another unique concept, developed entirely by Jenkins, was the practice of oral examinations. During the examination period, classes were suspended and students were called, one at a time, into the recitation room to be questioned by their professor. Emphasis was placed on questions that required lengthy explanations or on mathematical problem solving without prompting by the instructors.[30] Jenkins was convinced that the acquisition of knowledge was of no value without the concurrent ability to utilize and transmit this knowledge to others. Additionally, he required each senior to compose and deliver a speech on commencement day. The speech could be of the student's chosen topic but usually contained a patriotic theme. While this practice created a lengthy commencement exercise, it is doubtful that complaints were received from the proud parents.

By 1859 the academy added a classical department, as Jenkins realized that many graduates of Kings Mountain would not matriculate at The Citadel, and the program of studies must be diversified to help prepare students for other schools.[31] The faculty was expanded to seven instructors in 1860 despite the resignation of Professor Law, who departed Kings Mountain to open a similar academy in Alabama.[32] Law and Jenkins worked well together on the school's behalf, with no hint of the fierce competition that would later characterize their military relationship. The school completed its sixth year in 1860 with the same consistent level of discipline and behavior that characterized its early success. Kings Mountain dutifully attempted to open in 1861, but was soon forced to close its doors since most of its teachers and students departed to enlist in newly formed South Carolina regiments supportive of their state's decision to secede.

Chapter 3
Yorkville's Young Leader

From 1855 to 1861, while establishing the academy at Kings Mountain, the energetic Micah Jenkins also developed a reputation as a noteworthy civic leader in Yorkville, assisted in the founding of a new Episcopal church in the community, and courted and wed the beautiful daughter of a wealthy and prestigious upcountry planter. In January of 1855, as Kings Mountain Academy was about to open, Micah Jenkins journeyed downstate to Burwood, the plantation home of General David Flavel Jamison, near Orangeburg, South Carolina. He was exploring the addition of several new courses for the fledgling school's curriculum and sought Jamison's opinion.[1]

General Jamison, a graduate of the South Carolina College, was a member of The Citadel's first board of visitors[2] and widely respected in academic circles. Jenkins felt his support would prove important to successful initiation of programs for the academy. Jamison, a well-rounded man, was a distinguished lawyer, a respected planter with a two thousand-acre estate that employed the labor of 70 slaves, and a brigadier general in the state militia. He was also a highly regarded scholar who possessed an unusually fine library and had authored numerous articles, including one well-known treatise entitled *A History of the Life and Times of Betrand de Guesdin*.[3] He represented Orange Parish in the South Carolina House of

Representatives and was instrumental in the development and funding of the state's two military colleges. Jamison also represented the citizenry at several political conventions, including the Southern Rights Convention of 1852.

The Jamison family was hosting a coming-out party that weekend for their youngest daughter, Caroline, and Jamison insisted that Micah Jenkins join the festivities. The young captain entered the long drawing room as the first waltz ended, a striking figure in his uniform with its braid and gold buttons, and immediately was the focus of attention of many of the young ladies in attendance. He, however, had eyes for only one—the lovely Caroline Jamison.[4]

Caroline was a slender, beautiful young lady, the product of a wealthy and prosperous society. She was strong of character, energetic, and intelligent. Unlike many young women of her era, she was very well educated, determined, and forceful in the expression of her opinions and ideas.

Soon Micah Jenkins was traveling from Yorkville to Orangeburg on a regular basis to pursue his courtship of Caroline Jamison. He related to his brother, John, he was merely checking on their sisters, Abbie and Lydia, who attended a nearby boarding school. But soon Micah and Caroline announced their engagement and their plans to wed in December of 1855.[5] This sudden news touched off a flurry of strong reactions in both families.

Social convention at the time dictated that men should marry late in life, when financial and social status were firmly established; therefore, they usually married much younger ladies. John Jenkins was adamant that 19 years of age was far too early for his brother to make such a serious commitment. Micah's sisters, influenced by low-country class distinctions that excluded those not native to the costal islands, also expressed concern about the match, despite the obvious wealth and social status of the Jamison family. Elizabeth LaRoche, Jenkins's eldest sister, wrote that many on Edisto Island thought he had "no business to get married to an upcountry girl,"[6] and suggested he seek a wife nearer home.

A second point of dispute centered on their religious differences. In 1820, when the first Protestant Episcopal Church was constructed on Edisto Island, Micah Jenkins's father was one of its leading contributors, and in 1840 when a new, more elaborate structure replaced the original church building the Jenkins family donated the *Episcopal Prayer Book*.[7] Micah Jenkins adhered closely to family tradition and in May of 1855, shortly after his arrival in Yorkville, he and a group of gentlemen met at the Rose Hotel to formally organize the first Episcopal parish in that stoutly Presbyterian neighborhood. Jenkins was elected secretary-treasurer of the first vestry of the Church of The Good Shepherd.[8] The Reverend James D. Gibson of Savannah, Georgia, was called to Yorkville as rector.[9] Jenkins also invited Reverend Gibson to serve as chaplain for the Kings Mountain Cadet Corps, and the minister arrived in time to participate in the elaborate cornerstone-laying ceremony for the Garrison Building. Construction was begun on a church building and on November 18, 1855, the structure was consecrated. On that same day, Apostolic Rite of Confirmation added 15 individuals to the communion lists of the church.[10] Micah Jenkins, age 20, and his friend, Asbury Coward, were two of those confirmed.

Despite conventional disfavor of religious differences between a husband and wife, Caroline, an independent thinker, was not inclined to give up her family faith nor would she relinquish her affection for Micah. Although John Jenkins had taken a Presbyterian wife and converted to her faith, Micah's sisters were not ready to let their younger brother follow the same course. Elizabeth admonished him,

> Do not, my brother, make any promises about yourself Although you may promise not to interfere with her. I have seen a great deal of harm come out of such Promises, very

easily made, but when it comes to Quitting your father's church it is not so easy.[11]

Elizabeth's experiences are unlisted. Perhaps she is referring to the trials of brother John, but she was certainly outspoken as to Micah's marriage plans.

All of the objections to the early marriage did not originate with the Jenkins family. Among other considerations, General Jamison was dubious of Jenkins's career aspirations. While he admired Micah personally, he was unsure of the ability of a school headmaster to provide the style of life to which his daughter, reared with every luxury, was accustomed. Jenkins's career offered neither the financial compensation or the social status reasoned appropriate by the general. Jenkins was very sensitive to this point when he wrote Caroline that the way was open, the path, though difficult, could be overcome with iron will, and that his ambitious spirit would always establish high goals. And further "that he was young in years and could educate himself to, any point he might wish, and there were many roads which a determined mind might follow...but, education was a noble employment and it would suffice to say when one's life was almost done....I have done my duty."[12] Jenkins, obviously, gave little concern to wealth as he had always enjoyed its benefits and simply could not conceive of ever being needy. To Micah social class and distinction were natural assumptions and did not seem necessary to pursue. Jenkins, seemingly, felt he was free to enter whatever profession in which he found interest and meaning, and in educating young men he felt he could contribute to the common benefit. He thus assumed that Caroline would feel the same.

The general was very close to his daughter and she to him. Unlike her older siblings, he had educated Caroline, for the most part, at home. Of their relationship, she later wrote:

> I was his constant companion....My girlhood was spent
> almost entirely in his library....He was the embodiment
> of a devoted husband, a wise and tender parent, and a
> kind master.[13]

With this kind of father-daughter relationship, a marriage
without approval of General Jamison was unthinkable. No
matter who the suitor might be, Jamison was not eager for
such an early marriage for his favorite daughter, and he prevailed upon her to delay the wedding. Jenkins, in frustration,
wrote to Carrie that he did not understand why her father
must give permission as to the date, arguing that in his experience "that was always the point to be settled by the parties
involved and the old folk merely acquiesce."[14] The wedding
was postponed indefinitely, but Carrie was secure in her deep
understanding of her father. She may have agreed to his post-
ponement wishes, knowing full well that the general would
concede to her desires when he realized her seriousness of
purpose and commitment to Micah.

Elizabeth suggested that since Micah's wedding was postponed, perhaps he would agree to a six-month tour of the continent.[15] His brother, Edward, recently returned to Charleston
from a period of European medical study, added his encouragement for such an endeavor. Whether these suggestions were
career-motivated or simply a family attempt to further delay
the nuptials is hard to ascertain, but Jenkins was seriously
considering this proposal when General Jamison suddenly
relented and agreed to a wedding in the summer of 1856.

On July 3, 1856, Reverend Benjamin M. Palmer of the
Presbyterian Church of Orangeburg, South Carolina, united
Micah Jenkins, age 20, and Caroline Jamison, age 19, in marriage.[16] The ceremony was an elegant affair with numerous
friends and relatives in attendance.

The newlyweds then accompanied the Jenkins family to
Edingsville, the unofficial summer residence of wealthy Edisto

cotton planters.[17] More than 60 large, comfortable two-story houses with broad shaded verandas were at "the Bay," as Edingsville was called, as early as 1820. The houses faced the ocean at the dune line, where they caught the sea breezes that brought relief from the heat. The planters, unknowingly, had discovered a remedy from the "fevers" so common during the hot summer months. While they believed that the breezes prevented fever, actually the ocean breeze prevented the assaults of the mosquitoes that carried the dreaded fever. The beach houses boasted vegetable and flower gardens, carriage houses, and slave quarters. The entire beachside community was owned by the Edings family, who leased lots for home construction on a long-term basis at an annual rate of $400 per site.[18]

The high social season at Edingsville was summer, when all the island families were in close proximity. Swimming, sailing, fishing, and horseback riding were favorite activities. Also eagerly anticipated were the two- and three-day dance parties that drew scores of overnight guests from Charleston. Most planters rode home to their estates for several hours each day to monitor the progress of their crops, but returned for the evening meal. The Episcopal and Presbyterian churches erected small chapels on the beach to serve the spiritual needs of their parishioners during the extended summer. Undoubtedly, Micah and Caroline Jenkins were the social lions of that summer season.

In mid-August the newlyweds reluctantly departed the active social life at Edingsville, and journeyed upcountry, stopping at Burwood for a week. They arrived at Yorkville on September 1.[19] The two-story piazza wings on the Garrison building were not yet complete, so the newlyweds took rooms in the local hotel. When the teacher's quarters were completed in late October, they moved into their spacious new home.

The Jenkinses and Cowards established a close friendship with Reverend Gibson and his family. They enjoyed many pleasant evenings together engaged in discussion and debate. When an incident occurred in the summer of 1857 that forced the rector to leave his parish, both families were quite distraught. In a letter to his brother, John, Jenkins wrote, "I have some sad news to communicate, which I feel is my duty to do so. We have found Mr. Gibson unworthy and he leaves us this week."[20] At least one page was torn from the church record book at a vestry meeting, that page being removed and reported lost by Secretary Treasurer Jenkins on orders from the entire vestry.[21] In any event, Jenkins's substitution of the title *mister* for the usual *reverend* in his letter to John indicated his grave consideration of the incident.

By 1860, Mrs. Caroline Jenkins's name appears on a list of communicants of the Church of the Good Shepherd. Carrie had remained a Presbyterian for a time, but as their family grew, she joined her husband's church, becoming quite active in the ladies' relief fund, which amassed monies and clothing for the needy.

Micah Jenkins sometimes seemed to envision himself as a gallant knight protecting God's fair creation, and he often displayed such a tendency toward protectiveness of Caroline that might lead one to believe she was frail and incapable. This was far from accurate. While slim, attractive in appearance, and demure, Caroline was capable of an amazing toughness. She would bear five sons in their seven years of marriage, four of whom she would raise to manhood almost alone. She became adept at managing the business affairs of a household, a school, and an estate with a limited number of servants.[22] Their wartime letters would be filled with references to crops, livestock, when to plant, when to sell, and how to care for the servants. Jenkins rapidly came to respect and value her ability to manage their properties and conserve their dwindling resources. On numerous occasions he commented as to her handling of an emergency, confessing that he could not have done so well himself.[23]

Carrie's strong religious faith would sustain her through many disappointments and tribulations, including the deaths of a child, her husband, and her father within a few short months. That she and Micah were devoted to each other, there can be no doubt. Their wartime letters express how much both detested the separations required by Jenkins's long periods at the front, and both shared a belief that God would protect them. Despite the reservations of their families to such a youthful, early wedding, the couple enjoyed an unusually strong marriage based on mutual love and respect—a marriage unusual for the mid-1800s in that it was a union of equal partners.

For his relative youth, Jenkins took a surprisingly active role in the community life of Yorkville. In 1859 he purchased three hundred acres in the Yorkville area and planted this plantation the following spring with seven slaves dispatched from the family estates on Edisto.[24] In February 1860, Jenkins campaigned for, and was elected intendent, or chairman, of the governing board of the city of Yorkville.[25] This position was not demanding but primarily ceremonial in such a small town; however, Jenkins did have several interesting ordinances passed: a prohibition of firearm shooting, a prohibition of itinerant salesmen at the Yorkville market,[26] a restriction against livestock in the city streets,[27] and a prohibition of rioting and disorderly conduct. In the fall of 1860, a serious matter came before the council. Variola, or smallpox, had broken out in Columbia, and a regulation was passed that "no person who has been in the city of Columbia shall be permitted to enter into, tarry, or reside within the limits of the town of Yorkville until twenty-one days from the time he has been in said city."[28] The town marshal was given power to remove those persons, or fine violators.

Jenkins believed that public speaking was a beneficial exercise, both for the community and the individual speaker. On May 2, 1859, he delivered the anniversary address to the

Yorkville Lyceum, a speech that was widely acclaimed as attractive and accomplished.[29] He additionally spoke to the Associate Reformed Presbyterian Church in Yorkville on the duties of a Sunday school teacher on June 30, 1860,[30] quite an unusual honor for an Episcopalian.

On several occasions Jenkins served as a petit juror for the Court of Common Appeals, and he was one of five York district delegates to the Columbia Democratic Convention, which convened after the Charleston Democratic Convention of 1860 divided and adjourned without agreeing on a nomination for president.[31] This body sent delegates to the Richmond Democratic Convention that nominated John C. Breckinridge of Kentucky for the presidency, a candidate whom Jenkins actively supported in the presidential election. While Jenkins was not active or outspoken as an advocate of secession and he did not attend the Secession Convention, his father-in-law, D. F. Jamison, chaired the meeting, and his uncle, Joseph Evans Jenkins, participated. He surely was well aware of the proceedings, and once the ordinance of secession was adopted, he avowed that it was his duty, as well as that of every man, to support and defend his state's right to leave the union. So deeply involved in civic and militia affairs was Jenkins that when Asbury Coward was nominated for warden of Yorkville in 1861, Coward stated that his obligations at the school precluded his performing the duties of the office.[32] Probably, Coward felt that Jenkins's various activities and commitments made it incumbent on him to concentrate on their common educational endeavor.

From its inception in September of 1859 Jenkins was an avid participant in the development of a militia company in the Yorkville area, and an increasing amount of his time was committed to this activity. The initial volunteer company was known as the Jasper Rifle Guards, soon renamed the Jasper Light Infantry.[33] Jenkins was elected the unit's initial captain and he organized its lengthy bi-monthly drills. The Jaspers often enlivened drill by parading with the Kings Mountain Military Cadets in battalion level exercise. They then enjoyed the advantage of marching to the airs of the Kings Mountain Negro Band. In January of 1860 the state inspector general approved the company's organization and assigned it to the 34th Regiment of South Carolina Militia. In May the local newspaper praised the unit and described it as "composed of well-sized and handsome men, fully uniformed and cleverly drilled...prepared to honor their state."[34]

Jenkins instituted a summer militia encampment that enabled the militia unit to concentrate on its preparedness. The reputation of the Jaspers grew, and other militia companies borrowed drillmasters from its ranks. The summer of 1860 saw increased activity as regimental drills were mandated by the state. The 34th Regiment paraded as a unit for the first time on August 14, 1860.[35] Fall brought increased state funding for ammunition, thus target practice at various distances became an integral part of the company's drill. Jenkins offered silver cups and presentation rifles as prizes for those who became experts. The company met three days after Christmas 1860 to shoot with its improved rifled muskets. Before dismissal, a vote was taken relative to the unit tendering its services to the governor of the state in the present emergency. The vote, as expected, was almost unanimous in favor of state service.[36] All companies of the 34th were ordered to recruit to the full strength of 90 to 100 men, and in January 1861 drill was increased to once per week. Jenkins visited Charleston to offer his company's services to State Secretary of War Jamison and to purchase knapsacks, haversacks, fatigue suits, canteens, and other field equipment.[37]

Later that month, South Carolina officials ordered each battalion of militia to expand to regimental size and to conduct elections for field level officers. Jenkins was nominated for colonel of the regiment being raised in the ninth brigade district. He was highly endorsed by the *Yorkville Enquirer* and the *Carolina Spartan*, two local newspapers who jointly published an editorial that stated:

> We want an officer in every way worthy and well-quali-
> fied not only to lead us into battle, but to drill us in every
> department of the military service.... No man in this bri-
> gade area can be found who is more competent than Ma-
> jor Jenkins. He has constantly been involved in drilling
> recruits for the past ten or twelve years, and thoroughly
> understands not only the theory, but the practice of all
> minutea and complications of the various branches of all
> military tactics.[38]

Several other officers filed for the command, and, as was the custom, Jenkins traveled to the barracks of the various militia companies and addressed the soldiers. He wrote Carrie, "My prospects are good, there seems to be little doubt as to my success."[39] By early February his principal competitor, States Rights Gist, had withdrawn, finding support of Jenkins too strong to face, and on February 18, the soldiers met in their barracks or armories and cast ballots for regimental officers. The results were announced two weeks later and Micah Jenkins was elected colonel without opposition, receiving all 718 votes cast.[40]

At 4:30 a.m. on April 11, Confederate guns opened fire on Fort Sumter in Charleston Harbor. That same day, Micah Jenkins received orders for his newly designated 5th Regiment of South Carolina Volunteers to assemble in Columbia. Under the leadership of their 26-year-old colonel, the 5th entrained for the South Carolina capital and whatever lay beyond.

Chapter 4
Manassas to Williamsburg

On December 17, 1860, three days before the Ordinance of Secession was approved in state convention, the South Carolina legislature enacted an ordinance organizing a state military force and authorizing the governor to call for the arming of 10 regiments of 12-month volunteers. The 5th South Carolina, commanded by Micah Jenkins, was designated as one of these initial regiments, which were numbered consecutively 1 through 10. The legislature then authorized the organization of a regiment of regulars and a regiment of six-month volunteers. Thus in a confusing manner, three regiments were entitled to be known as the 1st South Carolina: one of 12-month volunteers under Colonel Joseph Hagood, one of six-month volunteers under Colonel Maxey Gregg, and another of regular state troops commanded by Colonel Richard Anderson.[1] To add to this proliferation, a number of private regiments or so-called legions were raised, including Orr's 1st South Carolina Rifles and Wade Hampton's Legion of combined arms.

Of the ten original 12-month regiments, eight were immediately ordered north to Virginia in the spring and summer of 1861, including the 5th South Carolina. The 1st and 10th South Carolina regiments were retained in the Charleston area to provide coastal defense.[2] Eventually the 10th South

Carolina, under Colonel Arthur Manigault, was dispatched west to perform hard duty with the Army of Tennessee, while the 1st South Carolina found its combat assignment in Virginia.

When Fort Sumter surrendered, several of these newly organized regiments were dispatched to the Charleston Harbor Islands, as a Union blockade of the port had been instituted and the landing of Federal troops was anticipated. The 5th South Carolina moved by train to the coastal city, then by boat to Sullivan's Island.[3] As the soldiers erected tents among the palm trees and sand dunes, Colonel Micah Jenkins was in the city recruiting drill instructors and seeking supplies and ammunition. Realizing that the various militia companies that made up the 5th Regiment had some experience in company drill, but were sadly lacking in maneuvering skills at the battalion and regimental level, Jenkins, assisted by volunteers from The Citadel's Cadet Corps, instituted a demanding drill program. One of the volunteers, Johnnie Whilden, was so adept that he was appointed regimental drillmaster.[4] Johnnie had been a favored pupil of Colonel Jenkins while a student at Kings Mountain Military Academy and was a recent graduate of The Citadel, having served as first captain of the corps of cadets. Whilden drilled the regiment three times a day despite humid conditions and frequent grumbles. Jenkins was pleased with the isolated island camp that precluded interruptions and numerous diversions experienced by those units stationed in or near the city. Even though Union gunboats sometimes sailed close inshore, little action occurred save an occasional cannonball tossed into the Confederate camp.

The 5th South Carolina remained on Sullivan's Island until late May. Jenkins then received orders to arrange transportation to Virginia where action was anticipated momentarily. In early June the 5th South Carolina entrained in Charleston for Richmond, Virginia, the Confederate capital. The trains moved slowly up the coast to Wilmington, North

Carolina, then via the Weldon and Petersburg Railroad to Richmond. One rider recalled the trip as less than pleasant, despite high spirits and wildly cheering inhabitants. The men rode primarily in open rail cars with coal smoke blowing back into their faces and frequent thunderstorms soaking the riders. He remarked that so many blackened faces streaked by raindrops reminded one of a troop of minstrel players preparing for a show.[5] Food was plentiful as citizens flocked to the depots with rations for their heroes. But Private J. W. Reid of the 4th South Carolina, which preceded the 5th, was concerned over the abundance of strong drink. He wrote to his wife:

> This trip beat anything I ever saw for non-discipline and insubordination....Whiskey was plentiful and cheap and every man had as much as he wanted, and a great deal more than they needed....I was glad when we reached Richmond....we still had Whiskey in abundance but it was not long before it was difficult to get.[6]

Reid, of course, reported that he did not participate.

After the lengthy trip, many of the men managed to slip away and view the bustling capital of the newly established nation. Richmond's population had more than tripled in a few weeks and its streets included visitors from every state of the Confederacy and many foreign countries. A more wide-open city was seldom seen. Within days the 5th was dispatched to encamp near the small Virginia crossroads of Manassas Junction, where the conqueror of Fort Sumter, General Pierre G. T. Beauregard was assembling a small army. Rumors persisted that Union Major General Irvin McDowell, with a large contingent, intended to march on Manassas and end the rebellion. Beauregard requested reinforcements from General Joseph E. Johnston's Valley Army and prepared for a confrontation. He formed the arriving regiments into brigades of three to five regiments. On June 17, David R. Jones of South Carolina was promoted to brigadier general and assigned a brigade of three regiments: the 5th South Carolina, the 17th Mississippi, and the 18th Mississippi. Five additional South Carolina units arrived at Manassas including the 4th South Carolina, which was assigned to Colonel Nathan G. Evans's brigade, and the 2nd, 3rd, 7th, and 8th South Carolina Regiments that were brigaded under ex-senator Milledge L. Bonham.[7]

John Whilden continued to conduct drills and when the 5th was ordered to Virginia, he accompanied Jenkins as a volunteer aide. While stationed near Manassas, Jenkins wrote President Jefferson Davis requesting that the young man be appointed a second lieutenant in his regiment, stating that "Mr. Whilden has been gratuitously assisting this regiment, since its formation near three months ago and his services have been very valuable."[8]

The terrain near Manassas was difficult for military operations. Bull Run, a small stream running west to east, presented a formidable obstacle, as its banks were rocky and steep.[9] But long-used and excellent fords were plentiful. Beauregard scattered his brigades up and down the banks to defend these fords.[10] The Confederate front followed the twisting stream for a distance of about eight miles, leaving some of the brigades separated by considerable distances. Jones's brigade was stationed at McLean's Ford, with James Longstreet's brigade on his left at Blackburn's Ford and Richard Ewell's brigade to the right at Union Mills Ford.[11] As Jones settled his men into camps behind Bull Run, he instituted brigade drills, again utilizing the expertise of Jenkins's young aide, Johnnie Whilden. Whilden performed so well that Jones added his letter of commendation for the young man.[12]

The organization of the Confederate States Army at Manassas was based on brigade structure, and all actions were planned for brigade-size units. The army commander intended to communicate directly with the various brigade commanders, a task that became complicated and cumbersome since

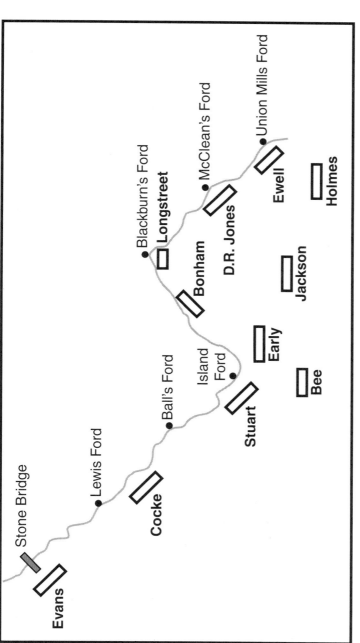

Confederate Positions along Bull Run

Confederate brigades were scattered along Bull Run protecting fords or bridges. At dawn on July 21, 1861, a large number of units were on the southern right anticipating an attack from that quarter.

his headquarters staff was quite unqualified and totally unprepared for this signal assignment. When the battle was
joined, all communication ceased, and the outcome was largely
determined by the instincts and military abilities of the various brigade commanders.[13] Union organization was equally
poor, and the battle that ensued along Bull Run was possibly
the most disjoined and bumbled action of the war, truly a clash
between two armed mobs.

Union Commander McDowell's strategy was to deliver a
series of feeling-out attacks on the Confederate right, masking his primary effort on the left near the stone bridge over
Bull Run. Meanwhile, Beauregard planned to contain the enemy on his left and to launch an attack on his right led by
Ewell's brigade and joined by those of Jones and Longstreet.
Thus, both commanders planned to deliver a right hook, which
if successful may have carried each army into the rear of the
other, virtually exchanging positions. McDowell was more
successful in carrying out his plan, but the performance of
select Confederate brigade commanders determined the outcome of the battle.

The Federal army advanced slowly from Washington,
reaching the Centreville area on July 17. The next day
McDowell sent a probing force toward Blackburn's Ford.
Longstreet's brigade, in a brief encounter, repulsed this column. Hereafter, Union troops occupied the high ground north
of Bull Run and were content to maintain a scattered, light,
artillery fire on the Confederates occupying the various fords.
Their mission was to hold the Southern forces in that sector
while the main effort was made farther west.

Beauregard's complicated attack plan on the right was to
be initiated by Ewell's attack at Union Mills Ford. As Ewell
advanced he would be joined in turn by Jones and Longstreet,
and the three brigades would sweep toward Centreville.[14] Several reserve brigades were to cross the stream and follow these
units. But as Union pressure near the stone bridge grew,

Beauregard pulled his reserve brigades and sent them to the point of danger. The brigades of Brigadier General Thomas J. Jackson, Brigadier General Barnard E. Bee, Colonel Jubal A. Early, and Brigadier General Theophilus H. Holmes along with Evans's men and the independent legion of Colonel Wade Hampton, bore the brunt of the fighting. With the timely arrival of reinforcements led by Brigadier General Kirby E. Smith, they were able to halt, and then eventually rout, the Federal column. Confusion reigned on the Confederate right. Staff officers dashed to-and-fro, searching to no avail for the army commander. Jones and Longstreet were anxious to advance, but Ewell did not appear. He never received orders to attack and dutifully remained at Union Mills Ford. Finally, orders arrived that the brigades on the right should demonstrate against the enemy by forcing a crossing of Bull Run. Jones immediately complied, and an impatient Micah Jenkins eagerly moved toward his first combat test.

Jones ordered his brigade to cross the stream and align in a front of two regiments abreast, with the third as a support line. Jenkins led the 5th South Carolina across and quickly formed, facing a wooded ridge called Grigsby's Hill, upon which Federal artillery with infantry support was visible. The 17th Mississippi followed and dressed upon the 5th on Jenkins's left. After a short delay the 18th Mississippi arrived and formed a reserve line. Federal artillery fire opened on the column when Jones ordered an advance up the hill. The shell bursts diminished as the brigade entered the trees, but the 17th Mississippi soon became separated from the 5th South Carolina in heavy brush. Both regiments continued to move forward, and as the trees thinned near the crest, the Mississippi regiment attempted to veer right to rejoin the 5th. As they approached, artillery fire caught the 17th, and a panic ensued. The right six companies of the 17th faced right and poured two rifle volleys into the 5th South Carolina, then broke for the rear, running over and carrying the 18th Mississippi with them in flight.[15] General Jones, furious and cursing, spurred his horse after the fleeing soldiers in an attempt to rally the Mississippians. Jenkins redressed the lines of the 5th South Carolina and continued to advance up the hill accompanied by two companies of the 17th Mississippi who attached themselves to his command. When Jenkins broke out of the trees at the hillcrest, he found himself with about six hundred men in the presence of four Federal infantry regiments, two batteries containing a total of eight guns, and a cavalry squadron.[16]

Uncertain of the fate of the remainder of the brigade, Jenkins decided to hold his position and await support. Closing ranks, the regiment exchanged fire with the enemy force for about three quarters of an hour. At this time, hearing no signs of support, Jenkins reluctantly decided to retire. But withdrawal could not be so easily accomplished. First Jenkins advanced part of his line toward the enemy guns and directed massed rifle volleys on the gunners. The Federal artillerymen fled over the crest and into the trees on the reverse slope. He then pivoted the regiment and advanced upon the Federal infantry, forcing their retirement over the crest; they, however, maintained good order. Slowly and deliberately, he then withdrew the column down the hill, still facing the Union position.[17] Upon reaching the ford, he encountered General Jones and the Mississippi regiments drawn up to defend the crossing. The Union force, regrouping to pursue Jenkins, was advised of Federal defeat on the left and immediately began a retreat toward Centreville. Initially, Jenkins believed his small force had bluffed the Northerners into retreat, but he later learned that the entire Union army was in rapid flight to the Washington, D.C., defenses.

Jenkins estimated his losses at 70 killed and wounded including the peerless Johnnie Whilden, who was slightly wounded.[18] The action, although brief, could have produced high losses. Jenkins was fortunate that the encounter was at close range, for after receiving some early punishment the 5th

South Carolina was able to negate the Federal artillery advantage by shooting down the gunners.

It is remarkable that Jenkins, the only officer on horseback on the field, survived the fight. This may have resulted primarily from poor enemy marksmanship, since the raw soldiers in both armies tended to fire high and without proper aim. The Mississippians informed Ben, Jenkins's body servant, the colonel was slain and his command cut to pieces. Ben was discovered at dusk, sorrowfully searching for his master's body on Grigsby's Hill.[19]

Colonel Jenkins was pleased over the enemy rout and joined the large number of Confederate officers who urged immediate pursuit of the beaten enemy. Heavy rains the following day prevented any meaningful follow-up, thus Jenkins and his men became involved in the gathering of the abundant Union equipment abandoned on the field.[20] Jenkins wrote to his brother and Carrie, stating:

> We should have pressed closely upon the heels of our victory and by this time Washington would be ours: but through delay we must fight the harder when the time comes.[21]

He, as others, proclaimed the victory as one of the most significant battles in history. Jenkins was extremely proud of the conduct and performance of the 5th South Carolina. While their portion of the fight was certainly minor, Jenkins's pride was somewhat justified. The soldiers had stood fast in the face of artillery fire and taken casualties without flinching. Many regiments, north and south, did not do the same in their first combat experience. Most of the victorious Southerners would, in the months and years to come, recall 1st Manassas as a mere skirmish when compared with the mighty clashes to come.

The unit remained camped along Bull Run for several weeks, enjoying the summer sun and the claims of Southern superiority. John Jenkins came to Virginia and toured the battlefield. He was overjoyed when Micah presented him with a Union army greatcoat as a trophy of the victory. But it became apparent that despite extravagant predictions the war was not over. Abraham Lincoln called for more volunteers and began to assemble a larger army. Soon Confederate forces advanced into northern Virginia to observe Union activity along the Potomac River. The 5th South Carolina, in company with the 4th South Carolina, marched northward to Germantown and camped near that pleasant little village.[22]

In early September, Jenkins was ordered to conduct a reconnaissance toward the Potomac River. With his regiment, a squadron of cavalry, and a battery of three guns, he marched 15 miles, approaching the Potomac at Great Falls. Sighting Federal activity across the river, he unlimbered the battery and began to shell the enemy soldiers. The artillery-less Union force sustained several casualties before withdrawing from artillery range. Jenkins's guns continued to play on the aqueduct that supplied Washington, D.C., with water, causing some minor but easily reparable damage. Major Asbury Coward, a member of General Jones's staff, voluntarily accompanied Jenkins on this expedition, enjoying himself immensely. At nightfall Jenkins rapidly withdrew his men, avoiding a Federal column that was dispatched to trap his small force. He was excited over this initial experience in independent command and exclaimed in a letter to Carrie that it was a neat, rapid raid with some Union casualties and much disruption.[23]

The Confederates remained in their Germantown camps throughout the fall, enjoying the apples, peaches, and other fruit with which the area abounded. Days were spent on camp chores and drill, with only an occasional alarm due to Union movements. On the 19th of October, the 5th received orders to return to McLean's Ford, and by November 1 the troops were busily constructing winter camps on the old Manassas battlefield. The South Carolina soldiers were surprised and somewhat unprepared for the rapid onset of winter in Virginia. They had moved north in the spring expecting a brief campaign and were without any cold-weather clothing or proper shoes. On November 18, a shivering Confederate private wrote:

> We are in plain view of the mountains, which are covered with snow. It was snowing here yesterday the whole day....A stormy wind is blowing and a colder day I never saw or want to see. It is a bad time in camp: every man is wrapped up in blankets and handkerchiefs, tied around their jaws and ears. And this is only the beginning of winter.[24]

Soon the harsh weather and unsanitary living conditions produced disturbing levels of sickness among the men. Medical facilities were so poorly regarded that most soldiers preferred to remain in quarters when sick, thereby increasing the spread of contagious diseases. A Mississippi soldier expressed his fear of hospitals when he stated:

> Unless they take me there when I am insensible or too weak to resist I will never get in one. They are the most loathsome holes that I ever visited.[25]

Influenza and dysentery swept through the camps, causing numerous fatalities. Large contingents were invalided home, often to stay. Those who remained grew hard and tough.

Beauregard, whose fame had soared with his victory at Manassas, became embroiled in a succession of disagreements with Jefferson Davis, president of the Confederacy. While the substance of his complaints about the Confederate Commissary Department may have been accurate, he made the mistake of writing letters critical of the Davis administration to several Confederate congressmen. Somehow these letters found their way into the *Richmond Whig*, a staunch anti-Davis publication.[26] Davis was not a forgiving man, and Beauregard was destined for replacement. Gradually the army was turned over to General Joseph E. Johnston.

In late September Davis visited Manassas, reviewed the army, and discussed one of his favorite projects with Johnston. The president, a stickler for administrative detail and organization, desired that regiments from the same state be formed into state brigades, with their commanders appointed from that same state whenever possible.[27] Johnston was not enthusiastic about the confusion such reorganization might cause in the face of the enemy, but after much debate he acquiesced to Davis's demands. He then stalled, delaying the actual implementation. However, the organization of the Confederate army was soon threatened from another direction, an act passed by the Confederate Congress.

In December 1861, Congress passed the infamous Furlough and Bounty Act, designed to encourage the large number of 12-month volunteers to remain on duty.[28] Enlistment terms for a majority of the 12-month soldiers were due to expire in early 1862. The Furlough and Bounty Act offered each man who reenlisted for the duration of the war up to a maximum of three years a 50-dollar bounty and a furlough of 60 days. Additionally, after reenlisting they could request assignment to a regiment or service branch of their choice. The soldiers could then hold new elections for company- and regimental-level officers.

Despite well-designed intentions, this act provided serious internal organizational difficulties. If the 60-day furloughs were honored in large numbers, the army would be substantially weakened and vulnerable, but if the promised furloughs were not granted, reenlistments might cease and the army could virtually disintegrate in the spring.[29] Additionally, the widespread election of officers could cause discipline problems, in that many competent but unpopular officers might not be elected and thus lost to the army. Fortunately, enough patriotic spirit remained that enlistments were high despite lengthy furlough delays, and the elections did not produce the overall feared consequences, although there were some glaring injustices and some excellent officers were deposed. However, the provision for transfers to other regiments or branches created so much confusion and discontent that in April Congress passed a conscription act. This action made all white males between 18 and 35 liable for three years' service. While laggards could sometimes find exceptions, the resolution was at least successful in providing adequate manpower for the Confederacy.

In December Colonel Jenkins obtained leave to return home and recruit volunteers. Despite his canvassing the state for new enlistees, he was also able to spend much of the 20 days with his wife and sons. Micah now understood that the war would be long and brutal, requiring years of his time, and he all the more treasured the brief respite around the fireside with his young family. By February 6 he was back in Richmond and, for several days, attempted to get an appointment with the secretary of war. He failed in his attempt to gain permission to recruit a legion similar to that organized by Wade Hampton. While in the capital Jenkins visited several sessions of the Confederate Congress, where he was shocked by the myopic, bombastic, and pompous behavior of the legislators.[30]

Upon his return to the regimental camps, Jenkins took advantage of the provisions of the Furlough and Bounty Act to pursue an idea of a specialized force. He organized a new regiment of qualified marksmen that became known as the Palmetto Sharpshooters.[31] This unit accepted all volunteers who qualified as riflemen and possessed the necessary physical stamina. Most enrollees were reenlisters from the 4th and 5th South Carolina regiments. The new regimental members were equipped with the long-barreled, British-manufactured Enfield Rifles and were provided with sufficient ammunition for extensive target practice. Several types of Enfields manufactured in England were sold to both Union and Confederate armies. The most popular weapon among Confederates was the long-barreled (39-inch) Enfield that fired a .577 or

.58 caliber bullet. Most of these rifles entered the South by blockade-runners. They were sturdy weapons with long shoulder slings and a brass-end muzzle stopper to keep out moisture.[32] The Palmetto Sharpshooters preferred these rifles, although a limited number of Whitworth Rifles were distributed to exceptional marksmen. The high-precision Whitworth fired the same caliber ball but of a smaller bore, and ammunition was difficult to obtain. The performance of the two guns was equal up to about 500 yards; beyond that distance the fragile Whitworth was vastly superior, and in the hands of an expert using a scope, could be effective at 1,500 yards.[33] The more serviceable Enfield proved preferable for combat purposes, utilizing ammunition standard to both armies.

The Palmetto Sharpshooters were expected to perform skirmishing duty for the entire brigade and Jenkins rapidly devised skirmishing drills and techniques. Regular drill proficiency was still maintained since the regiment would join the brigade line of battle when a major action occurred. The increased accuracy of the regiment's rifle fire became apparent in the next several engagements. On three separate occasions the Palmetto Sharpshooters collided with Union regiments in a one-on-one match and, each time, almost decimated the opposing regiment through increased speed of loading and accuracy of fire. This specialized regiment was probably the first such unit organized in Confederate service. They were, additionally, the first unit to develop drills based on accuracy of aimed fire rather than volume fire only.

In the winter of 1863–64, special sharpshooter battalions were developed in many brigades of the Army of Northern Virginia, with much of their training based on the experiences of the Palmetto Sharpshooters.[34] Individuals in these regiments were expected to demonstrate expert marksmanship at distances between 300 and 600 yards. Some talented soldiers learned to fire the Enfields at a range of 900 yards with accuracy. These battalions differed from Jenkins's regiment in that they were a combined unit with members selected from throughout a brigade and they returned to their original regiment for battle. They were extremely effective in the bitter trench warfare of the war's final year.

So depleted was the 4th South Carolina by transfers and illness that it was soon reduced from a regiment to a battalion of five companies.[35] In the newly instituted state brigade organization the Palmetto Sharpshooters were united with the 5th South Carolina and the 4th South Carolina Battalion, and the 6th South Carolina was soon added. In February General Jones was transferred due to poor health, and Brigadier General Richard H. Anderson was assigned as brigade commander. The 40-year-old Anderson was a graduate of West Point and a United States Army veteran. A tall, physically strong man, he was immediately well liked by the entire brigade. This native son of South Carolina was unassuming, quiet, and unselfish.[36] He was confident in his own ability and encouraged the initiative of his young subordinates. This trait alone would have endeared him to the impatient Micah Jenkins, but the two men rapidly developed a relationship based on mutual respect. Anderson's quiet, friendly demeanor in camp was misleading, for his boldness in battle became legendary. He was to rise to the rank of lieutenant general in Confederate service.

Gradually, Joe Johnston's Confederate army abandoned its base at Manassas Junction and moved down onto the peninsula formed by the York and James Rivers to support the trench lines at Yorktown already being defended by a small force under Major General John B. Magruder. The new Federal commander, Major General George B. McClellan, had assembled the first truly large army of the war (over 100,000 men) around Fort Monroe, on the Virginia Cape. His avowed objective was the capture of the Confederate capital by an advance up the peninsula.

The army that Johnston brought to Yorktown had changed a great deal since its Manassas victory. Not one of the brigades that had fought on the plains of Manassas had remained in its entirety and under the same commander.[37] The institution of state brigade organization and the shifting of many general officers changed the face of the army, for many officers found lacking at Manassas were transferred or released. The interval without action had also been utilized in improving drill and movement of large bodies of men, as well as in the institution of divisional organizations. Brigades were now grouped into divisions under major generals, who in turn would be directed by the army commander. This reduction of the span of control should have and probably did increase the efficiency of army operations, but the scarcity of competent staff officers and the still remaining large number of political officer appointees offset immediate gains that the divisional plan would later demonstrate.

The brigade of Richard Anderson left Manassas by train but arrived in the Yorktown area on foot, as the railway system simply could not handle the large troop movements. By late April most of the Confederate States Army were entrenched in lines near the old revolutionary battlefield.[38] But when Johnston arrived and surveyed the field he was not pleased, thinking the position a weak one. He was already flanked on his left by Federal gunboats that controlled the York River and was threatened with a like situation on his right. The guns of the Federal fleet could reach almost all of his trenches, and the possibility of a waterborne landing in his rear was a constant worry. Despite the objections of President Davis and his military advisor, Major General Robert E. Lee, Johnston determined to withdraw to a position closer to Richmond.[39]

On the night of May 3, 1862, Johnston's Confederates quietly spiked their heavy guns and withdrew from the Yorktown lines. The few available roadways were thick with heavy mud, which slowed progress, and Union forces were soon pressing the withdrawal.[40] McClellan had scheduled his long-awaited attack for the fourth and after finding the Confederate trenches empty, he ordered his troops to pursue vigorously.

About noon on the fourth, Johnston realized that he must somehow slow the Federal pursuit. He decided to occupy Fort Magruder, an earthen work located at the junction of the Hampton and Yorktown Roads, just a few miles from Williamsburg.[41] Generals Lafayette McLaws and John B. Magruder were instructed to place a brigade in the fort, and they promptly complied. Just before dusk Union infantry approached and were discouraged by a heavy volume of Confederate fire. After nightfall the two Confederate brigades were withdrawn, since they were scheduled to lead the army's retreat. General James Longstreet, commanding the rear guard, was then ordered to garrison the fort until the army was clear. Longstreet immediately dispatched the small brigades of Anderson and Brigadier General Roger A. Pryor, already camped west of Williamsburg, to return and hold the entrenchments. Micah Jenkins and the Palmetto Sharpshooters countermarched and in a driving rainstorm, led Anderson's brigade back to Fort Magruder.[42] When the marchers reached the fortification it was pouring rain and too dark to properly post the brigade. Realizing the fort was too small for his two brigades, Anderson placed Jenkins's Sharpshooters and six companies of the 5th South Carolina within the fort. The four remaining companies of the 5th and the Louisiana Foot Rifles were assigned to small redoubts on either side of the fort. The 6th South Carolina was placed in reserve.[43] The Confederates spent a long and miserable night in the fort. One soldier remembered how dark the night seemed as he strained to hear Federals approaching. Jenkins had his men awake and alert by 5:30 a.m., and they did not have long to wait.

At 6:00 a.m. Union skirmishers slowly approached Fort Magruder. Finding the works occupied they withdrew and

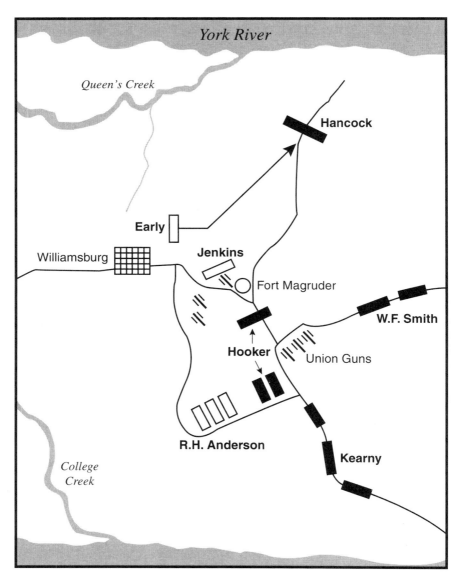

Williamsburg, May 5, 1862

Fort Magruder held the key to Confederate delaying action at Williamsburg. Located in the narrow gap between Queen's and College Creeks, the fort dominated all roads into Williamsburg.

Federal artillery opened with a sudden powerful roar. Two Confederate batteries that attempted to reply were hopelessly outgunned and silenced. The earth seemed to shake with the power of the Union guns and Fort Magruder was soon obscured with dust from the shell bursts. But inside the fort the earthen walls absorbed the shells and the defenders suffered only minimal casualties. The artillery batteries in Fort Magruder suffered most of the losses, as enemy sharpshooters were effective in shooting down those gunners who appeared while serving their weapons. Jenkins supplied assistance to the gunners in the form of volunteers from the Palmetto Sharpshooters.[44] Meanwhile Longstreet, in Williamsburg, heard the vicious bombardment and dispatched two additional brigades to Anderson, whom he placed in command on the field.[45] Anderson then turned over command of his brigade and Fort Magruder to his senior colonel, Micah Jenkins.

Despite an uncomfortable night, Jenkins and his men were amply supplied with ammunition and eager for a fight. Confederate soldiers who commented on the deafening noise of the artillery were surprised that so little damage occurred to the fort or themselves. They were learning the value of defense from behind earthen walls. At 9:00 a.m. artillery fire lifted and Federal infantry moved forward to the assault. Jenkins held his infantry fire until the Federals were within two hundred yards then, responding with heavy volleys of fire, repulsed the assault in 15 minutes. Again, heavy artillery fire was directed on the fort. Union commanders seemed convinced that artillery fire would eventually reduce the position and demoralize the defenders. But the Sharpshooters now knew the guns could not penetrate the fort and they confidently waited out the barrage. A division-size Union column moved toward Fort Magruder. Federal private Warren Goss of Major General Joseph Hooker's division described the second Union attack on the fort:

> We advanced along the edge of the woods and about 11
> o'clock a swarm of Confederates emerged from a ravine to
> the left of the fort. They opened a deadly and terrible fire
> and charged upon us with their peculiar yell. We took
> advantage of the trees and stumps and retreated rapidly
> back to the trees.... We were none of us to proud to dodge
> behind a tree.[46]

Jenkins had unleashed a carefully hidden vicious counterattack at the very moment that the Union soldiers began to waver
before rifle fire. Pursuing wildly, the Confederate counter-
punchers stormed into the edge of the woods and cut off a
four-gun battery whose infantry support had fled. Guns and
ammunition limbers were hauled by hand into the fort, and a
Confederate gunner in Fort Magruder stated with satisfaction, "We took their ammunition and shot it back at them."[47]
The additional fire of several batteries located near the fort
bolstered the rebel defense. Captain Stribling's four-gun battery, still located inside the earthwork, was particularly effective in a duel with Battery H, United States Artillery.[48] When
Battery H attempted to deploy, Stribling's Fauquier Artillery
was on target with its first salvo, cutting down a number of
men and horses. A second and third salvo created such panic
that the Union gun crews sprinted for safety and could not be
rallied. A reserve battery of New York Volunteers was ordered
forward to serve the guns.

A third Union infantry advance was sternly repulsed, and
the following counterattack again routed several regiments of
Hooker's division. Subsequent onslaughts were feeble and easily disbursed by artillery fire. Unable to carry the position by
assault, Union commanders searched for a means of flanking
Jenkins out of the fort. While Fort Magruder was not an impressive looking position, the Confederates enjoyed a distinct
geographic advantage. The peninsula was only seven miles
wide at this point and due to streams and marshes on the

riverbanks, only a three-mile-wide area around the fort afforded maneuverable terrain. Longstreet had provided Anderson with ample reserves, and as Federals marched to find flanking routes, Anderson spread these reserves to either side of the position to counter.

Late in the afternoon a brisk action took place to the left of the fort. When Hooker's division retreated after being repulsed by the South Carolinians, Major General Winfield S. Hancock's division appeared in a threatening position on the left. Anderson dispatched a brigade under Jubal Early to block Hancock's approach. Early's troops advanced through heavy woods unobserved by the Union general. Early correctly perceived his force to be on Hancock's flank and he requested and received permission to attempt to roll it up.[49] Initially, he met with success as several Federal regiments were driven in confusion, but his brigade became scattered in the dense underbrush. Two regiments cleared the woods and observed a Federal force positioned behind a rail fence. They impetuously charged, not realizing they were attacking an enemy brigade supported by artillery. The attackers were slaughtered, with the 5th North Carolina losing 68 percent of its strength in casualties.[50] Early became aware of the mistake and in attempting to halt the attack, was himself severely wounded.

With darkness the fighting ceased. As blue-clad lines of skirmishers approached Fort Magruder at dawn on May 6, they advanced through their own unburied dead. The previous day's action had continued so late into the night that casualties had not been cleared from the field. Private Warren Gross related a grisly incident in which he came upon a Union soldier aiming his gun over the branches of a tree at Fort Magruder. He remembered:

> When I called out to him he did not turn or move. As I approached I put my hand on his shoulder and looked into his face....He was dead, shot through the brain and still occupying his post after death.[51]

The Union army combed the battlefield, burying the dead, scavenging equipment, and capturing a few late-sleeping Confederates. But Johnston and his army were gone.

McClellan claimed a great victory, but the Confederate rear guard action had been near perfect. Union pursuit was delayed so well that contact between the two armies did not actually reoccur until they reached the environs of Richmond. Although the action at Williamsburg was brief, the fighting was vicious. The Union army suffered more than 2,200 casualties, with more than 1,500 of them in Hooker's division that had carried out the attacks on the fort. Confederate casualties were more than 1,000 with a majority in Early's brigade.[52] Jenkins's force suffered 10 dead and 71 wounded.[53]

The positive results of Jenkins's command efforts were soon recognized within the army. Longstreet commented on his fiery zeal and his determination in holding Fort Magruder.[54] Anderson felt his management of a brigade size force was outstanding and the timing of his counterattacks superb. Micah Jenkins was marked for increased responsibility and future promotion.

Chapter 5

Fame at Seven Pines

Micah Jenkins's determined Palmetto Sharpshooters served as the army's rear guard for several days; however, Federal pursuit after the clash at Fort Magruder was so lethargic that contact between the two forces was slight. Deplorable road conditions intensified the difficulty of movement. Heavy rains had inundated eastern Virginia all spring and the dirt roads became bottomless quagmires of mud. As the Confederate army struggled to convey its wagons and gun carriages through this morass, even the commanding general dismounted to lend a shoulder to the wheel.[1] The passage of Johnston's divisions produced such rutted conditions that the pursuing Union army could not follow in the same roadway and was forced to utilize field roads. Most Confederates recalled the retreat as a period of acute hunger. The Confederate Commissary Department, never very efficient, completely broke down under the deplorable road conditions and with thousands of soldiers moving west on a few tracks, the commissary wagons couldn't deliver supplies eastward from Richmond to the marchers. One Alabama soldier commented that his regiment proceeded on the march "as hungry as wolves."[2] A Confederate officer reasoned that the Union army would need its own rations since his men had stripped the countryside bare. Most local residents preceded the army to Richmond, leaving their homes and farms deserted and open prey for bands of roving, hungry men. Realizing that the Union army would soon occupy these farms, hungry rebels simply helped themselves to whatever food or livestock they encountered. A South Carolina private became so tired and hungry that he, like many others, left his unit and found a deserted farmhouse. Upon entering, he found an elderly slave preparing supper. Stating that the owners had fled and left him in charge, the old man fed the tired soldier and stood watch while he slept.[3]

Discipline was never strong in Johnston's army, and in retreat soldiers tended to lose their units and proceed alone or in small groups. Major General Daniel H. Hill attributed this undisciplined state to the newly instituted election process that, he felt, decreased the control of officers over soldiers. The lack of suitable rations created a need to forage for food that also certainly amplified this disintegration of military unit organization. Most of these soldiers were not deserters; they simply were on their own for a while looking for food. Dirty, tired, starving men began to arrive in the Confederate capital in large numbers where they slept in vacant lots and cooked on street corners. Provost marshals were soon busily engaged in arresting, sorting out, and returning the men to their proper units. As many as eight thousand soldiers, or nearly a division, were rounded up inside the city limits. At last, by May 9, most of the army reached the rail connections to Richmond and found rations waiting by the tracks.

Although no serious pursuit of the Confederate army occurred, there was a Federal movement to disrupt the withdrawal. McClellan, strongly reinforced while the armies were entrenched at Yorktown, decided in one of his aggressive moments to land waterborne troops behind the Confederate front. He dispatched Brigadier General William B. Franklin with his division up the York River on transports, attempting to cut off the marching Confederates. Franklin sailed to West Point, Virginia, on May 6 where he established a bridgehead well protected by Federal gunboats.[4] Once ashore, Franklin reconnoitered toward Barhamsville. The Confederate division nearest the Federal landing area, under Brigadier General John B. Hood, was ordered to oppose any further offensive action by Franklin. Hood, always an aggressor, attacked Franklin's outposts and drove the Union troops back upon the landing area. Only strong support fire from the gunboats prevented further action. Hood joked that his Texans wanted to charge the gunboats but could find no rowboats or rafts.[5]

As Johnston evacuated the peninsula, an equally significant event occurred on the James River. Major General Benjamin C. Huger, commanding the Confederate garrison in Norfolk, realized that his position was exposed and prepared for evacuation of that important naval base.[6] Huger burned the shipyard, blew up several ammunition depots, and marched his men out of the city. The Confederate ironclad warship CSS *Virginia,* based in Norfolk, was thereby forced to attempt a retreat up the river. The *Virginia* had posed a threat to the entire Union fleet in the Chesapeake Bay and even after her stalemate with the Federal ironclad USS *Monitor,* her presence had prevented Union penetration of the James River. Retreat proved disastrous for the *Virginia.* Every effort was made to lighten the ship, but she ran aground near the mouth of the Elizabeth River. After repeated attempts to free her were unsuccessful, she was blown apart by her crew to prevent capture.[7] The James River was now open, and the Union fleet responded rapidly. By May 15, a squadron of Federal gunboats approached Drewry's Bluff, only seven miles from Richmond.[8]

At Drewry's Bluff the river veers sharply eastward and then southward, forming an elbow-shaped configuration that contains a narrow channel.[9] A Confederate entrenchment entitled Fort Darling was hastily constructed on the bluff above the elbow and obstructions were placed in the channel. If Federal gunboats hoped to sail upriver and shell the capital, the fort must be reduced as well as the obstructions removed. About midday the Union flotilla, led by the armored gunboat USS *Galena,* approached Fort Darling. Anchoring below the obstructions, the warships prepared to force surrender of the fort by bombardment. But soon it was discovered that only the *Galena*'s guns could elevate sufficiently to reach the entrenchments perched atop 90-foot bluffs. Consequently, all Confederate fire was concentrated on the lone Federal flagship. Gun crews from the abandoned *Virginia* were serving the heavy guns in Fort Darling with remarkable accuracy. The *Galena* was struck by 28 projectiles and perforated 18 times.[10] Casualties were heavy on board the vessel, and her captain was forced to withdraw his flotilla downstream. Fort Darling simply could not be reduced by naval gunfire alone. General Johnston, who had already retreated to within 20 miles of Richmond, fell back to the city's suburbs to anchor his right flank on the James River opposite Fort Darling.

The Palmetto Sharpshooters, following their stint of rear guard duty, encamped about 30 miles from Richmond.[11] On May 11 Jenkins received orders to move his regiment across the river and establish a campsite adjacent to and supportive of Fort Darling.[12] A second Union attempt to capture the fort was anticipated, and it was feared this assault would include the landing of marines. He scattered his regiment down river below the obstacles. The soldiers amused themselves by firing on anchored Union ships whenever sailors appeared on deck. At least one gunboat captain fell victim to the bullets of the riflemen. An occasional dose of cannon fire into the woods was answered by shouts of derision. On May 25 the Sharpshooters crossed back to the north bank and, assisted by an additional unit, protected the construction of a twin fort on Chapin's Bluff. Jenkins reported that four guns were emplaced on the 25th and four more would soon be ready for action.[13] The twin forts and accompanying obstructions in the river effectively blocked all subsequent Federal threats from the James. The Palmetto

Sharpshooters enjoyed their two weeks along the river bank since duties were light, supplies substantial, and passes to visit the bars and brothels of Richmond were sometimes granted.[14] Constant skirmishing and artillery exchanges occurred farther north. Jenkins commented to Carrie that he could clearly hear the exchanges of artillery from his position at Chapin's Bluff and that he expected a major battle at any time.[15] In the city, panic reigned. The Confederate Congress adjourned, and most of its members left for home in haste. Various government agencies prepared to ship their papers and files to the west.[16] The packet boats, railroads, and stage lines to Lynchburg were crowded with the fainthearted. Even President Davis doubted the city could be held.

An encounter between the two armies seemed inevitable, for Johnston could retreat no farther. On May 20, McClellan began crossing troops over the Chickahominy River.[17] A sluggish stream, its bed consisted primarily of swamps and bogs full of snakes and fever, but it was the last major geographic barrier before Richmond. McClellan slowly inched his way forward, always probing, but never aggressively committing himself to an attack. General Daniel H. Hill wrote his wife that he did "not feel McClellan would venture to attack at all. His movements have been characterized by great prudence, not to say great timidity."[18] Hill's analysis was substantially correct. McClellan was an engineer at heart and he envisioned the siege-like investiture of the Confederate city fashioned on the European model of besiegement and capture. His vast train of heavy artillery was unloaded at West Point and shipped eastward by railroad. He planned to confine the opposing army within the city and then pound the capital into submission with his heavy guns.[19] McClellan believed this type of action could end the war with minimum casualties and he proceeded toward this objective in his methodical manner.

Johnston was urged repeatedly by Davis to initiate action with McClellan's army. Retreat had brought the Confederates so close to the city that the capital would be doomed if the Federal artillery was properly emplaced. Johnston must drive the Federals away from Richmond. Davis and Lee were discouraged with Johnston's progress. Lee argued that Richmond, as the capital of the state and the nation, must be held, and the only way to hold the city was to attack.

Johnston was at last pushed into action. He first decided to attack the right wing of the Federal army, northwest of the city. But McClellan shoved his left wing, consisting of two army corps, across the Chickahominy, and Johnston wisely changed his mind. If he could rapidly mount an attack on this somewhat isolated left wing, he could cripple the Federal army before McClellan could send assistance across the stream.

Johnston assigned 22 brigades of his growing army to carry out the offense.[20] Attack columns were rapidly assembled. Micah Jenkins brought the two regiments from Chapin's Bluff to rejoin Anderson. On the night of May 30, with the attack scheduled for the next day, thousands of nervous soldiers attempted to sleep in their makeshift camps. Suddenly, a tremendous storm struck the Richmond area, with strong winds lashing the tents, accompanied by heavy rains and lightning. The electrical display was so severe that soldiers in both armies were killed by lightning strikes.[21] While the discomfort was acute, the resulting flooded condition of the Chickahominy further served to separate the Federal army. Johnston grew confident, as even the fates seemed to predict success.

Three distinct roads fanned eastward from the environs of Richmond. Johnston planned to use all three in an assault on Major General Erasmus D. Keyes's IV Corps, entrenched at the crossroads of Seven Pines, and Major General Samuel Heintzelman's III Corps, scattered between Seven Pines and the Chickahominy bridges. Confederate Major General D. H. Hill and his four-brigade division would march directly out the Williamsburg Stage Road and assault Brigadier General Silas Casey's division of the IV Corps at Seven Pines. Major

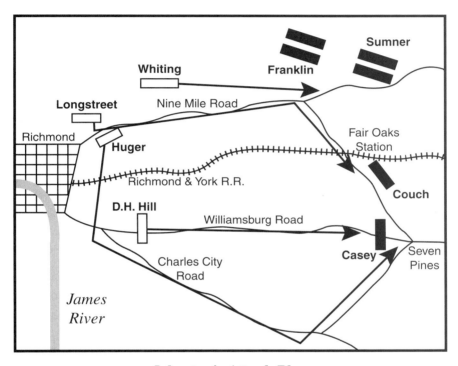

Johnston's Attack Plan

Worthy of Napoleon, Johnston's grandiose plan was poorly executed by a Confederate army which became noted for weak staff execution. While Whiting's division shielded Federals Franklin and Sumner from the action, three Confederate columns led by Longstreet, Huger, and Hill were to converge on Casey's camps at the crossroads of Seven Pines.

General Benjamin Huger and three brigades from the Norfolk garrison were to proceed out the Charles City Road, turn left and attack the southern flank of the Union army. Major General James Longstreet and his large six-brigade division would use the Nine Mile Road to move on the Federal right flank and drive a wedge between the two Union corps. In addition, Major General Chase Whiting and his division would follow and support Longstreet in the event that Union reserves were dispatched across the Chickahominy.[22] It was a reasonable and well-conceived battle plan, but one very difficult to coordinate. Johnston's desire to cripple McClellan by destroying a portion of his army before it could be supported was reasonable, but this three-pronged attack led by four general officers necessitated strong leadership and excellent communication. Joe Johnston was long on neither trait. Misunderstandings led to monumental confusion and disjointed efforts from the onset.

Hill's brigades were camped near their designated attack routes and their advance proceeded smoothly except for Robert Rodes's brigade, which was positioned by orders on the Charles City Road. Rodes had to march his men cross-country through knee-deep water to rejoin Hill and this momentarily delayed Hill's column. But this hardship was insignificant when compared to the misadventures of the other attacking columns. Huger and Longstreet were camped in such a fashion that each had to cross the other's path to reach their proper advance routes. Huger overslept and was late marching, but since Longstreet was determined to let Huger cross first, his brigades waited idly by the roadside. When Longstreet's men finally approached Nine Mile Road, Whiting's division already occupied the road.[23] Longstreet then split his division, ordering three brigades to assist Whiting and two, under Brigadier General James L. Kemper and Anderson, to countermarch on the Williamsburg Road and support Hill. Meanwhile, Huger tardily advanced on the Charles City Road, became confused and halted his column while awaiting further orders. His seven thousand men, although clearly within audible distance of the battle, remained idle and never fired a shot.

The morning passed slowly as Hill impatiently waited for the other two columns to attack. About 2:00 p.m., he could seemingly wait no longer. He released his brigades to advance, and the soldiers swept down the Williamsburg Road.[24] Newly appointed Brigadier General Samuel Garland, Jr., pushed his brigade forward on the left of the road, while Rodes's tardy troops kept pace on the right. Brigadier General George Anderson followed Garland, and Brigadier General Gabriel Raines's brigade supported Rodes. Garland, a trim, well-dressed, young Lynchburg, Virginia, attorney and graduate of the Virginia Military Institute, had been advanced in rank to replace the wounded Jubal Early. On the opposite side of the roadway, the lanky, mustachioed Rodes drove his Alabama brigade to keep abreast of Garland. Rodes, likewise from Lynchburg and a V.M.I. graduate, ignored heavy Union artillery fire as his men waded through swamps and bogs. Garland's impetuous men surged ahead scattering Union skirmishers and crashed headlong into Casey's raw Union division, driving a hole in the initial Federal defense line.[25] As the Union defenders hesitated, Rodes arrived and rashly stormed over the entrenchments. Both brigades suffered heavy casualties, but almost without pause, they advanced toward a second line of earthworks. Although the reserve brigades arrived to assist, strong Federal reinforcements slowed the Confederate advance. Realizing his two leading brigades had sustained substantial punishment and that his advance was being stalemated by Federal reserves, Hill searched for more units.[26]

Both Garland and Rodes, despite superb performances by their soldiers, were "fought out," and the supporting brigades were not equally aggressive. Encountering Anderson's brigade of Longstreet's division as they approached, Hill decide to launch his own flank attack. He had seen no evidence of Huger's advancing and probably recognized that the battle was his to fight. Likewise, from the north, Hill heard no indication of Longstreet's moving to offer assistance. As Anderson rushed forward, a seam appeared in the Confederate line between two of the attacking brigades. Anderson instantly took two regiments in to seal the front and instructed Micah Jenkins to search for a way around the Union right with the remaining two regiments. Jenkins, delighted with the opportunity, aligned his Palmetto Sharpshooters in front, closely followed by the 6th South Carolina under Colonel John Bratton, and advanced into a wooded area on the Federal right. As he cleared the woods, a Federal column was encountered, marching to reinforce the Union center. The enemy was in column of fours, and the rifle fire of the sharpshooters staggered and then disbursed the column. Jenkins swung the advance northward following a railroad track for several hundred yards. He turned southeast and charged into and over a surprised and outflanked Federal line, changed his front and then engaged a third enemy column at 75 yards.[27]

Gradually, this Federal line was pushed back to the Williamsburg Road.[28] Jenkins then dispatched Lieutenant Colonel J. M. Steedman, now commanding the 6th South Carolina in place of the wounded Colonel Bratton, onto the enemy flank and when they wavered, scoured the road with his other regiment. At this juncture, Jenkins realized he was well inside the Union front and in an extremely vulnerable yet critical position. He dispatched his adjutant, Captain Cato A. Seabrook, for reinforcements and decided to keep advancing. The Federal columns were shocked and confused to encounter Confederates this far behind their front, and Jenkins could not allow them an opportunity to concentrate on his two-regiment force. He advanced boldly up the Williamsburg Road, driving deeper into the enemy position.[29]

When Seabrook located Anderson, the general responded to Jenkins's request by dispatching the 5th South Carolina under Lieutenant Colonel A. Jackson to assist the attacking column.[30] Meanwhile, General Hill had arrived, and noticing the confusion in Federal ranks caused by Jenkins's bold assaults, he sent another regiment, the 27th Georgia from Brigadier General G. R. Anderson's brigade, to strengthen Jenkins.[31] When the two regiments arrived, Jenkins was engaged in a stand-up exchange of fire with the 23rd Pennsylvania of Major General Darius N. Couch's division at a distance of 30 yards. The reinforced Confederate force then charged into and over the hapless Pennsylvanians. A sister regiment rushed to assist the 23rd and was wrecked in 15 minutes, losing 263 men out of 574 engaged. One company of the Palmetto Sharpshooters took 139 prisoners from the two Pennsylvania Regiments.[32] Jenkins halted the advance, redressed his lines, and faced the advance of a fifth Union line of battle. W. D. Smith, captain of Company G, Palmetto Sharpshooters, described the action with the fifth Federal line:

> Someone called to Jenkins, "Colonel just look at them coming at the double quick." He replied, "We will meet them at the double quick!" He gave the command to change fronts on the twelfth company and I never saw on ordinary parade a prettier maneuver. Jenkins was magic. He could come nearer making his men work like machinery than any other man I ever saw.[33]

The final Federal line was shattered about 7:30 p.m., and as darkness fell, the bluecoats retreated to a new position some miles beyond Seven Pines. Jenkins reported the conclusion of his day's work:

> thus we closed our busy day at 7:40....the last seen of the enemy being his broken and disorganized squads of from five to twenty men, visible for one half mile over an extensive wheat field.[34]

The advance had been continuous from 3:00 p.m. until 7:40 p.m., or dusk. Jenkins's battalion had contested five separate and distinct lines of battle, whipping each; had passed over three lines of breastworks; and had taken four Federal camps, two hundred fifty prisoners, and three sets of enemy colors.[35] Jenkins had taken advantage of fluid conditions behind the Union lines to interpose his small force between Federal columns and coolly defeated each that he encountered. The woods and rough terrain prevented Federal forces from ascertaining the truly small size of his force.

Jenkins's "attack when discovered" strategy drove much larger enemy forces into confusion and retreat. The audacity of his offensive actions saved his command from certain destruction and permitted this small force, never exceeding 1,900 men, to change the face of the battle.[36] Federal General Philip Kearny, who strove in vain to stabilize his front, was able to note the effects of Jenkins's maneuvering on the outcome of the battle. He described the Confederate advance and corresponding Federal troop reactions:

> It was near 6 p.m. when our center and right...defended by troops with willingness, could no longer resist the enemy's right central flank attack, pushed on with determined discipline. Once broken our troops fled incontinently, and a dense body of the enemy pursuing rapidly, yet in good order occupied the Williamsburg Road.[37]

Union units had resisted, sometimes fiercely. Jenkins's regiments had suffered casualties of more than 700 men, including the outstanding colonel of the 5th South Carolina, J. R. Giles, who was among the slain. Colonel Bratton of the 6th was severely wounded, captured and imprisoned. Jenkins was wounded in the leg, but the injury was certainly slight, for he wrote his wife that his biggest personal loss was a pair of pants.[38] The soldiers who followed Jenkins were proud of their accomplishments in routing the enemy but also realistic. J. W.

Reid looked around the thinned ranks the following day and exclaimed, "If this battle is called a victory, then I never want to be in a battle that is not a victory."[39] A further tribute to Federal resistance was Jenkins's statement that "the colors of the Palmetto Sharpshooters had been holed nine times and three of its color bearers slain."[40] As Union soldiers broke and ran, the survivors of the hard fought brigades of Rodes and Garland joined Jenkins's regiments in the midst of Casey's divisional camp. A large numbers of Federal prisoners were gathered in by the Confederate units but Jenkins's command had been too busy to take captives, and a larger count of defeated Union soldiers attained their own lines in the darkness. The Confederate units availed themselves of the abundant food supply in the Federal camps and enjoyed a virtual feast. Food, uniforms, and blankets were scattered in abundance. The rebels rapidly appropriated all the available Federal army tents, which they needed badly. Perhaps the most valuable commodity, however, was the large number of new Enfield rifles scattered across the fields. When assigned Confederate agents arrived the next morning to collect firearms, they were surprised by the odd collection of old weapons abandoned on the site. Graybacks had gleefully "exchanged" their antique weapons with those discarded by the departed enemy.[41] Sometime after midnight, Jenkins, Garland, and Rodes were ordered to fall back and consolidate at the Seven Pines crossroads.

As the army regrouped on the battlefield, sagas relating high praise of the adventures of Jenkins and his column flowed about the camps. Captain Thomas Goree of Longstreet's staff wrote that within a few hours, Jenkins's command had "immortalized itself."[42] Major General Gustavus W. Smith, who wrote the army's official battle report after Johnston was wounded, was even more extravagant in his statements when he said:

> It is believed in the annuals of war that few if any instances of persistent, skillful, and effective battlefield

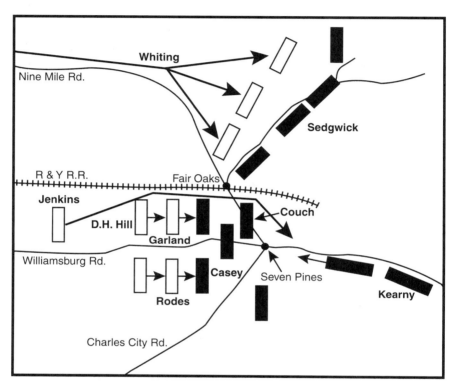

Battle of Seven Pines, May 31, 1862

Despite Johnston's four-prong attack plan, only Whiting and D. H. Hill's divisions saw action, fighting two distinctly separate actions. Jenkins's penetration along the railroad and into Seven Pines forced Federal withdrawal from their camps in that area.

fighting occurred like the May 31 action of the South Carolina Regiments under Colonel Jenkins.[43]

D. H. Hill and Longstreet both credited Jenkins's flank attack as keynoting their limited success. Both officers recommended that Jenkins immediately be promoted to brigadier general.[44]

Meanwhile, a second and separate action had been occurring farther north. The third Confederate column, now commanded by Major General Chase Whiting, had proceeded out Nine Mile Road and collided with Federal troops at Fair Oaks Station. Major General Oliver O. Howard's Union division was across the Chickahominy and marching hard toward Seven Pines when Whiting's leading brigade under Colonel Evander Law appeared in their front. Union artillery opened on Law's men who deployed for action. Whiting ordered Law forward, but as he advanced on the Federal guns, he was shocked to find Howard's entire division in line of battle. Repulsed, Whiting deployed three additional brigades and again advanced. Union reinforcements arrived and the battle became a slugging match, with neither side gaining a substantial advantage. Both forces demonstrated a willingness to attack enemy entrenchments in a straightforward fashion despite casualties.

Late in the afternoon, General Johnston, while observing Whiting's brigades go into action, was hit almost simultaneously by a minié ball in his right arm and a shell fragment in the chest.[45] He fell heavily from his horse, unconscious. Johnston was removed by ambulance, conveyed to a Richmond hospital as darkness fell over the scene and action ceased.

Of the 22 brigades scheduled to attack the two Federal corps only nine had seen action when night fell. Fully 30,000 Confederates had stood within earshot and listened to their fellows in arms fight two distinct actions. The Fair Oaks action had been a stalemate, while at Seven Pines the Federals had been splintered and driven for three miles at a cost of near 5,000 Confederate casualties.[46]

When Johnston fell, command of the Confederate army passed to General Gustavus Woodson Smith, his second in command. Smith knew almost nothing of Johnston's plans. Likewise, he had difficulty obtaining any accurate information on the whereabouts of the participants in the day's fighting. Consequently, Smith appeared befuddled and confused. On the following day, he authorized continued action against Federal positions, but after a second day of confused fighting and about one thousand casualties on each side, no appreciable results were apparent.

President Davis rode to the field and met with the new field commander in early afternoon. He found General Smith almost incoherent and unable to explain his plans or his objectives. Smith evidently almost cracked under the stress of sudden command pushed upon him in a battle already miscarried. At 2:00 p.m. Davis informed Smith that he was relieved and he turned over all Confederate armies around Richmond to his military advisor, Robert E. Lee.[47] Possibly this was the most significant action of the two days.

It was evident that neither army was prepared for the severity of fighting in a battle of this scale. Wounded Confederates soon flooded the streets of Richmond. Hospitals overflowed, as private homes and commercial establishments were hastily utilized. Volunteers from all social strata responded to the call for nursing aid. The space and buildings needed to care for the wounded formed the base upon which the huge Chimborazo Hospital complex would develop. This sprawling giant, when completed, would be described as the "largest military hospital in the history of this continent" and would serve much larger numbers of wounded in years to come when Richmonders were hardened to warfare.[48] Yet this first great wave of wounded, accompanied by the wagonloads of dead stacked like cord wood, shocked and saddened the citizens of the capital city. The Federal wounded were, if anything, in a worse situation. They were hauled by wagon and railroad boxcar back to the landings on the York River, where their stretchers were unloaded to await placement on the transport ships and conveyances to Washington or Baltimore. They lacked even the few comforts that the ladies of Richmond provided their Confederate counterparts. Medical staffs and facilities would grow and improve, and larger numbers of patients would be provided by subsequent battles, but perhaps nothing would compare with the impotent state of medical services following the battle of Seven Pines.

The dual engagements were characterized by a breakdown of Confederate army plans and strategies. Communication again fell apart and execution of battle plans was certainly as poor as the army's initial effort at Manassas. The greatly increased scale of action and the Confederates' initial attempt to conduct offensive action contributed heavily to the overall breakdown and confusion. Johnston had developed a good, if not exceptional, plan of attack, but had watched it fall apart from inception. He was unable to make any corrections or adjustments as his plans disintegrated. It was rumored that in mid-morning on the 31st, Johnston was heard to comment that he wished all the soldiers were back in camp.[49] It appears that once the plan was in operation, Johnston simply observed the ineffective management of his subordinates and made no effort to regain control or correct their mistaken efforts. The battle reports of major Confederate subordinates are conflicting and confusing, indicating that many of these officers did not understand their role and attempted to shift all blame to someone else.

There was certainly blame enough to share. This was also the first time the army had utilized the new divisional organization in combat, and understandably, this caused some mismanagement; however, the divisional commanders, with one lone exception, performed miserably. Huger, the most criticized, was late, indecisive, became confused, and stopped functioning.[50] He attempted to explain his idleness by referring to confusing messages that he had received from others, but remaining idle while others fought within earshot was unacceptable and inexplainable. Any advance by his division once Hill's troops were engaged would have resulted in complete Confederate victory. Longstreet's actions were equally mysterious.[51] Possibly becoming frustrated by the confusing marching orders, he split his large division, assigning brigades to two columns and exercised no further control of his troops. His reports blame Huger for the bungled battle, but it is difficult to ascertain any contributions Longstreet made to maximize Confederate efforts. Whiting's performance was deemed "too cautious" by Johnston. Goaded by Johnston's comments, he committed Law rashly and was expensively repulsed. Whiting was supposed to have supported Longstreet, but instead found himself blundering into strong Federal forces. While neither imaginative nor successful, he made no grievous errors and demonstrated a willingness to commit his troops, by far surpassing the efforts of Huger and Longstreet.

Daniel H. Hill, alone, demonstrated the ability to command and fight a division. Hill started his movements on time, kept his brigades under his supervision and committed them smartly to action.[52] When stalled, he committed his reserves and adjusted his deployment. He displayed initiative in using the support of Anderson and Jenkins to save a deteriorating battle. Hill's reading of the enemy's confusion and his response in sending reinforcements to Jenkins was indicative of his tactical skill. It was his fight, and unsupported, he did an excellent job.

Perhaps the most promising result for the army evolving from the Seven Pines action was the emergence of a group of aggressive, charismatic, young brigade commanders. These hard-driving, fearless colonels and brigadiers would become the backbone of the army. One of these was Robert E. Rodes, seeing his first action in command of his Alabama regiments. He had absolutely no fear and was cool and resolved as he led his brigade to the attack despite enemy fire, casualties, and difficult terrain.[53] Although severely wounded, he refused to leave the field until nightfall. Rodes demonstrated the kind of leadership that would later hold the mountain passes at South Mountain, lead Jackson's flank attack at Chancellorsville, and restore broken lines at a courthouse in Spotsylvania. Samuel Garland, newly promoted to lead Early's brigade, demonstrated the fiery leadership and disregard for personal safety that would become his trademark and by which he would fall at South Mountain. Garland's wife and infant son had recently died within days of each other, and it was rumored the intensely religious young man was purposely reckless.[54] Richard Anderson again displayed the quiet, steady leadership that would find him a lieutenant general and corps commander under Lee by war's end. His decision to split his brigades and fill a gap himself with one section while sending Jenkins around to the right with another was a key decision made by a man sure of himself and confident in the ability of his subordinates.[55] Micah Jenkins's performance was a surprise to everyone in the army but himself. He demonstrated the kind of aggressive nature tempered by cool judgment that would characterize his career with the army.[56] He was able to inspire his men by his personal bravery and exposure under fire. Some proclaimed Jenkins fortunate in that he assaulted a section of the Federal line that was loosely guarded and was able to penetrate easily, but it was that fortune which occurs when perseverance and aggression take advantage of opportunity. His strategy of constant attack confused the enemy and created uncertainty. His handling of his forces and his intuitive skills predicted future greatness.

Other brigade commanders fought their men hard at Fair Oaks. George Pickett, John Hood, and Evander Law gained the respect of the army for their gritty performance, which all but wrecked Howard's Union position. The army was changing, and its evolution would continue. Rodes at age 33, Garland at 30, and Jenkins at 26 were prototypes of the young stalwarts who would make up the core of the force known as the Army of Northern Virginia. They would provide impetus to the practice of promotion by ability and performance within the army, as the power of political appointees began to diminish. These three also refuted the theory that only West Pointers could be effective brigade and division commanders; all three were graduates of excellent state military academies. Many of the West Pointers were veterans of the old army and had held comfortable, risk free, United States Army positions. Initially, the Confederacy expected these men to provide military leadership, but Seven Pines found more effective performers among other, younger officers.

As Lee assumed command, the performers were rewarded, and those who did not measure up began to disappear. Joel Cook, a correspondent for the *Philadelphia Press* considered the misdirected shell that struck Johnston as the

> saddest shot fired during the war. It changed tactics. It took away incompetence, indecision, and dissatisfaction and gave skillful generalship, excellent plans, and good discipline.[57]

While Cook's statement referred to Lee's personal characteristics, it may well have also encompassed his utilization of the skills of his young officers. His ability to avoid Davis's political appointees tactfully and quietly while removing the incompetent allowed the development of the young leaders who, under Lee's guidance, changed the Army of Northern Virginia into a fearsome opponent.

Chapter 6

Seven Bloody Days

When Robert Edward Lee took command of the Confederate armies scattered around Richmond he was neither well known nor particularly highly respected. The 55-year-old Lee, a handsome Virginian of impeccable lineage and the son of "Light Horse" Harry Lee of Revolutionary War cavalry fame, was married to a descendant of the nation's first president, George Washington.[1] He was a graduate of the United States Military Academy, had returned there as superintendent, and was a 30-year veteran of United States Army service, having first gained fame as a young officer on the staff of General Winfield Scott in the war with Mexico. Since that conflict, his experiences had primarily involved engineering duties at important army posts such as St. Louis, New York, and Savannah. When the Southern states seceded, Lieutenant Colonel Lee was acting commander of the 2nd United States Cavalry stationed in Texas. Lee was extremely popular among his peers and acquaintances and also greatly admired by his old army commander, Scott, who offered Lee command of the Union army as the nation prepared for the rapidly approaching internal conflict.[2] Lee agonized at length but ultimately resigned from the United States Army to wield his sword in defense of his native state.

Since entering Confederate service, Lee's performance had been less than auspicious. His initial combat experience in the mountains of western Virginia versus Federal Major General William S. Rosecrans was a near disaster.[3] Lee was next dispatched to the South Carolina-Georgia Coast to plan and develop defensive strategies for containment of Federal forces that had occupied the coastal islands. Here Lee was quite successful in forestalling further advances and naval raids from these threatening island bases by a skillful technique of using interior railway lines advantageously. He was then ordered to report to Richmond as military advisor to President Jefferson Davis. While he surely preferred a combat assignment, Lee became quite adept in assisting the Confederate president. Tactful and diplomatic by nature, he quickly understood and gained the trust of the Confederate chief executive.[4] In addition, this assignment gave him an opportunity to observe and evaluate the performance of many of those officers in responsible Confederate command positions. He also became well informed on the disposition of men and materials throughout the Confederacy, information that would prove invaluable in the near future.

Initially, there was little reaction to Lee's appointment. The soldiers were fond of Joe Johnston, and Lee's reputation foretold no signs of greatness. His first orders to the army concerned the erection of entrenchments. He wanted earthworks, trenches, and gun emplacements constructed in a huge arc about the capital; strong lines that could be held by reduced forces, thus providing manpower for his offensive schemes. And he expected the soldiers themselves to do the digging, not to employ slaves to carry out the backbreaking task. Grumblers began to call Lee the "King of Spades."[5]

Some of the army's officers were misled by their new commander's serene, calm nature. While they appreciated his courteous and gentlemanly demeanor, they doubted that he possessed the necessary aggression to lead an army. Several days after Lee assumed command a number of Confederate officers expressed these views to Colonel Joseph Ives, who had served on Lee's staff in South Carolina. Major Edward Porter Alexander questioned the erection of such extensive fortifications and queried Ives as to whether Lee had the audacity to command an army. Would he be aggressive enough to run the risks and take the necessary chances to achieve success for Southern armies? Ives replied in a prophetical, stern voice:

> Alexander, if there is one man in either army, Confederate or Union, head and shoulders above every other in audacity, it is General Lee. His name might be audacity. He will take more desperate chances, and take them quicker than any other general North or South and you will live to see it, too.[6]

Lee's winsome personality and consistent daily managerial skills were so governed by his tremendous self-control that it was difficult for others to see him as a warrior. Even his principal opponent, General George McClellan, was disdainful of Lee's ability. On learning that Lee was in command, McClellan wrote a letter to President Lincoln in which he stated:

> I prefer Lee to Johnston....the former is too cautious and weak under grave responsibility....personally brave and energetic to a fault, he yet is wanting in moral firmness when pressed by heavy responsibility and is likely to be timid and irresolute in action.[7]

The basis of McClellan's evaluation is not known. The information he used to make such an unqualified statement possibly resulted from his old army contacts, but his assumptions cast doubts on his own later decisions. No appraisal could be more untrue or more reflect the appraiser's skill. A kind, gentle Christian, Lee, who expressed his concern for enemy wounded while in camp, could change dramatically when battle ensued. It was then that his eyes would flash with an almost angry light, and his unshakable self-confidence and indomitable will would quietly send legions to die to defeat an enemy. An

English observer, Francis Lawley, remembered Lee as two different people, one when in battle and another in camp. Lawley was almost frightened by Lee in the Wilderness when he came upon him and witnessed "the light of battle still flaming in his eyes."[8]

Suddenly, changes began to occur within the Confederate army. Supplies and equipment arrived on schedule, while favoritism in promotions and assignments disappeared. Officers were expected to be on duty and enforce discipline, and as a result, drunkenness and absenteeism were reduced. Alone, or with a single staff officer, Lee appeared on horseback daily, riding the lines and trenches.[9] Soldiers unaccustomed to a glimpse of their commander began to cheer when he appeared. Attention to detail improved at all levels, and subordinates began to appreciate the improved organization and communication.[10] The army may not have been certain as to what kind of fighter their new commander would prove to be, but it was immediately apparent that he was a master administrator and daily demonstrated his concern for the welfare of his soldiers. In just a few short weeks, the army changed markedly. Lee was in command.

One of Lee's early tasks was to consolidate and increase the army's size by bringing available soldiers to the capital from various points of the Confederacy. By adding brigades previously idle in North Carolina and Southside Virginia, he increased the number of all arms to about 67,000 men. When reinforced by Major General Thomas J. Jackson's Valley Army, fully 85,000 Confederates would face McClellan.[11] Lee the engineer clearly understood McClellan's approach to gaining the Confederate capital. The Federal commander intended to advance on Richmond post-by-post, moving forward when possible, fortifying his post, and awaiting attack. If no onslaught occurred, he would search for another opportunity to advance. Lee knew the roads were drying and would soon support

McClellan's heavy siege artillery. When these guns moved close enough, Richmond was doomed.

The Confederate commander dispatched his cavalry chief, Major General James Ewell Brown Stuart, with a select cavalry force on a reconnaissance toward White House Landing, testing Federal strength northeast of Richmond. Stuart rode northward probing Union lines and supply routes. Stirring up considerable pursuit, he brazenly decided to return by riding completely around McClellan's army. This spectacular feat accomplished, Stuart arrived in Lee's camp from the James River Road.[12] The flamboyant cavalryman gained much acclaim for his bold adventure, pleasing his vain nature, but Lee's purpose was also achieved. He ascertained two important pieces of information: first, that McClellan's supply base was still at White House Landing on the York River, and secondly, that only the Federal V Corps was north of the Chickahominy River and in a position to protect the road from White House.[13]

Meanwhile, Jackson's small army was marching and fighting its way to victory in the Shenandoah Valley. Lee decided to reinforce Jackson temporarily, affording him further opportunity, perhaps even offering the threat of an invasion of Maryland. Alexander Lawton's newly arrived Georgia brigade was moved via Lynchburg to the Valley with two brigades of Whiting's division soon to follow.[14] Jackson responded by conducting a brilliant campaign, defeating three Federal forces, and so threatening the opposing capital that reinforcement of McClellan's army ceased. Jackson then quietly slipped away and moved to join Lee north of Richmond.

The decision was made. Lee would turn the Federal right by assaulting the somewhat isolated V Corps, threatening the Union supply line, and forcing McClellan to leave his entrenchments and offer battle on open ground. Those critics of Lee who wondered if he would fight should instead have pondered as to just how and when Lee would attempt to force his will on his opponent. Lee would use four divisions: Jackson with his nine brigades would approach on the Union right; D. H. Hill with five brigades and Ambrose P. Hill with six would attack the center; and Longstreet's six brigades would move on the enemy's left.[15] Magruder and Huger's troops were to hold the newly constructed defensive lines south of the Chickahominy against substantial Union numbers. Both were somewhat nervous over their role, but Lee knew McClellan, and he felt there was little chance of a significant enemy move in that area.

On July 25, 1862, the Seven Days' Battle about Richmond began. The period was marked by three days of intense fighting, a day of relative quiet, then three more days of horrible conflict. The scope and fierceness of fighting was beyond the comprehension of most of the participants. The idealistic view of war as man's opportunity for glory and fame would disappear in the artillery blasts and rifle volleys exchanged along hot, steamy Chickahominy bottoms. After the Seven Days, both armies, as well as both nations, would face the reality of a lengthy, brutal, bloody conflict. Both Federal and Confederate armies were virtually untried before the Seven Days. Made up chiefly of volunteers, the armies represented patriots of their respective causes. But after thousands of these young men perished and thousands more were disfigured, the naiveté disappeared, and both could be deemed as professional armies. Sadly, the cream of the nation's volunteer youth died or grew wise to the horrors of war during seven summer days in 1862.

Oak Grove

Early on the morning of June 25 the thunder of cannon fire could be heard from the vicinity of the old Seven Pines Battlefield. With Lee planning an attack on the Federal right flank on the 26th he must have wondered if McClellan had anticipated his assault and was launching a spoiling attack directly where Lee was most vulnerable. From the rebuilt redoubts along Casey's old lines General Joseph Hooker sent two of his brigades, those of Brigadier General Daniel E. Sickles and Brigadier General Cuvier Grover, alongside Brigadier General John C. Robinson's brigade of Philip Kearny's division, straight west down the Williamsburg Road, blue-clad skirmishers forward. Their objective was a slight rise alongside the road marked by a grove of oak trees and occupied by Confederate pickets. McClellan had decided that the grove would be an excellent site for his siege guns.

Advancing astride the road Grover's brigade forged ahead, driving Confederate pickets. The two accompanying brigades were slowed in their advance by swamps and dense underbrush. As Grover's men reached the grove they struck a hornet's nest of opposition. Brigadier General Ambrose R. Wright's brigade of Huger's Confederate division suddenly counterattacked.[16] A brisk firefight developed, with neither side willing to yield. Since Wright's men were among those ridiculed by their comrades for nonparticipation at Seven Pines they had something to prove. Reinforcements arrived for both participants, and the conflict swelled in intensity.

The 25th North Carolina of Colonel Henry M. Rutledge, a newly arrived regiment in action for the first time, came up on the run to support Wright. As the dense smoke cleared they found themselves face-to-face with a Union regiment. The 71st New York under Colonel Thomas B. Hall was equally green and just as eager. Both regiments presented action fronts preparing to fire. The Carolinians fired first, a perfect volley, and the New Yorkers broke and ran.[17] Whenever two untried regiments met, the first to pull trigger was usually the winner. Some members of the 25th recalled that volley as the best the regiment delivered during the entire war. This encounter was typical of the day's action fought by numerous rookie regiments in each army. The action ebbed and flowed as the men charged forward eagerly, fought hard for a few minutes, and then often sprinted for the rear.

Hooker reported he was meeting tough opposition and asked for support. But strangely, about 10:30 a.m. McClellan sent word for all Union troops to return to their redoubts. A lull occurred until after noon when McClellan rode to the front. After considerable consultation he ordered the attack renewed. Blue-coated lines again moved forward over the same ground, soldiers attempting to avoid stepping on the untreated wounded. A second untried Confederate brigade, the men of Brigadier General Robert Ransom, Jr., disputed this Union advance. The engagement again disintegrated into fierce little battles between regiments or even companies. These rookie fighters in both armies were willing, even eager, but seemingly could not be controlled by their equally inexperienced officers. Lee, concerned over the use of so many green soldiers, approached the front in late afternoon. After observing for some time, he commented that for the most part the men fought better than their officers.[18] Confused clashes between units occurred until well after dark. Volleys were fired in the dark, often striking friendly troops. Colonel Alexander Hays of the 63rd Pennsylvania reported taking heavy casualties from nearby Union regiments.[19] Several Southern units penetrated too far forward and had to fight their way back to friendly lines. The struggle eventually sputtered out in the dark. McClellan was satisfied.[20] He had gained the desired grove of trees. It was a continuation of his post-to-post advance. Lee was probably reassured that a general assault was not in McClellan's plans. For about six hundred yards of ground, Union casualties were 625 and Confederate losses 441.[21] The first day of seven had concluded with more than one thousand casualties and no appreciable results.

Mechanicsville

Undaunted by McClellan's attack, Lee's offense would proceed as scheduled. If he could coordinate a successful onslaught by his four divisions on the Federal V Corps, he could then continue his drive onto the Federal supply line. The enemy position was an extremely strong one. The V Corps was entrenched not at Mechanicsville, but at Beaver Dam Creek, east of the village. During early June the Union army, like their Confederate adversary, had labored to construct extensive trench lines, redoubts, and artillery emplacements. At Beaver Dam Creek these elaborate preparations produced stout lines ably assisted by strong geographic features. The swampy creek was wide, waist-deep, and its banks rose steeply on the Union side. Artillery was sighted to fire directly into advancing soldiers or to either flank. Confederates would be forced to advance across open ground, wade through the swamp, scale a steep bank and assault strong entrenchments.[22] Brigadier General Fitz-John Porter, one of McClellan's favorite officers, commanded the V Corps.[23] Porter's corps of three divisions was strengthened by the addition of some 20 artillery batteries and a reserve infantry division.

Lee was aware of the strength of Porter's position and did not plan a direct frontal attack. Instead, he envisioned a turning movement against Porter's right flank, which would force the corps commander out of his strong entrenchments. Jackson's division, approaching Richmond from the north, was to move down on the Union right flank by 9:00 a.m. When this pressure began to disrupt Federal lines, A. P. Hill was to assault the Beaver Dam Creek lines, rapidly supported by D. H. Hill and Longstreet. Confederate soldiers were awake and preparing breakfast by 3:00 a.m., and as eight o'clock neared, all gray-clad divisions save Jackson's were in place.[24] The morning slowly passed as the army awaited Jackson, but Stonewall never appeared. For a variety of reasons, never properly explained, Jackson's men started late, moved slowly, became lost using incorrect maps, and then halted and made camp. Jackson seemed lethargic and unaware that his advance was the key to the day's action.[25]

About 3:00 p.m., A. P. Hill took matters into his own hands.[26] Without orders, he impetuously crossed his brigades over the river, dressed his lines and advanced through Mechanicsville. Accurate Federal artillery fire began to punish his lines, and Hill threw his three-brigade front at the unreconnoitered Union trenches. The result was disaster. Union Brigadier General George A. McCall had emplaced his division of Pennsylvania reserves in an excellent position above the creek, and they easily repulsed Hill, inflicting almost 500 casualties. A fourth brigade under Brigadier General Dorsey Pender tried to flank the Pennsylvanians assisted by Brigadier General Roswell S. Ripley's brigade of D. H. Hill's division, but they were even more abruptly repulsed. Confederate losses were near 1,475 men and still they did not dent Porter's line. Federal losses totaled around 400.[27]

Longstreet's division, including the South Carolina brigade under Colonel Jenkins, waited anxiously in the woods south of the river. About dusk Longstreet ordered Jenkins to move his men across the stream and take position opposite the Union works. Jenkins went forward in the darkness crawling near the stream to study the Union position. He was extremely concerned about attacking the forbidding trench line and he feared heavy losses.[28]

Despite good plans and the eagerness of the soldiers to fight, another Confederate offense had fallen apart. Mechanicsville seemed to be a stunning Confederate tactical defeat, but it was a defeat that by morning had become a strategic victory. During the early hours of darkness, McClellan, worried by the specter of Jackson somewhere in the woods on his right, decided that Porter must withdraw. At 3:00 a.m., he ordered the V Corps to give up the Beaver Dam Creek line and fall back closer to the Chickahominy River Bridges.[29] Porter smartly executed these orders and retreated six miles, forming a semicircular line about the valuable bridges. He was again in a strong geographic position, but without the advantage of prepared earthworks.

Lee had been checked initially. His plans had been executed only a little better than those of Johnston at Seven Pines, but he had gained the initiative when McClellan retreated, and he would not relent. Unbeknownst to Lee, when the Union commander determined to withdraw, he had also decided to abandon his supply base at White House. He thus conceded his ability to keep Lee off his supply lines and actually surrendered whatever opportunity he had to capture the Confederate capital.[30] The celebrated "change of base" was in reality a decision to end the Union campaign by withdrawing. McClellan's primary objective now became that of saving his army.

Gaines's Mill

Shortly after sunrise on June 27, Hill's gray-clad skirmishers cautiously approached the Beaver Dam Creek positions. To their surprise, the trenches were empty. Porter's V Corps had skillfully and quietly withdrawn during the night. Federal engineers had laid out new defense lines on the farm of Dr. Gaines, a local civic leader and ardent secessionist.[31] This second Federal position was in reality a bridgehead north of the Chickahominy, held by Porter's tired soldiers who were all in place by dawn.

Lee's objective for the 27th did not change: to press down hard on the Union right, exposing the primary Federal supply line. He could not know or believe that after one battle, which McClellan seemingly had won, the Union chief would abandon the campaign. Porter and his strongly reinforced corps were to hold Lee north of the river until McClellan could reorganize and begin his retrograde move back to the James.[32] McClellan was not concerned with the loss of his large inventories at White House; his siege guns were already on transports, and the mountains of ammunition and supplies were soon set ablaze. His resources were boundless, and he requested replacements be conveyed to his James River base.

Thus the 39-year-old Porter, McClellan's most dependable corps commander, was to hold for a day at Gaines's Mill. He was then to cross and burn the Chickahominy bridges and follow the retreating Union army south. The Gaines's Mill position was almost as strong as the previous trenches at Beaver Dam Creek. Again, the Federals were on elevated ground, with a swamp called Boatswain's Creek to their front. Attackers would be forced to cross open terrain, ford the swamp, and dash uphill to the assault. Three lines of temporary breastworks were erected on the plateau such that all three could fire at attackers, and 96 guns were emplaced along the lines.[33] In addition, McClellan's heavy guns across the Chickahominy could enfilade any attack on the Federal left. Confederate gunner Porter Alexander, who viewed Beaver Dam Creek as impenetrable, thought Gaines's Mill almost as strong.[34] Brigadier General Henry W. Slocum brought his division of the Federal VI Corps across the bridges to serve as Porter's reserve.

Confederates swarmed over the Beaver Dam trenches searching for abandoned equipment and picking up prisoners left behind in the hasty withdrawal. Soon they began to advance toward Porter. Longstreet's division moved down the Chickahominy while D. H. Hill swung north, searching for the Union right. A. P. Hill's men followed the trail of the V Corps and Jackson's awaited division was to fill between the two Hills. A South Carolina brigade under the energetic bachelor Brigadier General Maxey Gregg led A. P. Hill's advance.[35] Gregg's men were untried but eager. Shortly after midday, Gregg encountered a strong Federal skirmish line. Shaking out his regiments into battle line, he drove the enemy rapidly back. He arrived at the edge of a swamp and began to cross, when heavy enemy rifle and artillery fire halted his momentum. Wisely, Gregg stabilized his line, had his men lie down, and sent for Powell Hill. He had found the enemy.

Hill arrived and immediately began to prepare for an attack. Though not always careful, Hill was ever the aggressor. About 2:30 p.m. Hill's units moved forward, straight into a maelstrom of fire. So many Federal guns were firing on Hill's men that Union infantry officers complained that smoke prevented their men from firing accurately. They were taking casualties from artillery shorts.[36] Only Gregg's excited rookies got across the swamp, and the 1st South Carolina Rifles of Colonel Foster Marshall initiated a wild charge against the Federal guns. They met head-on the flamboyantly dressed 5th New York Zouaves, whereupon a fierce hand-to-hand struggle ensued. Reserves ran to assist the Zouaves, and the 1st Rifles were forced to retreat. The South Carolina regiment, in its first action, lost 309 men—57 percent of its roster.[37] The New Yorkers also suffered heavy losses. Federal reinforcements continued to stage sharp counterattacks upon Hill's discouraged troops until Lee, fearing a serious reverse, ordered Longstreet to demonstrate on the left. When he did so, using Pickett's brigade, Longstreet soon realized it was a futile gesture. He judged the position so strong it could only be carried by an all-out effort by all the Southern divisions. The terrain faced by Longstreet's men was the most imposing on the battle line. His troops faced a quarter-mile advance across open fields bisected by two streams, a line of sharpshooters, the swamp, and a hill, into three lines of breastworks crowned by artillery. Additionally, since Longstreet was opposite the Federal left, his brigades would be exposed to the heavy batteries south of the river. In mid-afternoon, Longstreet began organizing his division for the assault, expected to begin with Jackson's arrival.

But where was Jackson? Again he was late. His brigades were lost for a second time and when they did arrive, they were widely scattered.[38] When Jackson's initial units came on the field, they were utilized to stabilize A. P. Hill's fought-out units in the center. Brigadier General Richard Taylor's Louisiana brigade, known as the Tigers, suffered heavy losses in support of Hill without appreciable results. Brigadier General William Whiting's small division of Jackson's command arrived and was placed in reserve. Lee decided he must attack again, but simultaneously on all fronts. D. H. Hill was making progress slowly on the Union right, Longstreet was prepared and in position on the Union left, and Lee would use Whiting's two brigades under Brigadier General John B. Hood and Colonel Evander M. Law to directly attack the center.[39]

By 7:00 p.m. all available forces were ready, and the order was given to advance. Soldiers were instructed to load their rifles but not to stop to fire. They were to simply push forward until they reached the enemy trenches, fire a volley, and go in with the bayonet. Brigadier General Richard Anderson was assigned command of a division of several brigades, including the South Carolina brigade led in by Colonel Micah Jenkins. Jenkins rapidly aligned his brigade, consisting of the 5th and 6th South Carolina regiments, the 2nd South Carolina Rifles, and the Palmetto Sharpshooters, under the cover of trees.[40] They would form the left-hand brigade of Longstreet's front and would join Hood and Laws in line after crossing the swamp. Since the Union position was curved in a long arc, Jenkins would initially advance at an angle to Hood and Law. In the center, Hood started forward. A moment later Longstreet's front emerged from the woods and began to advance. It was apparent this was a last-ditch attempt to carry the Federal position, as the hour was late and the sun was almost down.

As the South Carolinians moved across open fields at double-quick, heavy enfilade artillery fire began to disorder their ranks. Jenkins, riding in front, halted the brigade, dressed the lines, and changed step to parade movement.[41] With measured tread the brigade continued, brushing aside

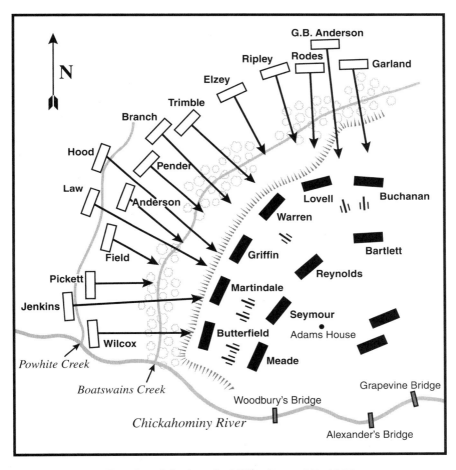

Battle of Gaines's Mill, June 27, 1862

About 7 p.m. the Confederate army, having been repulsed in previous attacks, launched a general assault on the Federal position atop the plateau at Turkey Hill. Jenkins's South Carolina brigade advanced from behind Powhite Creek, regrouped under cover of scrub brush at Boatswains Creek, then stormed uphill to unite with Law and Hood of Whiting's division to break the Federal line.

Federal skirmishers. Upon reaching the swamp they waded across, muskets held high. Enjoying some relief from Federal guns at the foot of the hill, Jenkins reassembled the men and led them into the open fields. The entire brigade then broke into double-quick and sprinted at the first Union trench line. Not a shot had been fired by the onrushing troops. As they approached within 15 paces, the enemy in the first line broke and ran, effectively masking fire from subsequent lines. The surging Confederate regiments halted on the parapet and delivered withering volleys into the fleeing Federals. Several Confederates reported the field so full of running Union soldiers that it was impossible to miss. Union soldiers fell in rows. Jenkins, on foot, waved them on, and they thundered into the second Union line on the heels of the panicked first-line defenders. Jenkins's left-hand regiment, the Palmetto Sharpshooters, was pinched out of action by the furious charge of

Hood and Law, which penetrated the Union center at almost the same moment. Jenkins was taking fire from several Union regiments on his right and decided to bring the Sharpshooters across the rear of his brigade to form a battle line facing the right flank. As he was attempting this maneuver, a regiment with closely furled flags approached.[42] Jenkins ran toward the advancing regiment and demanded "What Regiment?" Receiving no reply, he yelled, "Display your Flag!" The regiment turned to the front facing him. He immediately screamed, "Fire," to his

Marshalling his brigade in the tangled woodlands about Boatswains Creek, Jenkins led his men out into the open fields east of Gaines's Mill.

Photograph by Penny Swisher

Sharpshooters and threw himself full-length upon the ground. A sheet of flame burst from the Sharpshooters, and the entire front rank of the 16th Michigan went down. The Sharpshooters charged over Jenkins, and most of the Michigan regiment was captured. Shortly after dark, the regimental major and several dozen Michigan soldiers came out of the swamp and surrendered. The officer stated that since all his men had been killed or captured he wished to share their fate.[43] The colors of the 16th Michigan were captured and later presented by Jenkins to Governor Pickens of South Carolina, destined to hang in the state house in Columbia.[44]

Simultaneous with the breakthrough of Jenkins, Law, and Hood, a brigade of D. H. Hill's division under the indomitable Samuel Garland fought its way onto the Union right flank, and the entire Federal position began to crumble. Jenkins's brigade, intermingled with men of Law and Hood, raced for the Federal gun emplacements atop the hill. These artillery pieces had punished Confederate lines severely during the advance, and the Southern infantrymen did not easily forget. They shot down the Federal horses to prevent withdrawal and

Sweeping up the slope, Jenkins's brigade broke the line of Morell's Union brigade and captured the Federal guns arrayed along the crest.

Photograph by Penny Swisher

went into the batteries with bayonets. Confederate officers were forced to intervene, preventing the slaughter of Federal gunners.[45] As the soldiers regrouped among the captured guns, an unusual event unfolded which almost every soldier remembered above all other action on that bloody day. From approximately three hundred yards away, five companies of the 5th United States Cavalry led by Captain Charles J. Whiting launched a charge at the celebrating Confederate infantry. The Southern regiments closed ranks and opened deadly volley fire into the galloping riders. Fully a quarter of the cavalrymen were slain including six of seven officers, with the remainder driven rearward. The effect of the rifle volleys upon the horses was horrible to witness.[46] As Corporal Edmund Patterson of the 9th Alabama remembered, "We taught them a lesson, that when infantry are fighting they should keep out of the way."[47] Headlong cavalry charges against infantry in the European tradition were a revelation of past glory. The increased accuracy of the rifled musket doomed such attempts to costly failure.

Pursuit halted as darkness fell. Union soldiers struggled to reach the Chickahominy Bridges and protection of their heavy guns, which now fired indiscriminately upon the battlefield. Soon the night was alight with the fire of burning bridges, and as the gunfire ceased, the cries of the wounded could be heard.

Lee had achieved his victory, albeit at a heavy cost. The Union army suffered 6,837 casualties and lost 22 guns, but the total Confederate losses of 7,993 were higher. The number of Confederates killed and wounded was exorbitant, since they had assaulted fixed positions and also suffered heavily from the accurate fire of the superb Federal artillery. Captured Union soldiers numbered 3,000. Some Federal regiments, such as the 16th Michigan, were captured in their entirety due to the rapid collapse of the front, which isolated several units. A large percentage of the casualties in the South Carolina brigade were caused by Union artillery. Jenkins later wrote his wife that

> Artillery shells and canister so decimated our ranks, that I was unsure if enough of our gallant men remained to attain the initial enemy trench.[48]

June 28

The 28th of June dawned hot and hazy in the Chickahominy River bottoms. Federal wounded and stragglers were still being rounded up north of the river, but most units of the Union army had withdrawn southward. One of the most notable captives was Brigadier General John F. Reynolds, who had fallen asleep in what he believed a secure camp and was awakened by D. H. Hill's men exploring the battlefield.[49] Union equipment was scattered widely over the field. Rifles, knapsacks, blankets, canteens, and tents were in abundance and eagerly appropriated by the scavenging victors. Jenkins's letters to Carrie made use of United States Army stationery for the next six months.[50]

Confederate work details took over the distasteful task of burying the dead of both armies. While Union dead were buried in long unmarked trenches, Confederate casualties were identified whenever possible. The ladies of Richmond were again called upon to care for the long ambulance trains of wounded winding their way down the dusty roads. Federal wounded who escaped across the bridges crowded into a huge tent hospital at Savage's Station on the York River Railroad. But the transports at White House had departed, and as the Federal army moved southward, it became apparent that the wounded in the hospital would not be evacuated. Soon the roads behind the Union column were crowded with limping, gasping, wounded men. They gamely followed their retreating army until captured by advancing Confederates.

When McClellan ordered the Chickahominy Bridges burned, he effectively broke contact with Lee's pursuing Confederate soldiers. Lee was still anxious to fix upon "Little Mac's" intentions; not quite believing the Federal commander would give up his supply base so easily. Stuart was ordered to send a cavalry brigade, backed by an infantry brigade under Major General Richard Ewell, overland to the railroad, which he was then to follow to White House Landing.[51] When Stuart reached White House, the base was deserted and ablaze. Confederate horsemen salvaged oysters, ham, coffee, and fine Havana cigars to top an extraordinary meal.[52] It was thus apparent that McClellan had changed his base and was in fact retreating south to the James River.

Until Lee could get his four divisions across the Chickahominy and in pursuit, he had to rely on Magruder and Huger to impede the Federal retreat. He dispatched orders for these two officers to explore their fronts and attack the marching enemy if any opportunity was available. But both generals were hesitant, and the only action of the day occurred when Brigadier General Robert Toombs's brigade aggressively attacked and penetrated a Union screening force, only to be stopped by a Union "coffee mill" gun.[53] This was one of the few reported instances of successful employment of this early version of a machine gun.

Lee was anxious to pursue and punish McClellan. But he was surely aware that he could not expect much assistance from Magruder or Huger. He prepared his army for the next day's chase.

Savage's Station

The Confederate commander's puzzlement was clarified by Stuart's report that the Union army was committed to retreat to the James. Lee thus accepted the demise of his original plan to force McClellan into open combat without comment, but his disappointment was obvious and his commitment to pursue renewed. Longstreet with his division and A. P. Hill's hard-fought troops were sent southwest. They were to approach the capital and then advance east on the Darbytown Road, where it was hoped they would bisect the marching Union column. Their march was lengthy, and Lee could not expect them in action until the 30th. Jenkins's brigade marched early on the 29th, leading the long gray column. The sun rose hot and humid, and the soldiers toiled heavily on the dusty roads. But the cry to "close up" echoed up and down the column beneath the clouds of dust that towered skyward, marking their passage.

Meanwhile, what could be done today? Jackson, accompanied by D. H. Hill, attempted to ford the Chickahominy and follow the Federal army through Savage's Station, but was stymied by the burned bridges and so delayed that no contact occurred with the Federals. Magruder and Huger would have to slow McClellan's rapid southward movement in order for Lee to catch up. As usual, Huger started, stopped, and then withdrew. His orders were to join Jackson in attacking the Union rear guard. Since Jackson never appeared, Huger would not advance. Huger was so afraid of being wrong he did nothing, which in itself was the greatest error he could have made. Magruder moved forward hesitantly, his leading brigade under Brigadier General Joseph B. Kershaw making contact with elements of two Union divisions under Brigadier General William B. Franklin and Brigadier General Edwin V. Sumner near Savage's Station.[54] Magruder also delayed, waited for Jackson, but at almost 5:00 p.m. reluctantly allowed Kershaw to advance. Kershaw had many unbloodied regiments in his command, including the 7th South Carolina of Colonel D. Wyatt Aiken, whose only prior experience with gunfire was a duel between two officers.[55] But if Magruder was nervous, Kershaw was not. He lunged aggressively forward, penetrating the Union line. Unsupported, he was forced to retire after dark in the midst of a tremendous thunderstorm.[56] As he drew back, Union forces followed, and confused action flashed in the night until after 10:00 p.m. One Federal regiment, the 5th Vermont, penetrated between two Confederate units but had the misfortune of confronting at close range a Confederate regiment armed with shotguns. Virtually useless in open field fighting, the shotguns loaded with buck and ball almost decimated the Vermont unit.[57] Venerable Federal General Sumner slept through the action and when awakened stated he would attack and end the rebellion tonight if he was reinforced.[58] The old general was eventually forced to leave the field by General Franklin.

Lee was keenly disappointed that the pursuit had shown no profit. He commented to Magruder, "I regret that you made so little progress in pursuit of the enemy."[59] This comment was akin to a severe reprimand when uttered by the soft-spoken Lee. It is probably fortunate that his comments to Huger were unrecorded. Lee's display of temper at these performances, while not unusual, was seldom so openly observed. Federal losses totaled nearly 1,000 and Southern casualties about 500.[60] The Union army continued its march after dark toward its next obstacle, White Oak Swamp.

Frayser's Farm

The last day of June 1862 was again hot and windless in the swamps. Soldiers of both armies gathered in the shade when possible, and the few springs of decent water attracted long lines. The Federal army, stripped of all but essential equipment, was across White Oak Swamp and marching hard for Harrison's Landing on the James. Federal transports were already at Harrison's with new supplies of food and ammunition. The various roads used by the bluecoats convened at or bottlenecked in a small village called Glendale. Lee recognized the importance of the Glendale crossroads and drove his divisions toward an attack on the strung-out Union army somewhere near that point. McClellan was outmaneuvered and overextended. His position was vulnerable, and Lee was relentless in his assertion that the Union general must be made to pay for his retreat. Porter Alexander later wrote:

> Of the few times we were within reach of military success so great that we might have hoped to end the war with our independence....June 30, 1862 was probably our best opportunity.[61]

Lee again was faced with the problem of coordinating several widely dispersed columns. He ordered Jackson and D. H. Hill to continue to follow the Union rear guard, attacking aggressively whenever possible. Huger, with his fresh brigades, was closer to Glendale than the other Confederate columns and was to push straight down the Charles City Road. Major General Theophilus Holmes was to lead a third column out the James River Road, moving onto Malvern Hill, the likely Federal objective. The hard-marching brigades of Longstreet and A. P. Hill had already reached the city limits and turned eastward out the Darbytown Road toward Glendale. Thus, Jackson was to attack the tail of the elongated Federal column and Holmes the head, while Huger and Longstreet were to attempt to sever the column at Glendale.

Jackson started briskly. His men pushed southward through Savage's Station picking up stragglers and discarded equipment. They took over the sprawling tent hospital with its three thousand unevacuated Federal wounded.[62] When he reached White Oak Swamp, Jackson sent a scouting party across and found the enemy arrayed in strength. Ever the artillerist, Jackson brought up his guns and attempted to drive the Union infantry back so he could cross. This stirred up a violent reply from Union gunners and Jackson's batteries were driven to cover. Both Brigadier General Wade Hampton and Colonel Thomas Munford discovered alternative crossings to either flank, and urged Stonewall to turn the Union troops. Strangely, Jackson seemed to give up and moved no further.[63]

Huger slowly probed down the Charles City Road. His leading brigade, that of the diminutive Brigadier General William Mahone, was delayed by Federal engineers who had felled large trees across the road. Mahone attempted to cut his way through, but became frustrated and began to construct a new parallel road. Huger arrived at the front and, deeming progress too slow, attempted to drive away the Union engineers with artillery. He ordered up two batteries and unlimbered them in the only clearing he could find. When they opened fire, Union response was immediate and violent. Federal guns seemed sighted on the clearing, and they drove Huger's batteries from the position. Huger then withdrew his infantry, settling for a methodical long-range duel with enemy artillery.[64]

Alongside the James River, Holmes was confidently advancing his division toward Malvern Hill. When he reached sight of the hill he observed Porter's V Corps arriving on the crest. Holmes decided that a brief barrage would drive the Federals from their position, and he quickly unlimbered his batteries and opened fire. He was unaware of the Union naval squadron anchored in the James behind Malvern Hill. These vessels opened with their huge shells, stunning Holmes's men. Some of his untried regiments fled headlong in terror. His weak efforts were defeated by artillery alone, with a net loss of three men killed.[65]

Thus, the three Confederate columns were at a standstill by mid-afternoon. Fully 50,000 soldiers had made no substantial contact with Union infantry and accomplished almost nothing.[66] The superbly handled Union artillery, coupled with indecision on the part of Confederate commanders, had halted all three columns. Lee must have recognized that his artillery, or the long arm of his army, would require considerable reorganization if it were to compete with Union counterparts in the future.

Longstreet's column was nearing Glendale by the Darbytown Road. General Lee and President Davis had met minutes before and were following the lead brigade, that of Micah Jenkins.[67] As Federal shells began to fall around the riders and musket balls whistled in the tree leaves, Lee ordered the president to the rear. A doubled line of Union pickets was encountered, and Longstreet ordered Jenkins to drive them back. Jenkins reinforced his skirmishers with the 6th South Carolina and chased the Federals back upon their main column.[68] Longstreet hesitated, awaiting news of Jackson or Huger. About 5:00 p.m., Lee and Longstreet could wait no longer and decided they must advance on the crossroads if progress were to occur before dark. Longstreet aligned three brigades, with Jenkins in the center, to attack straight up the turnpike. Jenkins was astride the road while Kemper's Virginia brigade was on his left in heavy woods and Brigadier General Cadmus M. Wilcox's Alabama brigade on the right in more open terrain. The Union artillery, aligned almost wheel-to-wheel, was advanced slightly in front of its infantry support, affording a clear field of fire. The Union infantry regiments could move forward when the Confederates closed. Jenkins rode forward, observed the attack route, and whispered to his aide, Lieutenant Jamison, "My God, my poor men."[69] There was no room for maneuver. The assault must be made straight into the guns. As the Union artillery was well positioned and supplied, when the gray lines emerged from the trees, red flags fluttering, the guns opened with a tremendous roar of shot and shell. Major Thomas's later recalled:

> Staggering like a ship against the wind they moved on....Unceasing was the storm of shot and shell, terrible was the cry of the file closers, "Close up, Close up," as by ones, twos, fives, and tens the gaps were made by direct

and enfiladed grape and shell....Thirteen times the color
bearer of the Palmetto Sharpshooters was shot down....
finally they reached the breastworks and lunged over,
Colonel Jenkins's horse falling dead on the works.[70]

The battery directly to their front was the 1st Pennsylvania
Light Artillery, and they were indeed stern soldiers.[71] The
artillerymen served their guns until Jenkins's brigade was in
the battery. Refusing to surrender, they resisted with spong-
ers and rammers. A vicious hand-to-hand melee ensued with
swords, bayonets, and rifle butts, and the brave Pennsylvanians eventually were overcome. As Jenkins's brigade over-
ran the battery, capturing the six 10-pound Parrott guns, they
faced an immediate counterattack from a Pennsylvania brigade spearheaded by the 9th Pennsylvania Volunteers. This
sudden shock drove the Carolinians from the battery. Refusing to admit defeat, Jenkins rallied his survivors 30 yards
away. Pacing up and down the line he waved his sword, whose
point had been carried away by a cannon ball, urging one more
attack. Jenkins later disclosed that as he looked his men in
the eyes he was not at all certain they would follow.[72] But

*Moving in echelon left from the Darbytown Road Jenkins's South
Carolinians emerged from the woods at Frayser's Farm and
charged directly into the guns aligned before McCall's Union
brigades.*

Photograph by Penny Swisher

follow they did, storming back into the battery and meeting the Pennsylvanians hand-to-hand.

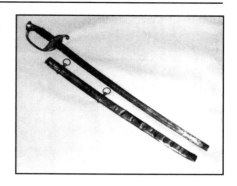

The fighting in and among the guns was as vicious as any experienced during the war. As the 9th Alabama approached on the right and added its weight to the fight, the Union troops were forced to give up the guns and flee. Confederate officers led by Lieutenant Jamison wheeled the captured guns about and fired into the backs of the flee-

Sword employed by Micah Jenkins at Frayser's Farm. The tips of both sword and scabbard were removed by a Union cannon ball while being worn by the colonel.

Courtesy of South Carolina Confederate Relic Room and Museum, Columbia

ing Federals. This caused some confusion in the second Union line, which was virtually backed onto the coveted crossroads. But the three attacking Confederate brigades did not have the strength to carry out another assault. The Palmetto Sharpshooters, already weakened at Gaines's Mill, carried 375 men into the attack and suffered 254 casualties—a 69 percent loss ratio.[73] The entire brigade lost 532 men out of 1,100 present for duty. Wilcox had suffered almost as severely. Kemper's brigade had advanced through the woods and, bursting forth with a yell, panicked the German Light Artillery, who fled without firing a shot. Yet despite Kemper's efforts, his brigade went out of control and sprinted after the fleeing Germans until abruptly halted by the Union second line. While suffering few casualties, Kemper's men were so disorganized that their irate commander was unable to reassemble his fighting unit.

The three brigades, despite sustaining heavy losses, had torn open the Union front, wrecking Brigadier General George A. McCall's division and capturing 26 guns.[74] The breach was

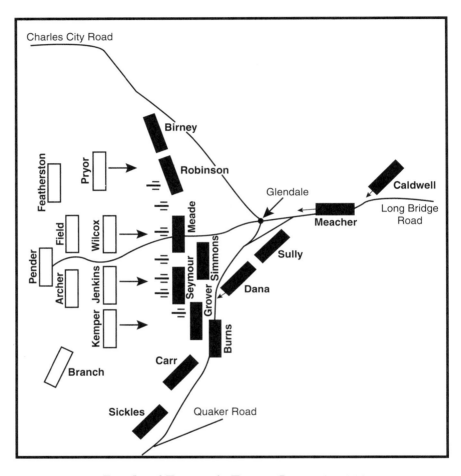

Battle of Frayser's Farm, June 30, 1862

At Frayser's Farm Confederate brigades attempted to sever Union lines reinforced by artillery that were protecting the Quaker Road. Had that artery been cut, the Union army would effectively been divided in two. Jenkins's South Carolina brigade charged across open fields, capturing a number of Federal guns, but were unable to take the road by which the Federals fell back to Malvern Hill.

narrow, and Federal pressure was rapidly building on each flank. Longstreet sent in two additional brigades to brace either flank and prepared to send his remaining two brigades through Jenkins and Wilcox to push for the crossroads. Philip Kearny's division was now holding the second Union line, reinforced by several brigades of Heintzelman's corps that had stolen away from Jackson's front. The Confederate brigades of Brigadier General Roger A. Pryor and Brigadier General Winfield S. Featherston stormed through the breach and fell on Kearny's line. Despite the odds they almost succeeded but were stubbornly forced back. Longstreet had no further resources and Kearny's troops held their invaluable line, bloodied but intact. A collapse of Kearny's line would have isolated five Union divisions and probably resulted in their capture or destruction.

Darkness brought a halt to the action, leaving scores of wounded crying in the woods and fields. Micah Jenkins and two staff officers returned to the field after dark, searching for a friend. By torchlight they stumbled through the slain, seeking Lieutenant John Dozier Lee of Sumter, South Carolina. Lee, an 1861 Citadel graduate, was a favorite of Jenkins's, having been transferred from Company B of the Sharpshooters to the regimental staff. Fiery and excited he had grabbed the Palmetto Flag and led the second charge into the Union guns, taking a round shot that severed both legs. He bandaged one stump to arrest the bleeding but died before he could tie up the other. Jenkins finally found and removed the body of his 21-year-old friend.[75] Federal units continued to pass through the crossroads, and sometime after midnight Kearny withdrew, leaving his dead and wounded. An extremely disappointed Robert E. Lee curtly remarked, "Yes, he will get away because I cannot have my orders obeyed!"[76]

Jenkins's South Carolina brigade was a shell. Lieutenant John Jamison, Jenkins's brother-in-law, was shot through both lungs while loading the captured Union field guns and invalided for life.[77] F. W. Poe, a private from Greenville, South Carolina, was recognized for picking up the regimental colors after every member of the color guard was down and leading the charge back into the battery. Jenkins lamented the heavy loss of life and the steep casualties among officers.[78] Major Anderson was killed leading the Palmetto Sharpshooters, Captain John Kilpatrick assuming command of that regiment. So gallantly did Kilpatrick perform that Jenkins recommended him for regimental command. Jenkins's survival was almost miraculous. Captain Thomas J. Goree, of Longstreet's staff, wrote of Jenkins:

> His horse was hit twice, his saddle blanket and a coat tied behind the saddle hit more than a dozen times, his bridle reins cut by a ball, his sword hit three times and broken, and he was wounded three times by shell fragments.[79]

Jenkins attributed his survival to the protection of a merciful God and grieved that so many of his friends had been

Honors from the battle flag of Palmetto Sharpshooters. Such honors were attached to the flag or flagstaff as a record of the engagements in which the unit had fought.

Courtesy of South Carolina Confederate Relic Room and Museum, Columbia

slain.[80] The action around the guns was so severe that Federal General George McCall remarked after being captured:

> It was my fortune to witness one of the fiercest bayonet charges that ever occurred on this continent. I saw skulls smashed with musket butts and bayonet wounds given and taken....[81]

Battle flag of the 6th South Carolina, one of the original regiments in the brigade led first by Richard Anderson then Micah Jenkins.

Courtesy of South Carolina Confederate Relic Room and Museum, Columbia

General Franklin admitted to the perilous and extended condition of McClellan's strung-out army. Franklin's corps faced Jackson across White Oak Swamp, and after Jackson seemed inclined to sit still, he stripped his command to send troops to the hard-pressed Kearny. Feeling that those troops made the difference in preventing a total military disaster, Franklin stated:

> In fact it is likely that we should have suffered a major defeat on that day had General Jackson done what his great reputation seems to make it imperative that he should have done.[82]

At a cost of 3,673 fallen soldiers, Lee had inflicted 3,797 losses on the enemy, captured more than 30 cannon, and "almost" cut the Federal army in two. But his plans had again miscarried. McClellan had been vulnerable, but had escaped. What if Jackson had forcefully crossed White Oak Swamp? Why did Huger hesitate? It should have been a tremendous Southern victory. Nevertheless, the brigades that went in at Glendale could but be praised for a supreme effort. Their valor and sacrifice almost overcame the lethargic and ineffective leadership of the three other Confederate columns.

Malvern Hill

A harassed Union field army filed quietly away during the night and by morning was in position on Malvern Hill, pleased to be out of the swamps and on open ground. Malvern Hill is actually a plateau that rises about 130 feet above the James River. Its slope is not steep, but ascends gradually over a half-mile distance. Fitz-John Porter, the first Union officer to survey the position, considered it the best with which the Union army had been favored. He commented:

> It was elevated and protected on each flank by streams or swamps....the hill was flanked by ravines, enfiladed by our fire....Our infantry and artillery had a clear sweep of fire in all directions for several hundred yards....the land over which an attacking force must advance was almost entirely clear and generally cultivated.[83]

Lee pushed his commanders to pursue. Longstreet's division, greatly weakened by the previous day's action, was held in reserve. Jenkins and his surviving soldiers tended their wounded and buried their dead, listening to the awful roar of the ever-present Union artillery.

Jackson was among the first to arrive at the foot of Malvern Hill. Scanning the position and realizing its strength, he first tried to attack with artillery. Finding two hilltops almost as high as Malvern Hill, Jackson attempted to assemble grand batteries on each, which he hoped could overcome the Federal position. Confusion and poor coordination among the army's reserve artillery battalions resulted in 17 to 20 guns being placed in each battery when 50 or more were requested.[84] Union artillery was again the winner, turning on each grand battery in turn and wrecking the Confederate artillery units. The Southern batteries had some success in punishing Union infantry, which was arrayed in ranks on the hillside, but they were no match for their Union counterparts and soon abandoned the field. Union naval gunfire from beyond Malvern

Hill was loud but generally ineffective, with most of the shells crossing Confederate lines to explode in rear areas. A near miss on an ambulance driver far to the rear brought a decided response:

> You damn son of a bitch! You haint got no eye and would as soon hit an ambulance driver as anyone else.[85]

Confederate brigades pressed closely around the base of Malvern Hill, and presently a confusing order produced a series of unwanted and costly assaults. Lee was determined to advance on the hill only when and if his artillery could establish dominance over the Federal guns. Brigadier General Lewis A. Armistead commanded a brigade in the center of the Southern position in a sheltered ravine from which he could easily observe the Federal lines. He was ordered to advance if the Union lines were broken or wavered as a result of Confederate artillery fire. Colonel Robert Chilton, Lee's chief of staff, dispatched a confusing general order to the remaining officers. General D. H. Hill retained a copy, dated July 1, 1862, which read:

> General D.H. Hill:
> Batteries have been established to act upon the enemy's lines. If it is broken, as is probable, Armistead, who can witness the effect of the fire, has been ordered to charge with a yell. Do the same.
>
> R.H. Chilton, A.A.G.[86]

In effect, this placed the attack decision solely in the hands of an inexperienced officer, who did not know he was making such an important decision, since he did not receive a copy of Chilton's order. Armistead advanced a regiment to clear skirmishers from a ravine in his front, and he was shocked when Mahone's men thundered by, screaming their rebel yell. A series of uncoordinated assaults were thus launched into the fierce artillery fire with little results save lengthened casualty lists.

The aggressive Samuel Garland, along with Rodes's tired men led by a fiery colonel named John Gordon did reach and get into the Federal guns, but were driven out by Union reinforcements. Frustrated Confederates lay down on the slopes of Malvern Hill until darkness brought a respite from the whistle of Union shells.

The Confederate army absorbed another 5,650 casualties at Malvern Hill compared to Union losses of around 3,000—a bitter defeat dominated again by excellent guns.[87] But when morning came, McClellan was again gone. He had moved his angry soldiers from their threatening position down to Harrison's Landing. There, in the unhealthy lowlands by the river, they were protected by gunboats but were in effect bottled up. If further action were to occur, the Federal army would have to initiate movements against strong Confederate positions. McClellan had saved his army, but now placed them in checkmate, a position from which they could be controlled by a handful of Confederates.

The Seven Days' Conclusion

A week of nearly constant marching and fighting was over. The ferocity of the fighting shocked even the most hardened of men. J. W. Reid wrote to his wife on June 29, "Each day is an echo of the one preceding it. Death and destruction are on all sides and there is no cessation of hostilities. We march and sleep on our arms at night...."[88] A second letter said simply, "The greatest battle of the age is over, and I am spared to write you."[89]

When Lee took command of the Confederate army, McClellan was almost inside the Confederate capital. When the Seven Days' Battles were concluded, the Union army was huddled under the protection of its navy on a bridgehead by the James River. Despite a horrific loss of many of its best and bravest, a strategic victory of great magnitude had been presented to the Confederate nation. Johnston and McClellan had jockeyed for days and weeks seeking an advantage; when Lee took command, the game changed. The huge destructive forces amassed by each government would now be used. Lee fought! Sometimes repulsed, often disappointed, he kept coming, his iron will fixed on predetermined objectives. Richmond natives hailed Lee as their city's savior, but he was personally disappointed. He felt the Union army had been within his grasp and should have been destroyed. But McClellan had survived.

The rank and file of the Union army emerged from the Seven Days with much to be proud of. In almost every instance the soldiers in blue had fought hard and well. Union artillery was superb and had actually saved the army on numerous occasions.

Lee's planning was exceptional, but execution of those plans remained generally abysmal. Subordinates were late, hesitant, and often confused. Staff work at all levels was poor, especially ineffective from Lee's headquarters. Confederate artillery, though bravely fought, was poorly organized and often mismanaged. As their Union counterpart, Confederate infantrymen demonstrated a tremendous ability and courage to extend every effort toward victory. Their willingness to assault gun batteries was amazing. While Lee endured the failure of subordinates with few comments, he analyzed and evaluated the performance of each. On July 3, Magruder requested a transfer and Lee promptly obliged. Soon Benjamin Huger was moved to the post of inspector of artillery. Whiting, Holmes, and others had held their last combat role with the army. Among the poor performers at divisional level, only Jackson escaped Lee's critical analysis.

Other officers who had reacted positively and demonstrated initiative were given more responsibility. A. P. Hill, though impetuous, willingly committed his troops to battle, and Lee liked a fighter. He was promoted to major general and assigned a divisional command. D. H. Hill, caustic and critical, led his division well. Longstreet had organized and managed his division well and was aggressive in combat. His steady, reliable performance led to his elevation to wing commander.

Even more promising was the leadership of many brigade and regimental officers. R. H. Anderson had met all expectations and was promoted to division command. John Hood, Evander Law, Samuel Garland, Robert Rodes, Dorsey Pender, and Micah Jenkins had been closely observed by Lee and were marked for higher rank. On July 22, Jenkins was promoted to brigadier general and assigned permanent command of the South Carolina brigade he had led since Gaines's Mill. Lee presented Jenkins's name to the president with the following statement:

> Colonel Jenkins has repeatedly been recommended for promotion by officers with which he has served and his conduct at Seven Pines was worthy of all commendation. He has also, in the recent battles, shown great skill.[90]

Lee desired that Jenkins's commission be dated from the action at Seven Pines, but it was issued from July 22. Jenkins had well demonstrated his ability to command a brigade. In every action in which he was engaged and often despite difficult circumstances, he executed the orders sent him, kept his soldiers well organized and under control, and showed a remarkable ability to remain cool under pressure. At Williamsburg he stoutly defended Fort Magruder, and his spoiling attacks completely disrupted the Union offense. At Seven Pines he was daring and resourceful, demonstrating his initiative in maximizing the disruptive effects of his small force behind enemy lines. At Gaines's Mill and Frayser's Farm he demonstrated the leadership qualities that inspired men to follow him straight into tremendous fire. He consistently showed the perseverance needed to pursue a task to completion.

Jenkins's principal fault to this point seems to be bravery under fire to the point of rashness. A common characteristic in an army led from the front and effective in inspiring men, this trait would prove expensive, perhaps ultimately fatal, to the army.

Colonel Micah Jenkins
Circa 1862

Chapter 7
From Manassas to the Blackwater

As Micah Jenkins affixed the three stars and wreath of a brigadier general to his lapel, the Confederate army was undergoing an extensive reorganization. Major General Benjamin Huger had been transferred; his division reassigned to newly promoted Major General Richard H. Anderson. Micah Jenkins thus succeeded to official command of Anderson's South Carolinians, the unit that he actually had led through much of the Seven Days' fighting. The now-veteran unit had suffered heavily at Gaines's Mill and Frayser's Farm and was sorely in need of replacements, as were most Confederate units. But there was little time for recruiting as Lee was planning a new and daring offense. The 1st South Carolina Volunteers and the 2nd South Carolina Rifles, two untested regiments, were summoned to Virginia from their home state and added to the brigade. The South Carolina unit then consisted of five and one-half regiments, although its total numbers hardly approached those of an 1861 four-regiment brigade.[1]

Jenkins's brigade was assigned to a newly created division containing the brigades of James Kemper and George Pickett and temporarily commanded by Kemper since Major General Pickett was still incapacitated from his wounds.[2] The division was placed in Longstreet's I Corps in Lee's new organizational pattern, which divided the army into two corps.

114

Lee temporarily dispatched Thomas J. Jackson's II Corps northward to screen Major General John Pope's consolidated Federal army in northern Virginia. The I Corps remained in the Richmond area to contain McClellan's army, still encamped at Harrison's Landing. When it became apparent that McClellan's isolated position precluded offensive action, and that his troops were rapidly being transferred via ship to Pope, Lee started Longstreet's corps moving northward. The new Confederate commander was determined to force Pope out of Virginia before a substantial portion of McClellan's troops could reinforce the bombastic Federal officer.

John Pope had inherited the remnants of three small Federal armies, each soundly defeated by Jackson in his famous spring campaign in the Shenandoah Valley. Pope organized these 51,000 men into three infantry corps, which he proudly entitled the Army of Virginia. He issued a series of confident, imperious general orders which virtually authorized looting and burning of private homes; and Lee was particularly anxious to rid the state of the braggart.[3] On August 15 Lee arrived in the small, quiet village of Gordonsville, Virginia, uniting with his two corps commanders in a discussion of how best to deal with Pope. The Federal commander had pulled his forces behind the line of the Rappahannock River into a stout defensive posture. Lee decided to flank Pope and cause him to retreat, perhaps attacking him en route.

He dispatched Jackson around Pope's right with the intent of gaining the Federal rear astride the enemy's supply lines. Longstreet's still-arriving divisions would hold the Rappahannock line until Pope fell back, and subsequently march to join Jackson.

Early on the morning of August 25 Jackson awakened his three divisions and by 3:00 a.m. they were on the march northwest.[4] Twenty-four thousand Confederate soldiers disappeared with Jackson behind the Bull Run Mountains. They would reappear the following morning, swarming through

Thoroughfare Gap and out onto the plains of Manassas, where Pope's rail junctions and supply depots were located. In two hot August days Jackson's foot cavalry marched 51 miles and descended like locusts on Briscoe Station and Manassas Junction. Telegraph lines were severed, trains wrecked, and piles of Federal supplies captured and enjoyed by the weary Confederate soldiers.[5] The ever-vigilant Jackson attested that all liquor supplies were destroyed.[6] Pope reacted quickly to the appearance of a force in his rear. He sent a corps to block Thoroughfare Gap and dispatched others to search for Jackson, who had retired into the woods near Groveton. Federal troops marched in the night as bonfires and exploding ammunition trains lit up the summer sky.[7] The next day Pope found Jackson entrenched in wooded terrain behind an old unfinished railway cut. By late morning Major General Franz Sigel's I Corps and Heintzelman's III Corps were probing Jackson's position. Earlier Longstreet's men had forced Thoroughfare Gap and, drawn to the roar of Jackson's guns, marched hard to unite with their fellow Confederates. John Hood's division arrived first and took position on Jackson's right, slightly curved inward toward the Federals. By midday Longstreet's entire corps was in position, and Kemper's division, including Jenkins's brigade, was dressed on Hood's right with the division of Brigadier General David R. Jones extending to their right.[8]

Pope, under the impression that Longstreet had not arrived, frantically tried to break Jackson's line on the afternoon of August 29 and the morning of the 30th. Longstreet's primary assistance to his fellow corps commander was the massed enfilading artillery fire of Colonel Stephen D. Lee's reserve artillery battalion. These well-handled guns achieved murderous results on the Union assault troops. After a final strong Union onslaught was repulsed, Lee and Longstreet agreed to attack the Federal left with the I Corps.

Colonel Andrew Coward, Jenkins's partner at Kings Mountain, was serving as a division staff officer and on occasion was dispatched to position certain brigades. He attested that almost everyone felt a decisive action would take place that afternoon. As he proceeded with his duties, Coward recalled:

> Passing a short distance to the rear of Jenkins' Brigade I came upon Jenkins reclining on the slope of a hill. Colonel Thomas Glover and Adjutant Cato Seabrook were seated nearby....I noted that Jenkins was holding a small book with a finger inserted to mark the place....he replied to my inquiry, "We have been reading and commenting on Paul's soldier spirit in the prayer book....God grant that at the end, to God and country, each one of us may be able to say with Paul, I have fought a good fight, I have kept the faith,"....When night fell Glover and five other South Carolina colonels were dead, Seabrook was slowly dying, and Jenkins was having a severe wound dressed by surgeons.[9]

At 4:00 p.m. orders were dispatched, "prepare to advance." By the thousands men threw down their books, playing cards, and letters, answering the call to fall in.[10] Jenkins's South Carolinians had rested in the woods all day. They eagerly dressed their lines under their faded red Confederate battle flags and blue Palmetto banners. Hood's division would initiate the advance and be joined by the troops of Kemper and Jones. Kemper aligned Eppa Hunton, now commanding Kemper's old brigade, to join Hood's right, with Jenkins on Hunton's right. The third brigade, under Montgomery Corse, was to follow in reserve.

The terrain was hilly with scattered heavy woodlands, crossed by steep ravines and small streams. Several large, bare hills dominated the area, with Chinn Ridge, the largest, dominating the Union left. Hood's men encountered early resistance as they collided with a forgotten and misplaced Union brigade, while Kemper's parallel advance was initially unopposed. A soldier remembered the advance as a glorious affair with "the line keeping perfect time and the colors showing red against the sky. No cheering or music accompanied the lines and the only sound was the clinking of equipment and the sound of footfalls in unison."[11] As Hood's men met resistance, Hunton moved his line left to assist and Corse moved forward to fill the gap. Jenkins's soldiers struggled forward through dense underbrush.

Four Ohio regiments under Colonel Nathaniel McCleans, with some artillery support, were the lone Union defenders on Chinn Ridge. But sharp-eyed Federal staff officers recognized the danger, and two additional brigades under Brigadier General Zealous Tower and Colonel John W. Stiles were dispatched as reinforcements. The branch valley leading to Chinn Ridge was a formidable obstacle to the Confederates, being covered with briars and undergrowth, almost impenetrable in places. This natural obstruction disrupted the Confederate line of advance as officers were forced to search for routes to ascend to the ridge. As Hunton and then Corse moved to the left joining Hood, Jenkins swung right up a defile, seeking a way up on the Union left. Hood's Texas brigade collided and drove through a Federal unit mistakenly stationed near the Chinn farm. In this confused action, the 5th Texas of Colonel J. B. Robertson virtually destroyed the 5th New York Zouaves.[12] The unexpected appearance of the Texans charging out of the tree line resulted in 300 Zouave casualties of the 500 engaged, with more than 120 slain.[13] Hood's men, supported by Corse's brigade and Brigadier General Nathan G. Evans's independent South Carolina brigade, surged en masse onto Chinn Ridge and discovered McCleans's Federals stoutly entrenched behind a rail fence line. After sustaining a furious resistance, repulsing several attacks, McCleans's Ohio brigade began to unravel. Suddenly, Tower's fresh brigade, followed by Stiles, appeared and extended the Union line.

At about this same time Jenkins was struggling to get his men out of the underbrush in the steep defile on Chinn branch. Finally, they cleared the obstacles and formed on the ridge; Hunton's Virginians arriving and forming on their right. The two brigades stormed onto the flattened top of Chinn Ridge and rushed the reinforced Union fence line. Captain R. M. Stribling's Fauquier Artillery located a clear position and began to lob shells into the Union line. As Jenkins led his men forward over Hood's wounded and slain, the blue-clad defenders opened such a heavy fire that the 1st and 6th South Carolina were stopped cold. Rallying, the entire Confederate force pressed forward to within 40 yards of the fence and opened fire. Like heavyweights, the two lines exchanged fire along a front almost 500 yards long at point-blank range. Survivors of Hood's and Evans's units joined the attackers as regimental and brigade lines became mixed. Smoke hung low over the field, so the combatants often could not see one another but simply loaded and fired into the smoke. One of Jenkins's men later wrote:

> We shot into this mass as fast as we could load until our guns got so hot we had at times to wait for them to cool....This mass of Yankees was so near and so thick that every shot took effect.[14]

The Federals suffered heavily. A member of the 13th Massachusetts recalled: "our men fell like ten pins before an expert player."[15] Both armies continued to pour soldiers into the cauldron on Chinn Ridge. As Jenkins's mixed force slowly forced the stubborn Federals from the fence line, a pair of fresh Confederate brigades arrived. Colonel Henry Benning and Colonel George T. Anderson led their cheering men into the action and turned the Union retreat into a rapid exodus as the ridge was suddenly filled with fleeing bluecoats. Into the midst of

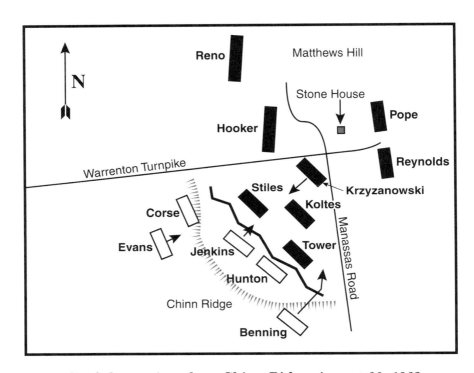

Confederate Attack on Chinn Ridge, August 30, 1862

In a late afternoon attack the Confederate divisions of Hood and Kemper overcame the frantic defense of Tower's, Stiles's, Koltes's, and Krzyzanowski's Union brigades. Despite high losses the Confederates broke the last resistance on the Federal left, assuring Union retreat from Manassas.

this confusion, Colonel John A. Koltes's fresh Union brigade arrived on the double. In a brave attempt to slow the Union retreat, Koltes ordered his men to charge directly at the exhausted South Carolinians. Volleys of rifle fire halted their advance, and when Koltes fell, Confederates closed about their flanks. Almost all the survivors were captured. Jenkins, already wounded in the arm, was hit again during this final exchange. His chest wound was at first thought to be fatal, but the ball turned as he was struck and continued down his arm, where it was removed from his elbow.[16]

As Jenkins was carried to the rear, Chinn Ridge was at last in Confederate hands. The cost was so high that the Confederate units which had carried the assault, were virtually incapable of further action. In Kemper's division, Corse had sustained 274 casualties, Hunton 234, and Jenkins 469. Hood lost 638 men and Law 324.[17] Federal losses were even greater, but the determined resistance of the stubborn blue infantry on Chinn Ridge gained the necessary time for Pope to partially reconsolidate his beaten army on Henry House Hill. Thus, the Union army was saved from total collapse and able to conduct an orderly retreat.

Losses among field-grade Confederate officers were unusually severe. Colonel John Glover, the outstanding commander of the 1st South Carolina, was mortally wounded. Young John Whilden, who had served Jenkins as a volunteer aide at 1st Manassas, was now a major in the 23rd South Carolina of Evans's brigade. Supporting Hood's attack, Whilden, by then in command of that regiment, picked up the regimental colors and charged directly into the enemy guns. He was shot five times and instantly slain.[18] While Jenkins lamented the loss of so many fine men, his personal grief was for the death of his adjutant, Major Cato Seabrook. Seabrook was a fellow native of Edisto Island, reared on an adjoining plantation. He was an outstanding teacher at Kings Mountain Military School, a close and dear friend, and had proved an exceptional adjutant.[19]

Jenkins's personal wounds were soon discovered to be less serious than first believed, and after initial treatment he was ordered home to recuperate. On September 6 he telegraphed Carrie that he was not dangerously injured and was on his way to Yorkville by train.[20] Colonel Joseph Walker of the Palmetto Sharpshooters took command of the thin ranks and led the brigade across the Potomac and into Maryland.

Jenkins's recuperation at commandant's quarters, Kings Mountain Military School, provided a much-needed respite. Experiencing little pain, he enjoyed the companionship of his wife and three boys: Micah, Robert, and William. He and Carrie traveled to visit Charleston on several occasions to purchase essentials and visit with old friends. On one trip, Jenkins encountered Andrew Coward at a wedding reception. The two men greeted each other warmly and discussed news of the war. Major Coward was temporarily without an assignment since he had served as an aide to General D. R. Jones, who became mortally ill and was forced to give up his command. Jones's division passed to another major general who, as was the custom, selected his own staff. Jenkins immediately recommended that Coward take command of the 5th South Carolina, presently without a colonel.[21] Both men were pleased at the opportunity to reestablish their close working relationship.

After almost six weeks' leave, Jenkins prepared to return to the army. In late October the Yorkville newspaper announced, "He looks and feels well, will do well and deserves the 'well done thou true and faithful servant' of his common country."[22]

Jenkins rejoined the brigade in November near Fredericksburg, Virginia, and found his command still attached to the division now commanded by Major General George Pickett. Jenkins's unit had again been bolstered by the addition of a newly arrived regiment, the Hampton Legion. The 4th South Carolina was so depleted that it was disbanded, and its remaining members incorporated into either the 1st, 5th, 6th, 2nd Rifles, or the Palmetto Sharpshooters.[23] The Hampton Legion was a unit of experienced infantrymen who were originally a part of Major General Wade Hampton's old combined arms force. General Hampton was now commanding a cavalry division. Recruiting had also increased the effective numbers, and by December the brigade totaled about 1,900 effectives.[24]

Jenkins's brigade, and in fact, Pickett's division, took little part in the battle of Fredericksburg. The bloody repulse of Burnside's Grand Army by the Army of Northern Virginia was so rapidly and easily accomplished that many Confederate units were not heavily engaged and many underestimated the ferocity of the battle. Pickett's units were assigned to a strong line of hills, so forbidding that a Federal attack was discouraged. By 2:00 p.m., when the assault on the Confederate right concluded and Union infantry began to advance on Maryes Hill, Longstreet directed Pickett to reinforce McLaw's division. Jenkins was dispatched by Pickett to assist Confederate infantry that was located in a sunken road behind a stone wall at the foot of Marye's Heights.[25] As they moved into position, Jenkins's soldiers sustained a few casualties from Union Artillery fire. Once Jenkins closed and could see the position, he realized the area behind the stone wall was already crammed with gray soldiers and that the Federal assault was, in fact, ebbing. He dispatched the Palmetto Sharpshooters to explore around the enemy flank, and some sharp skirmishing resulted before nightfall. Among the few casualties was a fatal wound sustained by Sergeant Major McKern of the Sharpshooters, a young man of talent from whom Jenkins expected much.[26] That night Jenkins sent Colonel Coward and the 5th South Carolina to relieve one of Kershaw's regiment in the sunken road.[27] A renewal of the Federal attack was expected at daybreak, so the Confederates gathered firearms and loaded spares until each man had four or five weapons. But sunrise revealed a field of Union dead and no resumption of enemy action. On the following day Jenkins sent troops into the city of Fredericksburg as ordered. He stated:

> Upon instruction of General Longstreet, I sent two companies of the 5th under Major Wylie of that regiment to scout the town, in doing which, being the first armed party to enter, they rendered certain the retreat of the enemy and captured some one hundred and fifty prisoners.[28]

General Jenkins was among the first officers to enter Fredericksburg after the Union evacuation. He was appalled at the wanton destruction resulting from artillery fire and widespread looting of private homes by Union soldiers. In a letter to Carrie he expressed thankfulness that she was remote from the ravages of war and added:

> I can well realize this fact after witnessing the pitiable condition of the people of Fredericksburg who have recently had their homes destroyed and are, many of them, now scared wanderers from their loved firesides, not knowing whether to turn. May God care for them and ever keep those I love from such a distress.[29]

By early December the brigade was established several miles outside the ruins of Fredericksburg. Whole forests disappeared as soldiers constructed log huts and searched for firewood. Despite extremely cold weather and scant rations, Jenkins reported his men warmly housed, healthy, and in great spirits. This was one of the few occasions in which the Confederate army established winter quarters with most of its divisions camped in close proximity. The soldiers enjoyed the social life. Frequent heavy snowfalls were a novelty to those from the lower South and snowball fights were a daily occurrence. Coward recalled one occasion when Jenkins called out his entire brigade and led them, flags flying and drums beating, to attack a nearby Georgia brigade.[30] Jenkins's industrious nature and desire to constantly improve his unit was not curtailed by the move to winter quarters. One innovation that he instituted was the establishment of examining boards before which all newly elected officers must appear before assuming their duties. If this board of review found the elected candidate unqualified for his assignment, the individual was returned to his previous rank and another election conducted.[31] This practice discouraged the election of officers based purely on popularity. Candidates began to prepare for the examination board review, and enlisted men began to view the elective process in a more serious manner. Soon many other brigades were using the examination board process.

The spirit of the army was high, as evidenced by an incident that occurred in the South Carolina brigade during Christmas week. A group of Palmetto Sharpshooters organized their own "provost" guard. Led by Private Earle Lewis, the "guard" donned stolen officers' uniforms complete with swords and sashes. They proceeded to the camps of two Virginia brigades, which reportedly had whiskey for sale. Stating that he was from Longstreet's staff, Lewis arrested the sellers and confiscated the whiskey. They released the prisoners and took the whiskey back to camp where the "guard" became roaring drunk. General Jenkins, when notified, ordered the brigade to fall in and proceeded to read a lengthy reprimand concerning drunken and disorderly conduct, while keeping the unit at attention in bitter cold and windy conditions.[32] One suspects that the actual culprits were never identified since the material evidence had surely disappeared.

On February 2, Jenkins again left for Yorkville to recruit replacements for his regiments.[33] Although he traveled about the state searching for recruits, he also enjoyed some time at home with his family. The large numbers of exempt men he discovered present in South Carolina discouraged and angered Jenkins.[34] While he and Carrie were at Kings Mountain the 6th Regimental Band, then home on furlough, appeared one evening and provided a concert for the young couple. Mrs. Jenkins hospitably received the fine musical group.[35]

In February Lee became concerned over reports of large numbers of Union troops being loaded on transports and shipped down the Potomac to Suffolk, Virginia. While Federals had possessed that city for some time, it was held with garrison troops, and no substantial strike force was available. Lee's army depended heavily on south side Virginia and eastern North Carolina for much of its hog and grain supplies.[36] A Union striking force in Suffolk or one of the North Carolina bridgeheads constituted a real threat to this supply source and must be countered. In February Longstreet was ordered to move two of his divisions to Richmond and prepare for action on the south side, from Richmond to the Cape Fear River in North Carolina. In addition to preventing movements from Suffolk, he must contain Federal garrisons at New Berne on the Neuse River and Washington, North Carolina.

Some Confederate units were already present in the area. Major General Samuel French commanded an undersized division near Suffolk, and Major General D. H. Hill had recently assumed command of the state of North Carolina and possessed several scattered brigades and cavalry units of unknown quality. In addition, Major General Chase Whiting was in charge of construction at Fort Fisher at the mouth of the Cape Fear River. This powerful fortress protected the important blockade-runners base in Wilmington, North Carolina. These commands and the divisions of Hood and Pickett were available to the I Corps commander to counter whatever Union threat might develop. Hill was already planning an attack on New Berne, and Longstreet dispatched some support, but the attempt was a half-hearted failure.

General Jenkins rejoined his brigade in Petersburg as they moved southward. The South Carolina brigade was soon transferred from Pickett's division to French's, as Longstreet attempted to strengthen that officer's weak force. French was

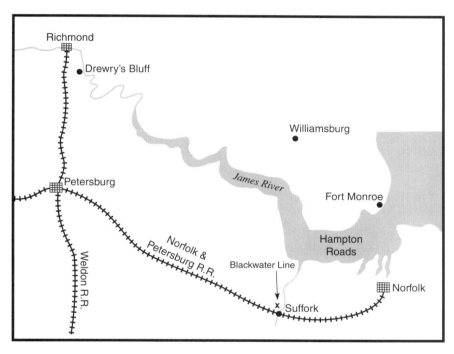

Southside Virginia

This area south of the James River was the scene of considerable maneuver in the spring of 1863. A Federal buildup was countered by Longstreet's brigades which attempted to prevent Union possession of this valuable supply area.

also in charge of artillery placement in the forts being constructed on the James River. Jenkins, as senior brigadier, was charged with divisional command when French was absent on his other duties.[37] Longstreet was aware of this and probably transferred Jenkins for that purpose, as he was somewhat concerned over French's ability.

Soon an incident occurred. Jenkins, acting in French's absence, ordered the other brigade commander, Brigadier General Joseph Davis, to move his earthwork lines to conform to those of the units on either side of his position. Davis, a nephew of Jefferson Davis, did not like the order and seemingly did not understand that whether he liked it or not he had no choice but to obey.[38] Davis had been an aide to his uncle and had recently assumed command of this outstanding brigade of Mississippians. He wrote a letter of protest to French's A.A.G., insinuating that he only took orders from the divisional commander. French attempted to handle the matter with tact. His reply assured Davis that both brigades were under his command, but that in his absence Jenkins as senior brigadier was acting as divisional commander and he must obey his orders.[39] Davis continued to argue and fume, but Longstreet declined to interfere or even address the charges.[40] There is little doubt that Davis carried his dissatisfaction to the president but he, likewise, did not officially respond. A seemingly unimportant incident, it was one which would have distinct repercussions for Micah Jenkins's army career.

Longstreet moved several divisions near Suffolk and entrenched them along the line of the Blackwater River. The Confederate right was amply protected by the Dismal Swamp, but the left flank rested on the James River and was vulnerable to raids and bombardment by the Union navy, which enjoyed total dominance of the waterways. Little action occurred, with the exception of demonstrations and artillery exchanges. The soldiers soon grew bored with life on the Blackwater line.

Nevertheless, if action was lacking, disputes between officers were not. A successful Federal waterborne attack on a Confederate fort produced charges and arguments. Colonel Hugh Connerly of the 55th North Carolina and General Law of Hood's division exchanged words over responsibility for Confederate errors. These statements led to a scheduled duel between staff officers of the two principals. The two duelists fired three shots apiece before listening to cooler heads.[41] Such actions exemplified the frustration of constant marching, countermarching, and preparing for actions that seemingly never occurred. Longstreet, in his initial experience at independent command, seemed hesitant, uncertain, and somewhat timid. His lack of direction allowed controversy to spark among the officers. In addition, the commander seemed reluctant to interfere in these disputes and allowed them to fester, rather than confronting the participants—forecasts of a weakness that would become gravely apparent in subsequent days.

Jenkins's boredom was relieved by a surprise visit from his wife. Caroline took advantage of a trip north by friends and accompanied them to the Blackwater. She returned after a few days, but Jenkins enjoyed showing her off to his brigade and, conversely, the brigade to Carrie.[42]

While returning from a meeting with Longstreet, Jenkins and a group of officers were crossing a large field. Colonel Coward became embroiled in a friendly argument with a staff officer from another brigade over the ability of various horses to jump a difficult fence line. Coward knew Jenkins's horse, Latta, was a spectacular jumper and he persuaded a reluctant Jenkins to allow him use of the animal to prove his point. Although successful, the jump proved so dangerous that Jenkins afterward approached Coward with tears in his eyes. He expressed to the colonel that his concern was for the welfare of both of his dear friends, horse and rider.[43] In late May the Army of Northern Virginia, having fought and won a great victory at Chancellorsville, began to gather and reorganize in its camps along the Rappahannock. The second Confederate invasion of Northern territory was about to occur, and Lee was consolidating his army. Longstreet, with Pickett and Hood's divisions, was recalled. When the soldiers began the long march that would end at a small town in Pennsylvania, only Micah Jenkins and Robert Ransom's veteran soldiers remained in Virginia. A visibly upset Jenkins wrote everyone imaginable, but to no avail. His brigade moved to Petersburg in late May to be available for defense of the capital, as only home guards now manned the city's entrenchments. Jenkins filled his days with long frustrated letters to Carrie and renewed constant drill of his troops. General D. H. Hill came up from North Carolina and Jenkins held a brigade review in his honor. The recently recruited and newly uniformed brigade presented an impressive sight, and Hill's praise was music to Jenkins's ears.[44]

On June 1, Union raiders were reported on the Pamunkey River, probing toward the capital. Jenkins paraded his brigade through the streets of Richmond, flags high and bands playing as he moved to intercept. Advancing north of the city on the third, Jenkins called forward several companies of the Palmetto Sharpshooters whom he deployed to skirmish with the Federals. When the Union force fled on contact, Jenkins accompanied the skirmishers, who chased the enemy for miles down dusty roads in soaring temperatures. Seeing that his men were exhausted, Jenkins halted his pursuit near a small railroad depot. While soldiers gathered around a spring for water, he dismounted and crossed the road, entering the depot. As the men relaxed in whatever shade was available, they suddenly heard the whistle of a train. Jenkins had telegraphed for a train to give his men a ride back to camp.[45]

It was then back to Petersburg for more drill and the boredom of camp life. Lieutenant Richard Lewis of the Sharpshooters was greatly embarrassed by General Jenkins one hot August afternoon. The Petersburg camp was near the city and was a favorite visiting spot of the young ladies of the area. Most of the young officers wore their best uniforms each day to take advantage of expected female attention. Young Lewis, being very shy, usually avoided contact with female admirers. On this particular day, Jenkins was entertaining a number of young ladies near his tent. He dispatched an order for Lewis to appear in his best dress uniform. When Lewis complied, Jenkins sent all other officers on assignments, mounted Latta, and rode away. Lewis was almost overcome. He stated:

> General Jenkins ushered me into a crowd of young ladies and scared me so badly that I dreamed about them all night.[46]

By September Jenkins was quite concerned over conditions at home. He was unstinting in his praise of Carrie's management of their affairs, but the truly profitable Jenkins plantations on Edisto Island were now being used to quarter and feed Union soldiers. Their last unoccupied plantation was sold for cash, and the slaves were sent to brother John at Adam's Run.[47] His only remaining property was his half share in the Military School at Yorkville and their only remaining home, the commandant's quarters. For a time Jenkins hoped to be assigned to South Carolina to be more available in assisting Carrie with family burdens, but this was not to occur for more active assignments awaited him.

Chapter 8

A Journey West

In the fall of 1863 a frustrated Micah Jenkins continued to fret over the endless assignment of his brigade to the Richmond defense lines. The Confederacy's very existence was threatened on all fronts, yet his strong South Carolina brigade remained inactive and uninvolved. As the Army of Northern Virginia retreated from Gettysburg and the Vicksburg garrison surrendered, the military situation became grave. Jefferson Davis, in consultation with the Confederate War Department, searched for an opportunity to strike a blow at Union forces with a favorable chance of success.[1] One plan that seemed feasible was to dispatch eastern army troops to reinforce General Braxton Bragg's western Confederate army by use of interior railway lines. The decision to implement this daring plan would recall Micah Jenkins to action and present him with some of the most difficult and challenging decisions of his career.

In southeastern Tennessee, Federal Major General William S. Rosecrans, by skillful maneuvering of his Army of the Cumberland, had forced Bragg's Army of Tennessee almost out of the state. Without engaging in a major battle, Rosecrans was poised outside Chattanooga, the gateway to Georgia and the route to highly coveted Atlanta. Bragg insisted that he needed reinforcements to contest Rosecrans, so Davis decided to send troops from the east with a respected commanding officer to assist. Lieutenant General James Longstreet had long advocated combining eastern and western soldiers for a chance at a significant victory, and after much discussion with Robert E. Lee, Davis ordered Longstreet to prepare to move westward with two divisions of his famed I Corps, Army of Northern Virginia, to unite with Bragg and clear Rosecrans from Tennessee. On September 8 the divisions of Major General John Hood and Major General Lafayette McLaws began to move from their camps on the Rapidan River toward various railroad depots.[2] Longstreet left George Pickett's division in the capital's defense works, since Pickett's units had been much weakened in the Gettysburg campaign. But Longstreet negotiated with Davis and Lee to make some changes in the troops who would accompany him west. In return for leaving most of Pickett's division, he requested and obtained a transfer of Jenkins's brigade from Pickett's division to Hood's.[3] Longstreet also was forced to send two brigades to Charleston, South Carolina, as a strong Union force was again threatening that city. He selected Brigadier General Henry Wise's inexperienced brigade out of the Richmond defenses and Brigadier General George T. Anderson's brigade, that was under strength. Jenkins heard rumors that he and his men might be dispatched to Charleston and he excitedly wrote Carrie of the possibility, but his strong, well-disciplined brigade was badly needed by Longstreet.[4] Jenkins was elated to be assigned to Hood's division and included in the western movement. His frustrations at the enforced idleness of his well-recruited and -equipped brigade had led to repeated requests for transfer to an active combat role.[5] Strangely, each request had been denied. Prior to the Gettysburg campaign Jenkins had appealed to the War Department but had been unsuccessful. Lee had supported Jenkins, as evidenced by a letter in August 1863 after the battle. He stated:

Dear General Jenkins,

I regret exceedingly the absence of yourself and your brigade from the battle of Gettysburg. There is no telling what a gallant brigade, led by an efficient commander, might have accomplished when victory trembled in the balance. I verily believe the results would have been different if you had been present.

Sincerely Yours,

R.E. Lee[6]

Likewise Longstreet, in his later writing on the invasion of Pennsylvania, would comment:

The Army when it set out on the campaign was all that could be desired, but it was despoiled by the loss of two of its finest brigades, Jenkins's and Corse's of Pickett's Division.[7]

The detached and enforced idle status of Jenkins originated from a level higher than Lee or Longstreet. The orders were issued by the War Department but there is little doubt the decision was that of President Davis. Just before leaving Virginia, Lee appealed one last time for the services of Corse's brigade, commanded at that time by Robert Ransom, and that of Jenkins. He wrote to Davis that they were "good and tried officers with veteran troops."[8]

Instead, Davis sent to Lee the brigades of Brigadier General Joseph Pettigrew and Brigadier General Joseph Davis, his nephew, who was as green as his soldiers. It seems not improbable that the younger Davis, anxious for combat, had influenced his uncle to substitute his troops for those of Jenkins.

But all the frustration was forgotten in the excitement of preparing for the rail journey. Longstreet and his staff, led by the capable Lieutenant Colonel Moxley Sorrel, initially organized the mass movement of nine infantry brigades and six artillery batteries to Chattanooga. The responsibility for providing rail transportation fell to two men: Major Frederick W. Sims, coordinator of railroads for the Confederacy, and Brigadier General Alexander R. Lawton, Lee's quartermaster general. Both were experienced and capable officers. Sims had been a railroad transportation agent in his native Georgia prior to the war. He served in a combat regiment until captured at the surrender of Fort Pulaski. After being exchanged in the fall of 1862, he was posted to the Railroad Bureau. Lawton was a West Point graduate who had ably commanded a brigade in Jackson's Valley Army and a division under Lee. He was so severely wounded at Antietam that he was not capable of returning to a combat command. Lawton also had prewar experience as president of a railroad line.[9]

The two men were fast friends and worked well together. They performed near miracles in assembling such a vast amount of rolling stock for the operation and also in coordinating the track schedule of 16 different railway lines. The original plan entailed forces moving directly to Chattanooga via the Virginia and Tennessee Railroad through Lynchburg, Bristol, and Knoxville. But on September 2 Major General Simon Buckner evacuated Knoxville when threatened by a Federal force under Major General Ambrose Burnside.[10] Furthermore, on September 9 Bragg strangely retreated from Chattanooga, allowing Rosecrans to occupy the city without opposition.[11] The severed rail line thus caused a complete overhaul of travel plans and threatened the strategic value of the operation, since speed of travel on interior railroads was the key Southern advantage.

The revised route of travel was by a system of railroads that led across North Carolina, through South Carolina to Augusta, Georgia, and on to Atlanta. There the troops would be entrained north to join Bragg somewhere south of Chattanooga. The travel distance thus increased from 540 miles on the original route to more than 925 miles. Additionally, the new route utilized a series of railway systems with differing railway gauges, and in most instances each system had its own depot in the larger towns. This required the soldiers to ride into a city on one line, disembark, march across town, and re-embark onto another system to continue. The original route would have used three railroads, while the new route utilized 16.[12] This increase in distance and time was largely responsible for the fact that of the total force, only five of the nine infantry brigades and none of the artillery batteries arrived in time for the critical battle along the creeks south of Chattanooga.[13] To ease strain on the railroads, Lawton and Sims divided the trains. Some were dispatched along the coast through Wilmington, North Carolina, while others were sent through Raleigh and Charlotte. At Kingsville, South Carolina, where the Wilmington and Charlotte lines rejoined to share a single roadbed, a tremendous bottleneck occurred. Trains were backed up for miles waiting their turn to proceed, and Mary Chesnut, an observer, commented on the rows of soldiers wrapped in their blankets like mummies, sleeping on the platform cars.[14] From Kingsville the trains moved to Augusta, where another march across town placed the soldiers on the lines to Atlanta.

It is truly remarkable that Confederate railroads of that period were capable of such a major military movement. Railroad equipment throughout the South was in deplorable condition and the tracks were worse. All civilian and industrial transportation was suspended as railway facilities were marshaled for the maximum effort; passengers were stranded in several states as schedules were altered and numerous trains canceled. Moxley Sorrel described the trains as

> passenger, baggage, mail, coal, box, and platform cars loaded to capacity and with even the roofs full of soldiers....laughing, singing, waving, eating, and sleeping.[15]

The movement was a great adventure for the soldiers, although sometimes full of dangers. Colonel Coward recalled that a

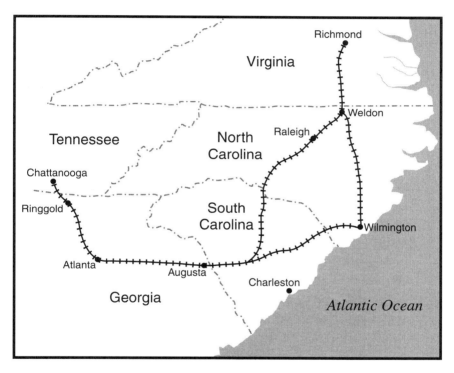

Route of the I Corps

The 925-mile journey across five states and numerous rail lines strained every sinew of the Southern railway system.

number of soldiers who slept atop the boxcar roofs lost their lives as they sat up and were swept away by overhanging limbs or railway trestles.[16] As the weather was pleasant, soldiers cut away much of the boxcars to enjoy the view. Large crowds flocked to meet the trains in the urban areas, and children and young ladies waved flags and cheered as the trains passed. Bonfires burned along the lines at night, throwing shadows on the moving cars. The various railcars, no matter how uncomfortable, were an improvement on the common mode of infantry travel. Richard Lewis of Jenkins's brigade was quite complimentary of the reception offered the Palmetto Sharpshooters as they traveled through Georgia. He remarked:

> The young ladies of Georgia were very enthusiastic in their reception of us in passing through the state, showering bouquets of flowers on us, cheering our hearts with their winning smiles and graces, and best of all, feeding our hungry souls with an abundance of everything good.[17]

Towns and villages along the route prepared tables of food for soldiers waiting to change rail lines. Moving large numbers of soldiers through highly populated and familiar areas, with the concurrent accessibility to alcohol and ease of desertion, was a nightmare for brigade, regimental and company officers. Jenkins and his staff worked diligently to maintain order and curtail excesses by exhilarated soldiers. For the most part the veteran troops were well behaved. There were stories concerning soldiers who missed trains and were stranded, to enjoy the hospitality of several towns. Columbia, South Carolina, was filled for days with gawking young Confederates. The provost guards soon recognized these absentees and placed then on later trains. The only serious incident of note was a near-riot in Charlotte when Benning's Georgia brigade determined to exact revenge on an unpopular newspaper editor by burning his establishment.[18] Jenkins took advantage of a brief respite in Charlotte to visit with Carrie and his young sons.

Coward joined the trains in Chester, south of Charlotte. He had been home on leave, sadly, to bury a child.[19]

A more serious problem occurred when the trains began to arrive in Atlanta. Sims and Lawton relinquished operational responsibility at that site and Colonel Jones from Bragg's staff took charge with a marked decrease in efficiency.[20] A single rail line, on which trains were shuttled back and forth on specific sections of track, led northward from Atlanta to Ringgold, Georgia, and Bragg's army. To further complicate matters, two brigades of infantry from Mississippi were also dispatched to supplement Bragg's forces and they arrived in Atlanta at the same time that Benning's Georgia brigade, the van of Longstreet's force, rolled into the city. Brigadier General Henry L. Benning and Brigadier General E. M. Law's brigades were moved north in time for the first day's action at Chickamauga on September 19, and other brigades arrived for action the following day. Trapped in the confusion in Atlanta; Jenkins's, Brigadier General Goode Bryan's, and Brigadier General W. T. Wofford's brigades missed the battle altogether. Longstreet's artillery under Colonel Porter Alexander did not even reach Atlanta until several days later. Major General John Hood had been seriously wounded during the second day's fighting at Gettysburg, and command of his division had passed to the senior brigadier, Evander Law, for the remainder of the action about the Round Tops and the subsequent withdrawal into Virginia. Law had seemed to perform well in the role, but Longstreet was not pleased and had openly remarked to that effect.[21] Hood had recovered sufficiently enough to resume command before the trains left Richmond, but for a time it was questionable if he could accompany his soldiers. During that period Longstreet had searched for an officer to replace him but Law was not considered. Thus were sown the first seeds of a bitter and senseless conflict.

Evander McIvor Law was a tall, sparse, fierce-looking young officer who developed into a vigorous and successful

brigade commander. He was born in the upcountry South
Carolina town of Darlington in 1836 and was educated at the
South Carolina Military Academy, graduating in 1856, one
year after Micah Jenkins.[22] Sorrel, writing in later years, spoke
of a bitter rivalry between Law and Jenkins dating back to
their cadet years,[23] but little evidence of such a rivalry exists.
Law's pre-war career closely paralleled that of Jenkins, and
upon his college graduation he was employed by Jenkins as
one of the five-man staff at Kings Mountain Military School.[24]
Law joined the school's faculty in January of 1857 and served
for more than three years as professor of belles-lettres. He
was widely respected as a teacher and was even invited to
provide the keynote address at an important observance on
June 28, 1860.[25] In July of that year he resigned his Kings
Mountain position to relocate in Alabama where he entered a
partnership to establish a military school in Tuskegee. Law
was active in militia affairs in Alabama, and when that state
seceded he enlisted as a captain in the 4th Alabama. Arriving
in Virginia in time to participate in the battle of 1st Manassas,
he was soon promoted to colonel of that regiment. He led the
4th through the Peninsula campaign and commanded a brigade in Whiting's division at the Seven Days' Battle. On October 2, 1862, Law was promoted to the rank of brigadier general
and assigned command of the Alabama brigade in Hood's division. He saw action at 2nd Manassas, Antietam, and led the
assault on Little Round Top at Gettysburg.

As the growing Confederate army waited south of Chattanooga and Rosecrans demonstrated in their direction,
Braxton Bragg, under pressure from the administration, decided to attack. Rosecrans's army was scattered all over the
mountains and coves south of Chattanooga, presenting an
excellent opportunity for a Confederate attack. But Bragg was
slow to move, and the Federal commander was able to reconsolidate his forces.[26] Bragg did not wait for the total force from
Virginia to complete its eight-day trip, and strangely, on the

night prior to the attack he reorganized his army. These two facts seem illogical, but many of Braxton Bragg's plans defy good reasoning. If his assault had occurred before Rosecrans's consolidation then his haste would seem reasonable; however, since that was no longer the case, a few days' delay would not have mattered.

Longstreet arrived about midnight and found he was assigned as a wing commander.[27] Lieutenant General Leonidas Polk would command the second wing. Longstreet was scheduled to lead an attack the following morning with whatever portions of Hood and McLaw's veterans were present, along with the divisions of Major General A. P. Stewart, Brigadier General William Preston, and Brigadier General Thomas Hindman, all from the Army of Tennessee.

On September 19 Bragg pushed his army across Chickamauga Creek and assaulted the Federal army. The two-day battle that ensued was one of the most disjointed, confused and fierce struggles to occur during the war.[28] It was contested in rough, thickly overgrown terrain and became an infantry fight with minimal opportunity for artillery or mounted troops. The outcome was determined by decisions of regimental, brigade, and divisional officers. Both opposing army commanders were virtually out of the action once they committed their forces to battle, which may have been fortunate for the Confederate army. The clash continued in the wooded terrain until Longstreet's fortunately timed attack splintered the Federal center. Rosecrans's army was forced into a headlong dash back to Chattanooga, and only a firm stand by Union forces under Major General George H. Thomas on Snodgrass Hill prevented virtual destruction of the Union army. Casualties were enormous in the mutual battering. Bragg suffered 21,000 casualties and the Federals sustained more than 16,000, killed, wounded, or missing.[29] The outcome was a decided Confederate victory but a fruitless one at best. Bragg wavered and then refused to pursue the beaten

Union army. Rosecrans withdrew into Chattanooga, and Bragg settled into siege-like positions about the city.

On the night of September 21 Micah Jenkins was frantically unloading his brigade from the boxcars at Catoosa Station, Georgia. His veterans could hear the roll of artillery fire from the north. Jenkins drove his troops through the cold Georgia night, passing streams of retiring Confederate wounded and listening to claims of Southern victory. As the Carolinians marched toward the field, controversy exploded in army headquarters. Wing commanders Longstreet and Polk, assisted by Lieutenant General D. H. Hill and Brigadier General Nathan B. Forrest, assailed Bragg, who was convinced the battle was over.[30] The subordinates were critical of Bragg's battlefield management and incensed by his failure to pursue the enemy. Forrest was so upset that he stated he would never serve under Bragg again in any capacity and, if forced to do so, would resign. Perhaps never before had a subordinate officer so berated a commander in such a fashion in the officer's own tent,[31] but Forrest was not one to avoid a face-to-face confrontation when he deemed it necessary. Bragg did not receive this criticism lightly. He struck back at those involved, especially Polk and Hill, relieving those two officers of their command.[32] Micah Jenkins, hastening toward the gory battlefield, knew nothing of these events.

John Hood, recognized as a hero of the battle, had again been wounded. Struck in the leg he had undergone amputation, and for a time there was concern for his survival.[33] Hood's division had been decreased to four brigades before leaving Richmond, since Anderson was detailed to Charleston, but only three—Benning's Georgians, Robertson's Texans, and Law's Alabamians—participated in the battle. Jenkins arrived the next day. When the division was complete, Longstreet appointed Jenkins, the senior brigadier, as acting division commander for the disabled Hood. Law immediately protested the appointment. There could be no argument as to which officer was senior, as Jenkins's promotion to brigadier general was dated July 22, 1862, and Law's October 2, 1862, and military seniority was closely observed in both Union and Confederate armies.[34] However, Law presented a strong case, insisting that he had seniority within the division. He had commanded the division in action at Gettysburg when Hood was wounded. He had also experienced action in every fight in which the division was involved since its organization. Jenkins, on the other hand, was recently transferred from Pickett and had never seen combat with the division. Longstreet decreed the command to be Jenkins's by seniority and said that Law would need a promotion to major general to supersede Jenkins. Certainly, Jenkins was pleased to receive a division, if only temporarily, but he saw immediately it was a difficult assignment. He was assuming command of a division that included an irate and vociferously protesting brigadier, two other commanders with whom he was unfamiliar, and he had no division staff other than a few officers borrowed from the regiments in his brigade. Law loudly proclaimed that Jenkins was benefiting by preferential treatment from Longstreet. But this affair was minor when compared to the storm that was about to sweep the high command of the Army of Tennessee.

Bragg and his principal lieutenants were soon embroiled in arguments, charges, countercharges, letters, and petitions. An anonymous petition was circulated that stated Bragg was unfit for command.[35] The authorship was wrongly attributed to Daniel Harvey Hill and resulted in the removal of that capable but irascible officer from future contributions to the Confederate cause.[36] Hill, brother-in-law of Stonewall Jackson, was a fiery combat officer, but testy in his relationships with other officers. He would not, however, become Bragg's whipping boy for a wasted victory. Polk, who did not perform well at Chickamauga and possibly deserved Bragg's censure, was also defiant. After suspension from his command, he journeyed to Atlanta with his staff and awaited results, confident

in his previous friendship with Jefferson Davis.[37] The principal participants immediately rushed letters to the president
and the War Department.

After repeated attempts at long-range mediation, Davis
decided to travel west and settle the bickering threatening
the internal structure of one of the country's largest forces.
On the 8th of October Davis arrived in Atlanta and spent much
of the day conversing with the suspended Leonidas Polk. The
following day the president, accompanied by Polk, traveled to
Bragg's headquarters in Marietta, Georgia. Bragg and Davis
met for several hours, and the president then invited the com-
plaining officers to join them. Davis was hoping to settle the
differences through a general discussion, but in a session particularly embarrassing to Bragg, the officers all disavowed
publicly any confidence in Bragg's ability to further lead the
army.[38] The results were, however, equally humbling to the
subordinates when Davis sustained Bragg as "worthy of confidence."[39] On October 10 Davis joined Longstreet for a ride to
the crest of Lookout Mountain. He questioned Longstreet at
length on the command situation and ultimately asked for a
recommendation: Who should replace Bragg should Davis decide to make a change in field commanders? Longstreet recommended Joseph Johnston and received a sharp retort from
Davis.[40] The sensitive chief executive could not overlook a long-
standing feud between Davis and Johnston, supposedly dating back to their West Point cadet days.

Longstreet then attempted to resolve the question of command of Hood's division. As it appeared Hood's wounds would
require lengthy convalescence, Longstreet recommended Micah
Jenkins for promotion to major general and permanent command of the division. Longstreet described Jenkins to Davis as

> a bright, gallant, and efficient officer of more than two
> years experience in active warfare, loved by his troops and
> acquaintances as well.[41]

Davis curtly refused, his reasons unknown. Longstreet then mentioned the possibility of promoting Law, stating that Jenkins would accept that decision for the good of the service, but Davis again refused.[42] The president departed for Richmond the following morning leaving Bragg firmly in command and the controversy over his abilities unsettled. Likewise, Davis's refusal to choose between Jenkins and Law also allowed that controversy to fester.

Jenkins moved Hood's division atop Lookout Mountain as a part of the Confederate lines about Chattanooga. Although the position was visually impressive due to its vast height, he recognized that it was not militarily sound and at once began to warn his superiors that the mountaintop position was really quite vulnerable.[43]

As the division established camps on the mountain, military positions and gun emplacements were laboriously scratched into the rocky surface facing Chattanooga. A serious problem was the lack of equipment and supplies. When Longstreet's soldiers entrained for the voyage west, no provision was made to deliver baggage, food, provisions, or even wagons. This lack of transportation prevented foraging for provisions or the distribution of the few supplies that arrived at the railhead. Logistical planning in Bragg's army was seemingly as lacking as battle plans. One member of Jenkins's brigade described the lack of supplies when he wrote:

> We have never experienced such a crisis in the way of rations...it being three days since an issue. The men are eating acorns, cracking them like hogs and with as much relish. One fellow picked up grain which the horses had missed and washing them fed himself.[44]

Constant rain and cold temperatures persisted through October, and the men suffered for want of tents or other decent cover. Lookout Mountain was soon stripped of its beautiful stand of chestnut trees. The soldiers used the wood to construct shelters, and the chestnuts became a major part of their daily diet. The newly uniformed and fully recruited South Carolina brigade sat on the crest of Lookout Mountain in the rain, shivering and starving. Sick lists and desertion rolls grew, and yet the soldiers waited. Accustomed to the direction of purpose and spirit of the Army of Northern Virginia, they and their young commander must have wondered over finding themselves in an army rife with dissension and characterized by indecision—truly omens of a dark, cloudy future.

Chattanooga, from the Confederate position atop Lookout Mountain, a long-suffering camp for the South Carolina Infantry.

Photograph by Robert Carter

Chapter 9

Lookout Valley

The weather remained wet and cold in southern Tennessee in October. The Confederates shivered atop Lookout Mountain, enviously observing their well-sheltered adversaries in the city of Chattanooga while the cold rain poured, day after day.

However Major General William Rosecrans, the Federal commander in Chattanooga, had problems more serious than shelter. His plan to clear Bragg from Tennessee that began with the capture of Chattanooga had never included a long-term sojourn in that Southern city. Provisions were not stockpiled for men or animals, and acute shortages became immediately evident. Federal troops were placed on half-rations upon the armies' withdrawal into the city.[1] William Smith, a staff officer, explained the situation as more serious than simply a lack of food. He stated that the army had not enough ammunition remaining for a single day's fight.[2] In effect the Union army was in a position from which it could not retreat, could not long defend itself, and would starve to death if left alone and isolated. Nashville was the nearest Federal supply base, and transportation from that site proved extremely difficult. Wagons from Nashville could easily reach Bridgeport, 26 miles from Chattanooga, but at that point the most practical route of access crossed to the south side of the

Tennessee River and meandered through Lookout Valley. The lone alternative was a rocky path over the mountains from Bridgeport to Chattanooga, on a narrow tract that was virtually impassable in winter due to the constant heavy rains.[3]

Although Confederate artillery did not command the road through Lookout Valley the route was clearly visible from the Confederate positions on Lookout Mountain. If not well protected, the route was vulnerable to Southern raids. On October 19, 1863, Ulysses S. Grant relieved Rosecrans of command and placed Virginia-born Major General George H. Thomas in charge of the besieged Federal army. Grant moved personally into the south Tennessee area and assumed direction of overall operations from his headquarters. Wherever Sam Grant led, action would surely follow. His first priority was the opening of the Nashville-Chattanooga supply route.[4] Although fearful of the hardships being suffered by the soldiers, he never considered abandoning Chattanooga. Grant stated years later that to give up the city would have been a "definite political disaster and a possible military one."[5] He felt a retreat from the city would cost the remainder of the army's artillery and, if pursued vigorously, retreat could possibly result in annihilation of the army. Thus the lone Federal option was to hold Chattanooga, resisting all pressures.

Jefferson Davis, having obviously not succeeded in his attempts to mediate the mutiny among the major officers in the Army of Tennessee, relied on the professionalism of Bragg and Longstreet to lead the Army of Tennessee. But tensions continued to build and the two officers totally ceased to communicate with each other. Longstreet's actions indicate that he considered himself and his divisions on detached service from Virginia to cooperate with Bragg, but certainly not an integral part of Bragg's army.[6] Bragg spent his days with the right wing of the army, yet when he did sent orders to Longstreet on Lookout Mountain, the corps commander was apt to ignore the directives.

Finally, Bragg made a move to reestablish command. He had received cavalry reports of increased Union activity in Lookout Valley and he traveled up the circuitous road to the top of the mountain to discuss with Longstreet a reconnaissance into the area. The valley below the Confederate position on the mountain was not easily controlled. It was about five miles wide, which precluded its control by Confederate guns from the heights, and was divided by a range of low hills, making observation difficult. Bragg repeatedly urged Longstreet to send troops into the area but the former did not respond. On October 25 an angry Braxton Bragg formally ordered Longstreet to send a force into Lookout Valley. Strangely, Longstreet bypassed Micah Jenkins, the acting division commander, and ordered Evander Law, whose brigade was nearest, to take two regiments and explore the valley as far as the foot of Raccoon Mountain.[7] When Law entered Lookout Valley he realized that its size precluded holding it with such small numbers and he sent for his other three regiments.[8] On the following day, Law, oddly, requested and received permission to leave his post and his regiments in Lookout Valley and visit the recuperating John Hood.

Meanwhile, Jenkins received a copy of Longstreet's orders to Law and immediately recalled the three added regiments.[9] Upon Law's return, he and Jenkins became embroiled in a heated argument over Law's orders and the actual purpose of the reconnaissance.[10] Jenkins insisted that the two regiments were intended as pickets to warn the army of Federal activity, while Law contended that he needed a larger force in the event of surprise by a Federal force. Longstreet's whereabouts at this time were as unknown as were his intentions. Bragg had forced the wing commander to carry out the movement for which he demonstrated little interest, and one might suspect the dispatching of Law was simply a means to satisfy Bragg and had no clear purpose. Law was certainly justified in his concern over being isolated with only a small force, but after weeks of inactivity he took leave. Jenkins was zealously following the specific commands of the lieutenant general in recalling the additional troops. He also felt that if Law needed more soldiers, Law should have contacted the division commander for authorization. Most of the blame seems to lie with Longstreet for his lackadaisical handling of Bragg's orders, but the incident only served to further alienate Law and Jenkins.

Rapidly developing Union plans would prove control of Lookout Valley more critical than the Confederate officers imagined. Prior to his relief, Rosecrans had initiated a plan designed to relieve the Federal supply crisis by use of the valley road. Major General William F. Smith was ordered to study all options and develop a plan of transporting materials through the valley, Bridgeport to Chattanooga. When the change in command occurred, Smith took his completed plan to Grant and Thomas, who immediately endorsed the idea without alterations.[11]

Brown's Ferry, a small landing on the south side of the Tennessee River, near the small town of Wauhatchie, was the key to Smith's two-fold plan of operation. The plan's first phase included the capture and fortification of Brown's Ferry as an essential anchor for the remainder of the operation. On the dark night of October 27, Smith moved with four thousand men to capture this initial objective. Eighteen hundred hand-picked men spearheaded the attack under Brigadier General William B. Hazen. They floated with the strong current down the Tennessee River on 52 pontoon sections or barges.[12] They quietly passed the rebel pickets at the foot of Lookout Mountain and neared Brown's Ferry, where they stormed ashore, drove off the few sleepy Confederate pickets present, and took possession of the ferry landing on the south side of the river. Meanwhile, Smith, with the remainder of the select force, marched out of Chattanooga, crossed the river and continued across Moccasin Bend to the north riverbank opposite Brown's

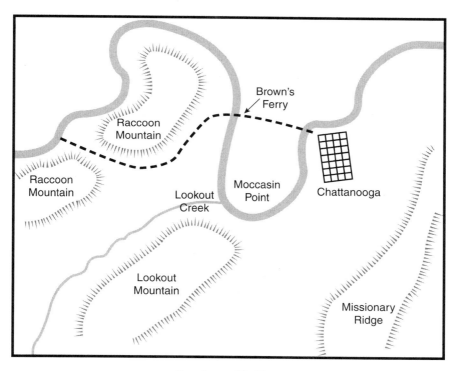

Lookout Valley

The Confederate encampment on Lookout Mountain overlooked and theoretically dominated the Federal army in Chattanooga. The movement of Federal supply wagons via Raccoon Mountain and over the Tennessee River at Brown's Ferry was easily observed but decidedly more difficult to interrupt.

Ferry. Smith's column carried a pontoon bridge that was hastily erected when possession of the opposite bank was assured.
Thus, on the morning of October 28 a surprised Confederate
army awoke to view a force of four thousand Federal troops
entrenched at Brown's Ferry with direct connections to the
main Federal force in Chattanooga.via two bridges and a short
march across Moccasin Bend. A well-conceived and ably coor-
dinated coup by the Federal staff.

The second phase of the plan, to establish northern control of the road from Brown's Ferry to Bridgeport, was possible due to actions initiated nearly a month earlier. On the
evening of September 23 Abraham Lincoln, alarmed over the
possibility that Chattanooga might be surrendered to Bragg,[13]
convened an emergency meeting of his War Department staff
to discuss relief for Rosecrans. It was determined that two
corps from the Army of the Potomac would be dispatched
west under Major General Joseph Hooker. If Lee could
weaken his army to aid Bragg, Lincoln reasoned, then the
Federal army in Virginia could release soldiers to aid their
hard-pressed comrades in Chattanooga. Taking a cue from

*Brown's Ferry as seen from the Tennessee River. Union troops
stormed ashore and captured this vital river crossing in a sudden
and well-executed coup.*

Photograph by Robert Carter

the Confederate railway move, the XI and XII Corps embarked by rail. Almost 20,000 men and all their baggage made the journey in six days. Despite a hazardous ride in which several serious accidents occurred, the van of the XI Corps arrived safely in Bridgeport.[14]

At daybreak on October 28 these newly arrived soldiers, stiff and stretching after their train journey, began to advance through Lookout Valley, observed by an alarmed Bragg and Longstreet from atop Lookout Mountain. Hooker marched unopposed the length of Lookout Valley and by 5:00 p.m. was encamped at Brown's Ferry.[15] A second Union column under Brigadier General John W. Geary, which consisted of the 2nd Division of the Union XII Corps, followed Hooker, escorting the wagons and pack mules of an extensive supply train. Geary halted and camped about three miles short of Hooker's force. This rapid movement from Bridgeport, following the capture and entrenching at Brown's Ferry, shocked the Confederate command. Union forces had now established a strong presence in Lookout Valley.

Longstreet may have recalled Bragg's repeated warnings of enemy activity in the valley; in any event he certainly realized that an immediate response was necessary, or the Federals would soon control the shortened supply route. Bragg encouraged his wing commander to use two or more divisions if a sortie into the valley were practical, but a continued lack of communication resulted in a confused exchange. Bragg later stated that he desired a two-division attack on Brown's Ferry striving to capture the outpost, whereas Longstreet simply wished to sever the Federal supply line. The two officers, therefore, did not even agree on the objective of the hastily planned night action.[16] Longstreet decided to use only the division of Micah Jenkins, whom he notified to prepare for movement at dusk.

At nightfall on the 28th the respective brigades moved with difficulty down the single, narrow path to the valley floor.

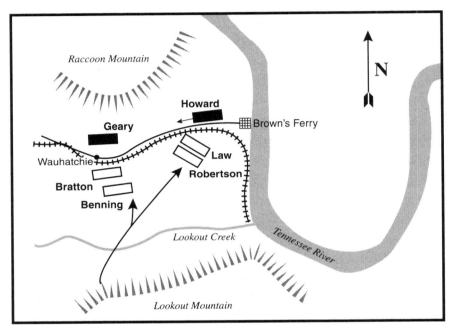

Night Action at Wauhatchie

On the night of October 28, 1863, Micah Jenkins took four brigades into Lookout Valley and attempted to overwhelm General John Geary's Federals encamped at Wauhatchie. General O. O. Howard's relief column marching from Brown's Ferry brushed aside Law's blocking Confederates and rescued Geary.

At the mountain's base they were forced to cross a stream on the remaining girders of two previously destroyed bridges. Longstreet accompanied the division to this point and, upon crossing the stream, divided the force into two battle groups. Evander Law, with his own brigade and that of Brigadier General Jerome B. Robertson, was to move down the valley and form a blocking force astride the road to prevent Federal troops at Brown's Ferry from interfering with the planned attack. Micah Jenkins, with his South Carolina brigade under Colonel John Bratton and Benning's Georgia brigade, would march to attack Geary's isolated camp. Jenkins assigned the larger South Carolina unit to deliver the attack with Benning held in reserve.[17]

After advancing some distance the South Carolinians deployed on a three-regiment front with two regiments in reserve. Under Bratton's direction, the line advanced over the low hills and collided with Federal pickets about 1:00 a.m. The pickets fell back onto Geary's awakening infantry and artillery, which was immediately assailed by Bratton. The Federal soldiers offered modest resistance at first, but after retreating through their camps, they resisted strongly. Bratton dispatched the Hampton Legion under Colonel Martin W. Gary, heretofore in reserve, around the Union left flank.[18] At the same moment, the Palmetto Sharpshooters fiercely assailed and folded back the enemy right.[19] The division of bluecoats was thus forced into a "U" and its position was quite critical. Joseph S. Fullerton, Union brevet brigadier and corps staff officer, described the assault as "a terrific onslaught on Geary's division, forcing us back to a point that we were assailed on three sides."[20]

The fighting was confusing and severe at all points. Major Grimes, who led the 1st South Carolina after the fatal wounding of Colonel John Kilpatrick, related in his report the extreme difficulty of maneuvering the regiment and maintaining contact with flank regiments on such a dark night.[21] Flashes

New York Monument on the site of the night action at Wauhatchie. Jenkins's regiments were forced to retreat when Geary's Federals received reinforcements.

Photograph by Robert Carter

from the volleys of rifle fire provided the only illumination by which officers could check alignment. Colonel Coward of the 5th South Carolina was impressed by the vigor of Federal resistance. He stated that after advancing through the Union camp, his regiment was greeted by such a severe fire they were stopped cold.[22] He responded by having the 5th lie down in a slight depression and return fire until the Hampton Legion could turn the Federal flank. Federal colors and a large number of wagons and mules were captured in the drive through the camps, but this booty would not long remain in Confederate hands. At the moment when Geary's force seemed bent to the breaking point, Jenkins received word that Federal troops were attacking Benning's reserve brigade directly in his rear.

Hooker had dispatched a relief force from Brown's Ferry that had broken through Law's blocking position and was threatening to cut off Jenkins from his only retreat route. Jenkins called off the attack with reluctance. The wagons and materials were set afire where possible and the livestock scattered. Jenkins then concentrated his force and began to extricate his units from the valley. Remarkably, he was successful. Jenkins credited the steadfastness of "Rock" Benning and the excellent control of his regimental commanders for the successful retreat.[23] The pitch-dark conditions also were a welcome aid, as enemy columns moved about firing volleys in all directions. Confederate commanders exerted superior fire discipline and avoided the Union forces, which were of greater menace to themselves. A disaster was averted but casualties among the South Carolinians were high. Of 1,800 soldiers entering the action, 358 were reported as killed, wounded, or missing. Among the slain was the outstanding commander of the 1st South Carolina, John Kilpatrick. Lieutenant Lewis later described his conversation with Jenkins and the latter's reaction to Kilpatrick's loss:

> Jenkins said....It feels like one half my heart is gone with the last pulsations of Kilpatrick. Never has a friend been more true and sincere to me, or could one's loss so completely desolate me: feeling as if the strongest link of friendship in the army has been severed—no longer that advisor to appeal to in all matters.[24]

But what had occurred with Law's two brigades? They had proceeded up the valley and established a stout position on a small hill near the road. When firing was heard from Geary's camp, Hooker acted promptly. He dispatched Major General Oliver O. Howard with a relief force to Geary's assistance. As Howard's men marched down the road, they were fired upon from a small hill to their left. Howard turned his men, charged the hill, and drove the Confederate force from their position.[25] No further resistance being offered, he regrouped his troops and proceeded to Geary's relief, blundering into the rear of Jenkins's assault force. Howard reported few casualties, as most of the 416 Federal losses were sustained by Geary. Law reported a loss of 15 men in his brigade. Micah Jenkins, in his official report, quoted this low number as proof of inadequate resistance by Law.[26]

The confusing night battle was concluded, having produced some stout fighting at the point of assault, much marching in the dark, but no appreciable results. The failure of the Confederates to disrupt the Union buildup resulted in a secure Northern supply route and eventually a Federal breakout from Chattanooga. By October 31 Jenkins reported that fully 20,000 Federals were in the valley, and the only trail down the mountain was controlled by Federal artillery.[27] On October 31, Jenkins wrote to Moxey Sorrel expounding on the poor defensive position of the Confederate army on Lookout Mountain. He felt the brigades were too few in number and too scattered to be mutually supportive. Since the Federal force in the valley was now so strong Micah reasoned that

> it is natural to suppose they will use these troops....and the many trails of access would lead me to believe they can overcome any of our scattered positions before reinforcements can arrive.[28]

He enumerated the trails, the distances between them, and the number of troops at each vulnerable point. His appraisal would prove disastrously correct in the subsequent battle above the clouds.

In any evaluation of the action in Lookout Valley, most of the credits to the principals involved would fall on the Federal side. Smith's plan was daring and well developed. Grant's coordination was superb and the execution by Smith, Hazen, and Hooker outstanding. While Geary's decision to halt and camp three miles from the main column may be questionable, he was alert and fought his men well when attacked. Hooker's response to the Confederate night attack was immediate and decisive, a totally well-planned and -executed operation by the Union army, perhaps a warning that Union operations would be more direct and more frequent.

The Confederate performance was not so creditable. Micah Jenkins had organized and delivered the attack on Geary's division with authority and dash, and when threatened, had removed his force in an exemplary manner. Evander Law did not perform as well with the other half of the force. He possibly did not place his two brigades in the proper position astride the road. Had Law been in the correct position,

Howard's relief column would have directly encountered their direct fire: instead the column was fired upon from their left. Law, for whatever reason, did not offer stout resistance to Howard and thus placed the entire division in serious jeopardy. He did, however, evacuate his troops without undue loss. The low casualties sustained by the blocking force attested the less than spirited resistance effort.

When Major Latrobe of Longstreet's staff questioned Law as to why he abandoned his position so quickly, Law became furious. He stated that the position was not abandoned and demanded a court of inquiry.[29] Law defended the withdrawal by claiming to have received confusing orders from Jenkins after the two forces separated, but the actual orders from Jenkins are clear. Lieutenant Jamison attested to the delivery of two orders to General Law on the night of October 28. The first was delivered personally to Law and requested him to strengthen his left by moving men from his right, since it was essential that the road be held; further, he was told to hold the position until he received further orders from Jenkins. It appears that Law's force never blocked the road, or if so, the force was aligned at an oblique angle. The second order was delivered by Jamison to Captain Hamilton of Law's staff, stating that Law should hold his position until Bratton withdrew and that Jenkins would notify him when to withdraw.[30] From the meager resistance, it would appear that Law either assumed he was faced with an overwhelming force, or he placed his men in an incorrect position and was simply brushed aside before he could correct the mistake. Longstreet, in his official report, attributed the failure of the attack to Law's lack of effort and his strong feelings of jealousy concerning Jenkins's command of the division.[31]

In January, Jenkins, who had been quite sick, finally replied in writing to the inquiries of Major Latrobe concerning discrepancies in the reports filed by Law and himself. Jenkins certainly knew of Law's request for a "court" and had read

Law's report of the action. In his report to Latrobe, Jenkins stated:

> I should perhaps have taken official notice of the disobe-
> dience of General Law, had it not been for my knowledge
> of his dissatisfied feelings in reference to my having com-
> mand of this division as his senior, and my belief that the
> contrary course on my part might tend to harmonize this
> division and to advance the best interests of the service.[32]

It is likely that Longstreet wished to have charges filed against Law and through Latrobe was exerting pressure on Jenkins to pursue this end. Jenkins's determination not to file charges was a decision he would surely regret.

However, Longstreet's leadership in the operation is open to more serious questions. Just what was his objective in or-dering the night attack? Why did he send one division into the valley to attack an enemy of unknown size? Did he envision the operation as a division-size raid or a serious attempt to seize and occupy a possible Union supply route?

Longstreet sent Law with two brigades of about 1,700 men to block a Federal force of close to 12,000 at Brown's Ferry.[33] The relief column under Howard was probably near 7,000, and even if Law had reached the correct position and conducted an aggressive, determined defense, it is doubtful he could have prevented a Federal breakthrough. Jenkins was dispatched with 2,400 troops to attack Geary's 4,000. While Jenkins thought he had the advantage of surprise, in fact the Federals were alert and resisted at once. Colonel William Oates of the 15th Alabama, Law's brigade, did not hesitate to point an ac-cusing finger at Longstreet when he stated:

> No greater remissness in a general was ever exhibited
> than Longstreet exhibited in sending Jenkins with one
> division to attack two corps of the enemy. By his negli-
> gence the lives of brave men were sacrificed.[34]

If Longstreet recognized the significance of Union activity in the valley, then he should possibly have committed several divisions to a dawn attack with the objective of inflicting a severe defeat on the Federals and discouraging further use of the supply route. Since the road could not be controlled from the mountaintop, a force large enough to capture and hold the valley was required. The defeat or capture of Geary's force would not establish Confederate control of Lookout Valley.

Longstreet and Bragg were certainly surprised by the sudden display of Union initiative and dash. They were accustomed to the lethargic and methodical shifting of large numbers of troops that characterized Rosecrans's leadership. The swift, decisive Federal movements to attain control of the valley indicated a change in Union style. They may not have known that Grant, the boldest of Federal field commanders, was in charge. But aggressive enemy action demanded an equally aggressive and decisive reply. While some small tactical advantage may have resulted from the destruction of Geary, there appears to be no clear strategic objective from the moment the corps commander ordered Jenkins to move his division down the mountainside and into Lookout Valley.

Chapter 10
Problems in East Tennessee

In October Jefferson Davis suggested a daring new course of action to General Bragg. Concerned over the continued Federal position astride the railroad at Knoxville in the upper East Tennessee Valley and unaware of Grant's gradual concentration of his forces in Chattanooga, he viewed Bragg's siege as a stalemate and concluded that a swift thrust to capture Knoxville would endanger the Federal army in Chattanooga and might force an evacuation of the city.[1] Davis proposed that Bragg send Longstreet with his two divisions up the East Tennessee Valley to defeat Burnside and capture Knoxville before winter weather prohibited campaigning. Thus the rail line could be reopened establishing direct communication from Richmond with the Army of Tennessee.

Why send Longstreet? His corps was posted on the extreme Confederate left. A movement by the right flank meant that Jenkins and McLaws would be forced to withdraw their divisions from Lookout Mountain, cross the rear of the entire Confederate position, and initiate an advance on the army's right. In addition, these two divisions were perhaps the worst prepared to conduct a lengthy march in the Army of Tennessee; each being extremely short of wagons, horses, and mules, having left their trains in Virginia. But since the purge of general officers following the post-Chickamauga command crisis,

162

Longstreet was Bragg's only remaining subordinate with sufficient experience to undertake such an independent assignment. It also separated Longstreet from Bragg. In his correspondence with the president, Bragg spoke of the conflict between the two and remarked that sending Longstreet to East Tennessee would be "a great relief to me."[2] Davis may have anticipated that Longstreet, once free of Bragg, might demonstrate some of the leadership qualities he had evidenced under Lee in Virginia. Whatever the reason, the luckless Army of Tennessee was reduced by two divisions at precisely the moment Grant was reinforcing the Union army by three corps.[3] Bragg seemed to feel his position on Lookout Mountain was invulnerable, despite the visible Union buildup and the warnings of General Jenkins and others. If the personal differences between Bragg and Longstreet were the primary reason for the division of the army, the consequences were grossly unfair to the Confederate soldiers who would fight and die in a vain attempt to hold Lookout Mountain in November. Grant, in his subsequent report on the Battle of Chattanooga, spoke of the detachment of Longstreet and his two divisions as critical to the later Union success.[4]

Late on the evening of November 4 Jenkins and McLaws began to withdraw their men from the rifle pits on the crest of Lookout Mountain, accompanied by an artillery battalion under Colonel Porter Alexander. The total contingent was about 12,000 men, which Longstreet considered grossly insufficient. He commented: "We will thus expose both (my force and Bragg's army) to failure and really have no chance of success."[5] But he seemed so elated to leave Bragg's control that he offered minimal protest.

The conditions for the actual withdrawal were terrible. One soldier reported that

> Our regiment left the mountain in the middle of the night.
> We were on picket duty and were the last to leave. It was

the most awful night man ever spent on the tramp. It
rained in torrents and was so dark and gloomy you could
not see your hand and the trails were knee deep in
mud....Many arms and legs were broken by soldiers falling off the mountainside in the dark.[6]

Micah Jenkins remarked that the marching conditions and
lack of rations were the worst he had ever experienced and
that he hoped the East Tennessee Valley would be a more
bountiful region.[7] Jenkins pushed his troops to reach the railway at Tunnel Hill Station since his men were to be loaded
before those of McLaws. But the overworked railroad suffered
a complete breakdown, and the lines of hungry, wet men were
forced to camp about the railhead waiting for the trains. A
member of the Palmetto Sharpshooters wrote that his company had been lying around Tunnel Hill Station for three days
and only one brigade had been entrained. He added that no
rations had been issued during that period.[8] When the trains
finally arrived, they were made up of flatcars, and the soldiers suffered severely, riding in the cold and windy conditions.[9] Vainly the gray-coats attempted to erect bulkheads
against the wind. As the trains arrived in Sweetwater, the
weather cleared and boxcars of rations were discovered sit-
ting in the rail-yard. The foodstuff was swiftly confiscated and
thankfully devoured. Jenkins's division, the South Carolina
brigade in the van, then led Longstreet's small army into East
Tennessee.

The East Tennessee Valley is in reality an upland plateau located between mountain ranges, an extension of the
Shenandoah Valley of Virginia, which runs generally southwest from Bristol on the Virginia-Tennessee line to Chattanooga near the Tennessee-Georgia line. It is bordered on the
east by the formidable Smokey Mountain range that separates
Tennessee from North Carolina. On the west, lesser mountains shield the valley from fertile middle Tennessee. Several

streams of appreciable size bisect the valley, including the flood-prone Tennessee and Holston Rivers. A winter campaign on such a plateau could expect to encounter harsh weather conditions characterized by sudden changes. The area had never been thickly populated, as its soil was thin and rocky. Large plantation-style farming was impractical and small-scale agriculture required perseverance and hard labor. The residents lived in near isolation, and many were pro-Union. They had voted against secession when Tennessee left the Union, and in at least one instance had attempted to secede from the Confederacy.

A Confederate army short on rations and moving through this area could expect little support from a populace that, if not outright hostile, was certainly not supportive of the Southern cause. Jenkins expressed concern early in the campaign over the lack of commissary support and the tendency of his hungry soldiers to forage for food. He observed that scavengers often became looters and that once soldiers were turned loose on the populace for food, all kinds of deplorable behavior would follow.[10]

Major General Ambrose Burnside, commander of Federal troops in the valley, had established cavalry outposts on both sides of the Tennessee River below the village of Loudon.[11] His infantry was centered about Knoxville but scattered throughout the valley, with outposts at Loudon in the south and Bristol in the north. Rumors of Confederate invasion necessitated that Burnside keep his army at a high degree of readiness; however, by late October heavy rains had so diluted the roads and swollen the rivers that the Union commander was convinced the year's campaigning was over and he began preparing winter quarters.[12]

As the South Carolina brigade toiled up the muddy road toward Loudon, Jenkins learned from scouts that a crossing of the swollen Tennessee River at that site would be a hazardous undertaking. A Federal cavalry regiment guarded the

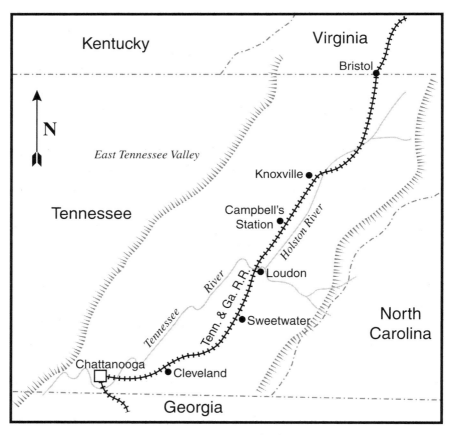

East Tennessee Valley

The East Tennessee Valley runs generally southwest to northeast through an upland plateau cut by two large rivers, the Holston and the Tennessee. A winter campaign in such an isolated valley was an extremely hazardous endeavor.

proposed river crossing and accompanying infantry was encamped nearby. In addition, the river was high and running
with a strong current. Jenkins decided to detach and advance
a small force forward, attempting a coup by suddenly taking
and holding a river crossing. Erecting a pontoon bridge he
would then rush his leading brigade across. "A" company of
the Palmetto Sharpshooters under Captain Alfred Foster was
selected for the delicate and dangerous task of securing the
crossing. One soldier of this unit described the task:

> We went over in boats, which were conveyed quietly by
> the men to the river and launched, taking an officer and
> eighteen men into each boat....All, for a time was silence,
> nothing to be heard but the rippling of the water against
> the sides of the boats, and each moment was counted as
> we expected to hear the splashing of minies into the
> water....But on landing we captured a few picket posts
> and the yankees skedalled.[13]

The remaining Palmetto Sharpshooters followed and the pontoon bridge was rapidly thrown across the river. Soon a brigade was across, then another. As Jenkins deployed his
available soldiers, Federal skirmishers pushed forward, followed by long lines of blue-clad infantry. After several hours
of heavy skirmishing, the enemy fell back about nightfall.
Burnside had undoubtedly hoped to catch the leading Confederate brigade in the process of crossing the river, but rapid
deployment of the pontoon bridge and spirited efforts by the
two leading brigades prevented this dangerous ambush.
Burnside briefly considered a night attack on the bridgehead,
but when his cavalry scouts reported large numbers of rebels
across the river, Burnside canceled the attack and ordered a
retreat.[14]

Early the following morning, Jenkins began to pursue.
The Hampton Legion led, deployed in a skirmish line, closely
followed by a brigade. Jenkins reported:

My instructions being to press upon the enemy's rear and
if possible to bring him to bay, thus giving McLaws' Division, moving on a parallel road, an opportunity to strike
the enemy in flank or rear.[15]

Lieutenant Colonel Thomas M. Logan admirably handled the
Legion and despite deplorable road conditions he maintained
contact with the Federal rear guard for the next three days.
On several occasions the opposing force halted and deployed
for battle, sharp exchanges of fire resulting. Logan's men captured several artillery pieces and some prisoners, but on each
occurrence the Union force detached itself by forced night
marches, admirably screened by cavalry. Both armies were
exhausted by the constant marching on the mud-filled roads,
but the retreat and pursuit continued. Burnside was forced to
abandon most of his wagons and baggage in order to utilize 12
to 16 horses for each artillery piece. Many of his guns were
saved in this manner. He issued orders to burn the wagons,
but scores were simply left in parks alongside the road. The
edible contents of these vehicles was welcome succor to
Jenkins's hungry men, as were the large number of Union
field tents that would ultimately shelter the Confederate army
during the coming winter months.

Longstreet had ordered McLaws to pursue on a parallel
road in an attempt to cut off Burnside's force. His division
advanced unopposed, but the Federal cavalry scouts provided
Burnside with constant reports of McLaws's progress. Near
the small town of Campbell's Station a crossing road con-
nected the parallel routes. Hoping to force a general engagement at that point Jenkins increased his pressure on the
Union rear guard, Colonel William Humphrey's Michigan
brigade. Jenkins requested a battery be advanced forward to
open on the enemy column. Delighted, Colonel Alexander accompanied the battery and commented on an exchange with
Federal artillery:

...we got in a sharp and pretty artillery duel over some nice open ground unusually favorable for it, during which one of our guns, a twenty pound Parrott exploded, but fortunately without killing anyone.[16]

The artillery exchange forced additional Union infantry to deploy in order to protect their guns. Jenkins rushed brigades to the front, deployed, and prepared to attack the enemy at once. As he surveyed the Federal position, Jenkins decided to attempt a movement on the enemy's left as he expected McLaws to arrive on the Union right at any moment. Despite sharp enemy artillery fire and muddy roads, he ordered the brigades of Law and Anderson to move by their right around the Union left. Jenkins's old South Carolina brigade faced the Federal center and continued to press forward against the enemy. Law's brigade led the movement onto a line of low hills. He was instructed to advance far enough that when the two brigades deployed, the last regiment of Anderson's brigade was aligned with the Federal guns, which were finding ready targets in the Confederate center.[17] At that point the two brigades were to attack the Union flank.

The terrain was difficult, being hilly and covered with scrub pines and cedar, and there was considerable delay in moving the troops into position. At about dusk Law reported both brigades ready, and Jenkins immediately ordered the assault. When Law released his men, his brigade dashed forward at a left oblique and collided with Anderson's advancing brigade. By this time it was quite dark, and the attack ground out in chaos and confusion. The Union artillery limbered and withdrew, followed by their supporting infantry. By a strenuous all-night march Burnside's forces reached the defenses of Knoxville on the next morning. Burnside reported the action at Campbell's Station as "A sharp but brief affair in which he suffered 300 casualties and estimated Jenkins' loss at 175."[18]

The Union commander had positioned a blocking force on the road by which McLaws was expected. This force withdrew as a rear guard, and McLaws arrived about thirty minutes after Jenkins's abortive attack—too late to influence the outcome or cut off the enemy retreat.

Micah Jenkins, disappointed and frustrated, angrily confronted the two brigade commanders. Law claimed that one of his regimental commanders had made a mistake of direction, and in the darkness the other regiments followed. For the first time in his career, Jenkins truly lost control in rebuking Law and Anderson. In his battle report his remarks were even more pointed. He stated:

> Brigadier Law stated that his brigade had been misled by the mistakes of his regiment of direction in closing the interval between it and Anderson's Brigade on its left. I do not conceive that a regiment of direction should have been so instructed as to leave such a change in direction discretionary, and the immediate directing presence of the Brigade Commander, by whom the position of the enemy had been seen and examined should have corrected the mistake at its inception.[19]

This was extremely harsh criticism of a brigade commander, but Jenkins, always the perfectionist, could not understand what he perceived as a lackadaisical handling of troops. Jenkins prepared his assault columns meticulously, always identifying the exact point to be assaulted. He could never understand officers who did not prepare to this level. Certainly he was disappointed that despite all the efforts to pursue and punish the enemy, Burnside had escaped with slight loss. A successful attack could have been very rewarding. The Federal guns and a substantial portion of their infantry would surely have been captured. With McLaws's appearance on the Union right, Burnside may have faced destruction of his entire force.

Jenkins had made some difficult decisions, and some were open to his critics. Law and his supporters felt the attack should not have been made at nightfall. But Jenkins's three days of frustrated pursuit and his instincts told him that the enemy would not have been there come morning. A more prudent course of action might have involved positioning the troops and attacking at dawn, but his aggressive nature would not wait, and his judgment that Burnside would retreat was surely correct. The only possibility of punishing the Federal force was the assault at dusk. Several regimental commanders thought Jenkins was asking the impossible in ordering a night attack over such difficult terrain. Certainly the task was difficult, but to overcome the superb tactics of Burnside in retreat, the difficult was demanded. A commander usually receives only the level of effort from his subordinates that he demands. Jenkins asked for that effort from Evander Law, but it was not forthcoming.

The following morning the reunited Confederate army moved in pursuit of the enemy, reaching the outskirts of Knoxville by mid-afternoon. The Union position at Knoxville, based upon previously prepared Confederate entrenchments, was unusually strong due primarily to its excellent defensive terrain features. The Holston River bisected the Federal line. North of the river, the town of Knoxville was located on a narrow tableland or ridge about 150 feet above river level. On both sides of the river were several high points that were fortified by the Federals. To abandon the hilltops south of the river would have invited artillery domination of the entire position.[20] On the highest point, Fort Sanders was erected. This redoubt was named for Brigadier General William P. Sanders, who lost his life while skillfully directing the Federal cavalry screen that successfully impeded the Confederate advance.[21]

The heights on the south side of the river were considered so vital to the Federal position that a pontoon bridge was constructed connecting these forts with the city. When a rumor of Southern raft construction was received, an iron cable was attached onto the upstream side to prevent the severing of this vital supply and communication link.[22] Within several days all Federal outposts were withdrawn into the defense works and an actual siege began.

Longstreet met with Jenkins, McLaws, and Alexander to consider which portion of the Union lines seemed most vulnerable to assault. Any major successful penetration would be disastrous for Burnside since his position astride the river would be almost impossible to evacuate. Fort Sanders was a logical assault point to consider. It was mounted on strong terrain but the results of its capture would be decisive. If the fort fell and Alexander's guns could be positioned on that site, the remainder of the Federal lines would be untenable. Burnside would be forced to surrender or attempt a difficult breakout to the north. That Burnside agreed on the vital position of Fort Sanders is attested by a sortie that he permitted on November 24. As Confederate trenches grew nearer, a fierce sortie was staged by the 24th Michigan, who captured and occupied an undefended portion of the rebel trenches for a short time. However, a counterattack cleared the trench, and caused heavy casualties.[23]

Thus, Fort Sanders was selected as the point of assault. A plan was developed to attack the fort at daybreak on November 25 after a concentrated bombardment by Alexander's batteries. The earnest young artillery commander worked diligently to locate his 34 guns to bear on the fort's earthen walls. Several of the guns were selected to serve as mortars by placing them in pits.[24] Jenkins was very concerned over the assault plan. He felt the forts walls were too steep to be easily scaled and argued that ladders and fascines be constructed to assist the soldiers in crossing the ditch and climbing the walls.[25] Additionally, a strange and unique obstacle had been constructed in front of Fort Sanders. When the fort was erected, the small trees covering the area were cut to provide clear fields of fire; with the stumps, two to three feet high, all that remained. Brigadier General Orlando M. Poe, having discovered a number of reels of telegraph wire at a nearby depot, had the wire strung from stump to stump and interwoven to create a menacing looking obstacle.[26] When Jenkins approached Longstreet concerning the assault plan, the commanding general responded angrily. Jenkins was a favorite of the commander, but in this instance he was scolded for questioning the assault plan. In a note to Jenkins, Longstreet stated:

> Keep your men at their work, and do not listen to the idea of failing, and we shall not fail....No men who are determined to succeed can fail....Let me urge you not to entertain such feelings for a moment.[27]

The attack was postponed when Longstreet received a message that Bragg was sending reinforcements. Two brigades under Brigadier General Bushrod R. Johnson and Brigadier General Archibald Gracie, Jr., were withdrawn from the Confederate lines opposing Grant's growing army in Chattanooga and sent north to Knoxville. Exactly why Bragg dispatched this force is difficult to ascertain. Perhaps he reasoned that the additional troops would bring a speedy conclusion to affairs around Knoxville, and Longstreet could return with the entire force prior to any movement by Grant. Several additional days were wasted by cold rain, and fog.[28]

The actual attack was to be carried out by McLaws's division, which had seen little action since leaving Chattanooga. Three assault columns of about one thousand men each were selected to make the attack.[29] Jenkins was to provide one brigade under Anderson, which was to follow McLaws's columns into the fort and roll up the Union trenches extending to the right. Anderson's men would not advance until the fort was secure.

During the days of delay, Longstreet changed his attack plan. He decided to attack at dawn with no artillery preparation, relying instead on surprise. Alexander protested vigorously. He felt his guns were well placed and could achieve significant results. Longstreet brushed aside Alexander's concerns much as he had the earlier protestations of Jenkins.[30] One suspects that Longstreet may have been overconfident. He probably did not feel that the relatively green Union troops could resist an attack by his veteran infantry. It is somewhat ironic that McLaws would later face charges for lack of proper preparation for the assault. He was accused of not providing ladders, axes, and scaling materials, the very preparations for which Jenkins had begged and been chastised by his commander. The Federal garrison of the diminutive fort consisted of about five hundred men. Elements of the 79th New York, the 29th Massachusetts, and the 2nd and 20th Michigan were assembled in the fort with 12 cannon.[31] Brigadier General Edward Ferrero commanded the position, including the entrenchments extending to either side that contained ample reinforcements if needed. After sundown on November 28 the assault columns were quietly moved forward into the rifle pits facing Fort Sanders. They spent a miserable night in temperatures around the freezing point and a cold rain. At dawn three signal guns were fired, and the columns dashed toward the fort. Sharpshooters, who fired over their heads at the fort's parapet, actively supported the attack. The soldiers picked their way through the telegraph wire obstructions and leaped into the ditch surrounding the fort. There the trouble began. The 11-foot ditch and 13-foot parapet formed one continuous wall, as the berm had wisely been cut away.[32] Additionally, the earthen walls had frozen during the night and the slope of 45 degrees was virtually unclimbable. When several officers and the colorbearers of the 13th and 17th Mississippi and the 16th Georgia did manage to climb the wall, they were either shot or pulled inside and captured along with their standards. Prior to the assault, the fort's gunners had prepared a number of shells with short fuses. These were put to effective use. Twenty-one-year-old Lieutenant Samuel Benjamin of the 2nd United States Artillery used his cigar to light the fuses and tossed the shells into the ditch, where they exploded among the trapped Confederates. The mass of soldiers milled around in the ditch as the defenders tossed bombs, rocks, and cannonballs into their midst. Sergeant Frank Judge of Company D, 79th New York, watched one brave attacker struggle up the face of the wall. Under a hail of bullets, Judge rushed out the embrasure, seized him by the collar and pulled him and his flag within the fort.[33]

After 20 minutes Longstreet sounded a recall. But retreating was more difficult than attacking. Soldiers were exposed to enemy fire from the fort as well as trenches on either side as they dashed for the safety of their own lines. A large percentage of the Confederate casualties occurred during this difficult retreat. Some soldiers refused to expose themselves and surrendered while in the ditch. Anderson thought he saw an opportunity to aid McLaws and sent his brigade to bolster the attack, but was likewise repulsed. Confederate losses were estimated at eight hundred killed, wounded, or captured and three Confederate colonels—Colonel S. L. Ruff of the 18th Georgia, Lieutenant Colonel H. P. Thomas of the 16th Georgia, and Colonel Kennon McElroy of the 13th Mississippi—lay dead in the ditch before the fort.[34] The repulse was absolute, and the inexperienced Union soldiers gained much-needed confidence from repelling the veterans of the I Corps of the Army of Northern Virginia.[35] One Federal officer described the repulse as Fredericksburg in reverse, and although the attack was not nearly the scale of Burnside's ill-fated assault on Marye's Hill, the results must have provided a measure of satisfaction to the heavily bewhiskered and much-criticized Union commander.

Micah Jenkins, fiery and aggressive, rushed to Longstreet and obtained permission to organize a second attempt utilizing his division.[36] He immediately set about collecting ladders, boards, and axes to cut steps into the earthen wall. Alexander carefully rechecked his already-sighted guns in preparation for a preliminary bombardment. Both young officers were convinced that they could succeed, but during the afternoon

Longstreet received a message that Grant had stormed the heights at Lookout Mountain and Missionary Ridge, and that Bragg was in full retreat into northern Georgia.[37] After the battle Grant dispatched a large Federal force under Major General Philip H. Sherman to relieve Burnside. Jenkins and Alexander argued that a successful assault would force Burnside's surrender long before help could arrive. But Longstreet, cut off from Bragg's army and on his own, determined not to risk an additional attack. His army was short on supplies, and he made plans to lift the siege of Knoxville. General Poe, in later writing on the siege from his personal perspective, agreed with Jenkins in that he felt the initial attack on Fort Sanders failed only because the soldiers were not provided with scaling materials. He disagreed with Jenkins and Alexander, however, on the outcome of a second attack; he did not believe an artillery bombardment would have damaged the fort and also commented on the heavy reinforcements sent into the fort by Burnside after the first attack. Poe was convinced a second assault would have resulted in an outcome similar to the first.[38]

Longstreet's army lingered on the outskirts of Knoxville for several days until he was certain of Sherman's advance. On the night of December 4, the Confederate force quietly left the Knoxville lines and moved north by forced march to Bean's Station. The night march was extremely hard on officers and men. The weather was bitterly cold, and the column was forced to ford a number of waist-deep streams. Since fires were not allowed, ice clung to the boots, pants, and clothing of the soldiers.[39] Morale was extremely low. The campaign into East Tennessee, which had begun with such promise, concluded with the humiliating defeat at Fort Sanders. Jenkins, amazed at the dedication of the soldiers under such adverse circumstances reported:

> The campaign was rendered severe due to a lack of shoes....but all was borne with commendable cheerfulness

and high spirits by the men. There was a tendency to straggle and a most disgraceful spirit of plunder, which by stringent measures has been restrained and corrected.[40]

But Jenkins observed that grumbling and continued dissatisfactions among the officer corps were of greater concern. He found that the dedication shown by the men was lacking in their officers.

....that the spirit of the men, instead of being encouraged and sustained against the hardships....some, from whom the country had a right to expect more, on the contrary expressed a lack of support of the army's efforts.[41]

As the army moved north the roads dried and progress improved. By late December Longstreet's small force was preparing winter quarters near Morristown, Tennessee. Snug encampments were constructed in the wooded mountain valleys. Soldiers used the ample supply of United States Army tents, which they floored with pine boards and equipped with stone and mud chimneys for heat. Supply efforts improved, and spirits began to rise despite several heavy snows. Colonel Alexander reported that "bushwhackers" caused some problems. Although they never took prisoners, several groups of pro-Union sympathizers watched the camps in hopes of cutting off the small parties of forage wagons dispatched for rations and wood.[42] Since insufficient cavalry was available to disperse these bands, infantry guards were assigned to accompany the wagons. Soldiers who were warm, dry, and well fed enjoyed the snowstorms, which provided lazy days with no action and little duty.[43]

On the 21st of February, Jenkins received leave to return to South Carolina and he left in high spirits, anxious to see his wife and sons. On Longstreet's orders he turned over the division to Major General Buckner, who was well received by the soldiers. But on March 9, newly promoted Major General Charles Field arrived in camp and assumed command of the division. Field was dispatched by the War Department in an attempt to settle the differences between Law and Jenkins as it was believed neither could successfully lead the division with the other in brigade command. Field had experienced considerable action in the early years of the war and had led a brigade in the II Corps. Severe wounds had prevented his holding a combat command for some time. He was a stern disciplinarian, and his severe punishments made him, initially, extremely unpopular with the soldiers. Jenkins returned to the army on March 20, having enjoyed several weeks with his family and stopped in Greenville, South Carolina, on his return trip to testify in the court-martial of General McLaws. Upon reporting for duty, Jenkins was immediately assigned to command of his South Carolina brigade. The brigade members were pleased by his return to that post. One soldier stated:

> All await his return with pleasure and satisfaction as the brigade has had many different commanders and is going to ruin very fast. It will need such a commander as General Jenkins to bring it back to its former efficiency and discipline.[44]

Jenkins returned to brigade command with renewed spirit and determination. He had been frustrated over the absence of success during the fall campaign and abhorred the infighting among officers for which Longstreet's command had become noted. Surely he was disappointed that he had not received the desired promotion to major general and divisional command, but the visit home lifted his resolve to complete the struggle to which he was committed. He immediately set about preparing the brigade for future action, and he established a relationship with General Field that depicted the Christian character of both men. Daily drill was reinstituted, and new recruits were added to the regiments. Rumors were adrift that Longstreet's force would soon return to the Army of Northern Virginia. Many of the veterans were anxious to be rid of Tennessee; even the commanding general seemed eager to return. As Moxley Sorrel later observed: "while it was more honorable, possibly, to have a separate command, he preferred being under General Lee, as it relieved him of responsibility and assured confidence."[45]

The controversies among officers make it difficult to assess the performance of Micah Jenkins as a divisional commander. He never led the division in a major action, but it would seem his ability was such that he would have performed well at that level. His pursuit of Burnside's force up the East Tennessee Valley was well planned, energetic, and aggressive. His precipitous commitment to battle at Campbell's Station may have appeared rash, but his assessment that a morning attack would be too late was correct. His performance at Knoxville was precise and diligent, and his assessment and recommendations on the Fort Sanders attack were exacting. He exerted excellent control of his division, although hampered by the animosity of Law toward himself and Longstreet and that of Longstreet toward Law. It would seem that Jenkins had earned promotion, but Longstreet's partisanship toward protégés like Jenkins and Kershaw only made their advancement more difficult, as Longstreet's quarrels with other officers reduced the value of his recommendations to Davis and the War Department. It appeared, and was believed by many, that Lee's "War Horse," when given independent command, was unable to manage his subordinates. He seemed biased toward some and vindictive with others. The results were not favorable for the officers involved or for the Confederate army.

Chapter 11
Crisis in Command

As snow and winter cold curtailed military operations in the mountains of Tennessee, the crisis in Confederate command heated up. Lingering disagreements and feuds erupted into open arguments, and the principals involved—Jefferson Davis, James Longstreet, Lafayette McLaws, Evander Law, and Micah Jenkins—would voluntarily or coincidentally contribute to a number of actions which resulted in unbecoming consequences for themselves and the struggling Confederacy.

Jefferson Davis, chief executive officer of the Confederate States, was a complex, proud, and talented individual. He enjoyed a vast background of experience in both civic and military affairs and he demonstrated strong, resolute leadership during the infant nation's struggle for survival. His stiff determination and dogged persistence served the cause well. Another man with less willpower might have folded when faced with some of the disappointments that Davis routinely encountered. But Davis also had certain weaknesses, and some became glaringly apparent as the matters in East Tennessee expanded. Davis, a graduate of West Point, had served with distinction as a commander of Mississippi volunteers during the Mexican war, and he considered himself quite a military expert.[1] He often remarked that he could replace any Confederate general with the exception of Robert E. Lee. Federal

Commander Ulysses S. Grant, however, in later writings, was not so complimentary. He felt that Davis's military expertise was actually a boon to Union efforts on occasions.[2] Grant contended that Davis knew only enough militarily to interfere with his generals.

Davis brought some disturbing tendencies from his army days to the Confederate White House. Seemingly he could not separate ability and friendship. He consistently overrated the military ability and expertise of his old army friends to an unrealistic level.[3] Likewise, he deferred the recommendations of those who disagreed with his judgments or policies. Albert Johnson, Leonidas Polk, and Braxton Bragg were among those whose friendship he prized from earlier days and whose abilities he highly valued.[4] On occasions these friends merited his support, but when they did not, he was unswerving. He simply would not remove or censure these officers despite their failures or even incompetence. A case in point was his relationship with Braxton Bragg, whose vacillating and bumbling leadership of the Army of Tennessee resulted in a number of defeats and several barren victories. Yet Davis retained Bragg in command of that proud, potent army until it was nearly destroyed by casualties, desertions, and crumbling morale. When finally forced to relieve him, Davis brought him to Richmond to serve as military advisor to his office, actually increasing his military influence. Contradictorily, officers such as Joseph Johnston, P. G. T. Beauregard, and D. H. Hill were so mistrusted by Davis, due to their opposition to his policies or theories that their contributions to the Confederate cause were considerably less than their abilities would indicate. Davis consistently related personal loyalty and national loyalty.

A second disturbing propensity of Jefferson Davis was an overpowering belief in the infallibility of his personal judgment. This trait quickly discouraged those officers bold enough to present contrary opinion or offer advice. This inflexible tendency to disparage those not in agreement appeared in his discussions with James Longstreet during his visit to the Army of Tennessee. Bragg had complimented Longstreet's role in the battle of Chickamauga, so Davis expected Longstreet to, in turn, support Bragg. When Longstreet joined the other officers in recommending Bragg's removal, Davis became disturbed. Further when asking for Longstreet's recommendation as to a possible replacement for Bragg, Davis was angered at Longstreet's endorsement of his old adversary Joseph Johnston.[5] These unexpected replies indicated to Davis some disloyalty in Longstreet.

A third relevant Davis trait was a tendency to postpone decisions.[6] When he was perplexed over a question, he would sometimes ignore the matter in hopes that the problem would solve itself. His refusal to endorse Longstreet's suggestion to put either Jenkins or Law in charge of Hood's division is another case in point.[7] Davis simply would not adopt either of the general's suggestions. Instead, he left for the capital with the matter unresolved. Further controversy would have been avoided by the promotion of one of the officers and the transfer of the other. Lee, who was politically astute in his dealings with Davis, could perhaps have convinced the chief executive to resolve the matter. Officers who performed poorly or created dissension in the Army of Northern Virginia were not brought up on charges; they simply and quietly appeared in a less demanding role in another theater of operations.

"Old Pete" Longstreet, West Point graduate and veteran army officer, brought his own characteristics to the fray. He had risen very rapidly in Confederate service to the rank of lieutenant general. Longstreet and Stonewall Jackson, his sometime rival, commanded the original two corps of the Army of Northern Virginia. On every field upon which that army had fought and bled, he demonstrated his skills and steady leadership. Douglas Freeman, Lee's biographer, described Longstreet as blunt, solid, systematic, and an outstanding administrator and tactical leader, yet Freeman found

Longstreet lacking in strategic skills.[8] Longstreet possessed enormous physical energy, never showing fatigue, but he seemed not to be the same soldier when in independent command. He was openly partial in his support of fellow South Carolinians Micah Jenkins and Joseph Kershaw. At times he was outspoken in his opposition to the promotion of Virginians in Lee's army, and he could be petty and vindictive toward those who opposed his choices.[9] His manipulative efforts to promote favorite subordinates were surely an outgrowth of his observations of Lee's systematic rewarding of the young lions of his own army. Aggressive young commanders were promoted in the Army of Northern Virginia, while other Confederate commands were filled with those who did not meet Lee's standards. But Longstreet possessed neither the influence and the insight, nor the tact of Lee. Every move that Longstreet made, seemingly met with opposition. His most obvious shortcoming was his refusal to deal openly and fairly with his subordinates.

Lafayette McLaws, short and portly, was an old army officer of some distinction. He graduated from the United States Military Academy with Longstreet; in fact, the two had been friends since boyhood in northern Georgia.[10] McLaws was promoted to major general early in the war based on his organizational ability—administrative skills that were highly valued by the Confederate army in the weeks after 1st Manassas. His combat leadership record was more suspect. His division had always performed well in defensive fighting, but their commander sometimes hesitated in delivering a blow to the enemy. Most in the army considered him competent but not growing as a divisional commander.[11] It may have been that McLaw's initial abilities were his best traits and as younger officers around him matured and developed in the profession of arms he appeared to diminish. His best performance was a solid defensive fight at Fredericksburg, and he certainly was never as electrifying as Robert Rodes at Chancellorsville or

South Mountain, Stephen Ramseur at Spotyslvania, Evander Law at 2nd Manassas, or Micah Jenkins at Seven Pines. He was never quite prepared to accept the risk of losing for the chance of a significant gain.

After Jackson's death when the Army of Northern Virginia was reorganized into three corps, McLaws expected, as senior brigadier, to be promoted to corps command. When A. P. Hill was promoted over him, he complained bitterly to Longstreet and Lee. McLaws had long been an admirer of Longstreet, but after the Battle of Gettysburg he seemed to change his mind. Shortly after returning to Virginia he wrote his wife an appraisal of his superior's ability: "He is a man of small capacity, very obstinate, conceited and selfish. If I can, it is my intention to get away from his command."[12]

McLaws was aware that Bragg had considered him for promotion after Chickamauga and that Longstreet had not endorsed the recommendation. Longstreet's private opinion was that McLaws had lost his nerve as a combat officer at Gettysburg.[13] McLaw's conduct during the East Tennessee campaign was so lethargic and slow that he was reprimanded several times. Perhaps unfairly, Longstreet attributed the unsuccessful attack on Fort Sanders totally to McLaws. Of much more serious consequence was his inept pursuit of Burnside up the East Tennessee Valley. A competent, professional performance by McLaws on the march up the valley would, almost surely, have resulted in a Confederate victory and removed the cause for the costly mistakes at Fort Saunders.

Evander McIvor Law was young, ambitious, and aggressive. He had earned early promotion in Confederate service through exemplary performances at Seven Pines, 2nd Manassas, and other battles in the eastern sector. He was hard driving, demanding of his troops, and extremely sensitive to his reputation. At Gettysburg he led the division after Hood was wounded and led it fairly well, despite Longstreet's criticism that he should have captured Little Round Top. These critical comments were public enough that Law certainly knew of them and probably provided the basis for the growing animosity between him and his commander. He became further incensed by Longstreet's continued advocacy for Micah Jenkins to lead the division. Some officers accused Law of dragging his feet while serving under Jenkins. A statement attributed to Law that "he could not be expected to furnish silver spurs for Jenkins's new uniform as major general" incensed Longstreet.[14] The separation between Law and Longstreet gradually became irreconcilable. In an attempt to gain support Law began to delve into the political arena. He actively sought the support of Hood, who he felt had the president's ear. He also attempted to ally himself with McLaws and others to discredit Longstreet, much as the corps commander had participated in the uprising against Braxton Bragg. Law was a valuable and brave brigade commander who, upon perceiving himself as unappreciated by his superior, allowed his frustrations and anger to affect his performance. Sadly, these actions curtailed his potential advancement and future effectiveness.

Micah Jenkins also brought his character and personal traits to the melee. First and foremost a product of the wealthy elite, reared and accustomed to the natural assumption of command, he easily assumed a role of leadership. While not outwardly arrogant, he surely believed himself the equal of any and superior to most. Like Law, he was extremely sensitive to criticism or questions by others as to his ability and performance. He was certainly ambitious, as evidenced by the many letters to his wife expressing his desire to achieve promotion and at one point despairing of his ever being promoted to brigadier. He also complained of inactivity while on the Blackwater line, because such inaction gave no opportunity to achieve further promotion. He was brave to the point of rashness and he strove for promotion as a reward for courage and performance. His promotion to brigadier general after Seven Pines was as close to a promotion for valor as the Confederate Congress awarded. Asbury Coward, his friend, classmate, and partner, when questioned as to Jenkins's ambitious nature answered as follows:

> Was he ambitious? Yes, he was full of ambition, free from all sordid or selfish taint—an ambition for high achievement in the cause of humanity and country, the noble ambition of exalted souls.[15]

In May of 1864, the *Charleston Mercury* addressed the ambition of Micah Jenkins in an editorial:

> He was ambitious of distinction and strove to win it; but he raised himself over his rivals by no meanness or indirection, and practiced no arts of advancement save the honest arts of resolute will and earnest endeavor.[16]

Jenkins seems to have suffered an internal struggle of conflicting values. His ambitious drive for recognition and advancement conflicted with his deep belief in the Christian virtues of modesty and demureness. For above all Jenkins was a devout Christian. His belief in a godly purpose for his life was all encompassing. He sought advancement that was merited by performance. His bravery under fire, his exacting almost perfectionist handling of troops, and his dogged persistence to achieve designated goals were characteristics that had dominated his civilian life. Each of his commanding officers praised his military performance, and he had grown rapidly as a military leader. But his strong ambition, though straightforward and honest, became a liability when supported in partisan fashion by Longstreet. Like Law, he was naïve to the politics of army life, whereupon political influence was often more important than performance. The weapons of political conflict were skillful infighting and the exertion of pressure from obtuse sources. Micah Jenkins had little knowledge of such weapons.

On the 16th of December Micah Jenkins filed charges against Brigadier General J. B. Robertson, commander of Hood's old Texas brigade, based on Robertson's conduct of a minor action at Bean's Station. He specified that Robertson, while under orders to advance his brigade rapidly, had called a conference of his regimental commanders and allegedly stated that there were only three days of food remaining, and he no longer had confidence in the present campaign. Further, Jenkins alleged, Robertson commented that he would no longer obey verbal orders from Jenkins or Longstreet and would request all further orders in writing. Jenkins appropriately charged that Roberson's actions were prejudicial to good order and military discipline.[17] Longstreet endorsed the charges and suspended Robertson from command of the famous brigade, long noted as the shock troops of Lee's army, but now much weakened by unreplaced casualties. Robertson was assigned to command the reserve troops of his native Texas and left the army for the West. While a brave officer, Robertson was an average brigade commander, and the charges and resulting dismissal might have been considered routine but for the controversy that was to follow.

On December 17 Longstreet relieved Layafette McLaws from command of his division on the grounds that "he had exhibited a want of confidence in the efforts and plans which the commanding general had thought proper to adopt."[18] Longstreet was displeased with McLaws's exceedingly slow progress up the East Tennessee Valley in pursuit of Burnside, but all the charges were based upon the failed attack on Fort Saunders. The major charge was neglect of duty with three specifications:

(1.) Poor arrangement and handling of sharpshooters in the attack.

(2.) Not choosing select troops to make the assault.

(3.) Centering the attack on an incorrect point as well as failure to provide ladders and fascines to assist the soldiers in crossing the ditch and scaling the walls of the fort.[19]

In February a military court was convened in Greenville, South Carolina, to consider Longstreet's charges. Proceedings and specific testimony have been lost, but as a result of the proceedings, McLaws was found not guilty on specifications one and two and guilty on the third. A strange conclusion when one considers that Longstreet expressly forbade the exact preparations for which McLaws was convicted. He was suspended from command and rank for 60 days, but the guilty specification was reversed by the War Department, and McLaws was returned to duty. He was, however, transferred to an administrative post and never returned to a combat command. Deserving Joseph Kershaw was promoted to major general and assumed command of McLaws's division.

On December 19 Evander Law approached Longstreet and submitted his written resignation. His stated purpose was to obtain a transfer to the cavalry, and he requested a leave of absence to personally deliver this resignation to the War Department. Longstreet approved both requests with obvious relief, for he had commented to Moxley Sorrel that the division would continue to suffer with both Jenkins and Law serving within it.[20] Soon after Law departed, Longstreet heard rumors of a petition being circulated among the Alabama regiments in his brigade requesting transfer to another theater under Law's command.[21] Longstreet immediately filed charges against Law, accusing him of resigning and obtaining leave under false pretenses, while at the same time petitioning with his brigade to seek service in Alabama. The formal charge was spreading discontent.[22] It was soon reported to the commanding general that Law had arrived in Richmond but had not presented his resignation to the War Department. Old Pete fired off another charge against Law, that of conduct unbecoming an officer and gentleman.[23] Specifically, he charged Law with stealing and destroying the already accepted request for resignation. Actually, Law had arrived in the capital and met with his convalescing former superior, John Hood, who convinced him not to submit the resignation but to return to his brigade in Tennessee. Law journeyed back to the army, and Longstreet placed him under arrest. Law returned to Richmond to defend his conduct directly to the War Department. He was successful, and in the late spring, Longstreet was informed that the charges were dismissed. Law was to be restored to his brigade command. Upon his return Law was arrested again by Longstreet, who in a letter to Lee stated: "I can not maintain discipline and spirit if Law could return to duty without trial."[24] Lee supported Longstreet's request for a trial in correspondence with the president,[25] but Davis berated Longstreet for having offended against good, military discipline, in arresting an officer who had been released by the War Department without any new offense having been alleged.[26]

This strange affair thus concluded with Law returning to his Alabama brigade in the division now led by Charles Field.[27] Longstreet complained bitterly to the War Department over the assignment of Field but was promptly informed that President Davis had made the appointment and his continued questioning was an insult to the chief executive.[28]

These three cases, occurring in rapid succession, were blatant signals of growing demoralization in Longstreet's command. While each case might stand on its own merits, altogether they reflected poorly upon Longstreet's leadership skills, a fact of which no one was more aware than he. The charges against Robertson were justified and probably long overdue. His dismissal was not disputed by the Confederate command. The confrontation with Law was an outgrowth of that officer's continued animosity toward Longstreet and Jenkins over his frustrated claims for the command of Hood's division. Law's behavior and actions from the date of his resignation were both unethical and unprofessional. Longstreet's harsh response was to be expected. The commanding general was criticized for not resolving the Law-Jenkins rivalry earlier, but evidence points to Longstreet's several attempts to settle the conflict, for which he received little support and no assistance. The dismissal of those charges seemed more a reprimand of Longstreet by the president than a statement of Law's innocence. The case against McLaws seems much less substantial. McLaws actions in the valley and at Fort Sanders were no more lethargic than his leadership had been for some time. It appears that Longstreet had carried McLaws without complaint for a period and decided to dismiss him when the Fort Sanders attack failed. A poor combat officer McLaws might have become, but Longstreet's charges were of equal quality.

Micah Jenkins was substantially involved in all three cases, although inadvertently in the last two. His reputation and potential were as surely injured by the controversy as that of more direct participants. He initiated and testified as to the charges against Robertson. He was called to testify in the court-martial of McLaws, although the substance of his testimony is unknown. But it was in Longstreet's case against Law that Jenkins suffered real discomfort. Law's defense, when explained in Richmond, centered on Longstreet's prejudice toward Jenkins and the efforts made by the commanding officer to obtain a major general's rank for Jenkins. The rumor persisted that the charges against Law were designed to remove Law as a rival and award Jenkins the division. Micah Jenkins's reputation as a general officer of real potential was curtailed by the specter of excessive ambition. While ambitious he was, as were most, he hardly deserved the discredit he received as a result of the conflict between Longstreet and Law.

Chapter 12
Into the Wilderness

As the vestiges of spring sunshine brought a slow melting of winter snow and ice from about the snug camps of Longstreet's I Corps in Zollicoffer, Tennessee, rumors abounded. The veteran gray-back infantrymen were certain they would soon be recalled to the Virginia army and, to a man, they eagerly anticipated such an order. Most were tired of the gloom and obscurity of their East Tennessee Valley camps and the strong Union sentiment in the area which left them isolated and unappreciated.[1] Micah Jenkins, ill and in constant pain, shared their desire to leave Tennessee. A campaign that had begun with such promise in the fall was now frustrating and discouraging. Hard marching, severe fighting, and merciless weather conditions had been endured with little appreciable results. Jenkins had developed severe carbuncles on his back, probably caused by the lack of a proper diet. The pain was so severe that he could not mount his horse, and he had become thin, pale, and depressed.[2]

When orders reached Longstreet on April 11 to return his corps to the Army of Northern Virginia, he immediately began to move his brigades toward the railhead.[3] Troop movement was, as usual, slow on an antiquated railway. Only about 1,500 men a day could be entrained.[4] However, when the infantrymen reached the railhead, they were surprised to find comfortable passenger coaches waiting, a far cry from the deplorable cattle cars that had carried them westward or the flatcars in which they had departed Chattanooga.

Once loaded, most brigades traveled rapidly, reaching Charlottesville, Virginia, within two days. When the South Carolina brigade reached western Virginia, General Jenkins was so ill that the regimental surgeon sent him home to Yorkville, accompanied by an aide.[5] His brigade enjoyed several days in Charlottesville roaming around the University of Virginia, and some soldiers even visited Thomas Jefferson's home, Monticello, on its nearby mountain. When the troops were formed to leave for Gordonsville, they enthusiastically paraded through the city, an event they long remembered. The ladies of the college town had never witnessed such a grand display of Southern troops and responded accordingly with food and cheers.[6] The brigade was soon in comfortable camps near Gordonsville, drawing adequate rations. On the 29th of April, 1864, General Lee reviewed the I Corps. The unit presented a somewhat ragged appearance, as coats, hats, and shoes were lacking or ragged, but their rifles and cartridge boxes shone brightly, a sign of veteran infantry. From the rowdy reception accorded their gray-bearded commander, it was obvious that morale had returned.[7]

Several days later, a gaunt Micah Jenkins rejoined his command, still unable to ride but duty-bound to take his part in the coming campaign. While at home, Jenkins was bothered by premonitions and dreams. He and Carrie had lost a newborn son to fever in the fall while he was campaigning in Tennessee, and this bothered him greatly. While traveling to Columbia in search of uniforms for his men, he conversed at length with his friend, John Thomas, about recent rumors. Some—namely Captain William Blackford and Colonel Sorrel of Longstreet's staff and Brigadier General Law and Colonel Oates of Law's staff—complained that Jenkins was overly ambitious and loved the act of war for the glory he could earn regardless of the outcome to others. Jenkins sternly disavowed these claims. Thomas later reported that Jenkins told him that

> He recognized his duty and would do his best to fulfill that duty, but that he detested war itself as he had witnessed too much of its death and suffering....further, that all he really desired was peace so that he might return to enjoy his home and fireside with Carrie and his little boys.[8]

Micah and Carrie talked often about the future, and on this trip Jenkins seemed to be putting his business affairs in her hands. Their son, John, many years later, quoted his mother as stating that his parents' last farewell was a tearful one, and that his father had told her he "had a dream that he would ride into the next battle....but not ride out."[9]

Jenkins rode back to Virginia with Reverend B. M. Palmer. They openly discussed the serious state of the war, and Palmer commented on Jenkins's Christian nature and unostentatious piety. Palmer was much concerned over Micah's obviously deplorable health and parted from him with an audible prayer that "God would bless him, keep him, and restore him in safety to those whom he loved."[10]

Throughout the war, Jenkins's religious faith had remained steady and strong, as so often expressed in letters to his wife. He believed in a strong and protective God who could and would protect him from all danger and also care for his wife and children.[11] In May of 1862, however, Jenkins wrote of his confidence that if God took him, that same God would protect his family.[12] Chaplain James McDowell believed that Jenkins's religious faith grew stronger and deeper as he witnessed the horrors of war. He saw increased concern by the general over the spiritual welfare of his soldiers.[13] Jenkins constantly welcomed chaplains to his tent and enjoyed his discussions of the scriptures with these men of the cloth.

Unlike Stonewall Jackson, Jenkins never believed that God's hand would determine the outcome of the horrible struggle, yet he firmly believed that a just God would stand by the upright and faithful. His faith was Old Testament, rooted in the teaching of the Episcopal Church on Edisto Island. This faith revealed to a man his duty from which he dare not recoil. He was convinced he was carrying out God's will and mission in the midst of chaos and death—a true soldier of Christ. But as the war progressed, he seemed to sense his survival less likely.

Jenkins's closest friend, Asbury Coward, who knew him as well as any man, attested to Jenkins's strong Christian values. He commented that "from his confirmation, Jenkins was a regular communicant....until his life's end....at home or in camp or on the field of battle, his Bible or his prayer book was always in reach."[14]

Immediately upon arrival at camp near Gordonsville, Jenkins sent for his brother Edward, then serving as a surgeon with the Confederate Hospital Corps. Together they drew up a power of attorney by which Jenkins granted his brothers Edward and John the responsibility of his estates and the care of his wife and children in the event of his death.[15] This action actually confirmed his premonitions of his own demise.

As the Confederate army prepared for the spring's anticipated campaign, major changes were occurring within the opposing Union army. Grant's success in the West convinced President Lincoln that he was a general who would fight and could possibly end this long war. On March 9, 1864, Ulysses Grant was commissioned a lieutenant general and placed in command of all the armies of the United States.[16] He moved east at once and established his headquarters alongside Major General George G. Meade and his Army of the Potomac. Although technically not in command of that army, he remained in its encampments for the remainder of the war; and as the campaign progressed it became known by its adversary as Grant's army. The first indication of change was an order by Grant that all sutlers wagons were to leave the army and

officers were to discard their excess baggage.[17] Veteran Confederates were highly indignant at hearing this order as they
considered Union sutlers their personal property and were
accustomed to acquiring many of their supplies from this
source.[18] But far more important dispatches were soon leaving Grant's tent. With the extraordinary powers accorded him
by Lincoln, Grant began to exert pressure on all of the Confederate field armies on the assumption that Davis could not
strip one area to strengthen another, and any discernable
weakness could be exploited.[19]

Grant's sweeping plan for 1864 was national in scope. He
required Meade's huge Army of the Potomac, reinforced by
Ambrose Burnside's IX Corps, to move against Lee's Army of
Northern Virginia, engage that army and keep it engaged. A
second Union army under Major General Benjamin F. Butler
would advance up the James River from Fort Monroe in an
attempt to capture Richmond or force Lee to weaken his army
to protect the capital. Another force commanded by Major
General Franz Sigel would move south into the Shenandoah
Valley, cutting off that Confederate supply source. Out West
Major General William Sherman, now in command of Federal
troops at Chattanooga, would move southward in an attempt
to destroy Joseph Johnston's Army of Tennessee. Finally, an
army led by Major General Nathaniel Banks would move on
the city of Mobile, Alabama, on the Gulf Coast.[20]

All five armies were to move in concert, exerting maximum pressure on all fronts. The wide advantage in numerical
superiority enjoyed by the Federals would then be used to maximum efficiency. Union forces now had a leader with a clear
purpose and direction. He intended to engage and fight his
Confederate opponents on every front until a decision was
reached. With his manpower and material advantage, Grant
thought the outcome inevitable. James Longstreet, Grant's
friend in the old United States Army, warned other Confederate officers when he stated:

> We must make up our minds to get into line of battle and
> to stay there, for that man will fight us every day and
> every hour until the end of this war. In order to whip him
> we must out-maneuver him, and husband our strength
> as best we can.[21]

Grant could maneuver, but tactical guile was not his
strength. His ability to understand and exploit his strategic
advantages constituted the basis of Grant's eventual greatness as a military leader. As Grant stripped down his army, it
was obvious to all but the greenest recruit that a long, ardu-
ous campaign was about to begin. When he crossed the Rapidan
River, his army would number 119,000 men, magnificently
equipped and well supplied.[22]

In contrast, Lee's army south of the river was experiencing acute shortages. Even with the addition of Longstreet's
Tennessee veterans, Confederate strength still numbered only
65,000 effectives.[23] Lee may not have known how severe the
manpower discrepancy was, but he certainly knew he was at
a disadvantage when he wrote to his son:

> Our country demands all our strength, all our energies.
> To resist the powerful combination now forming against
> us will require every man at his place. If victorious, we
> have everything to hope for in the future. If defeated, noth-
> ing will be left for us to live for.[24]

However, there were other shortages as serious to Southern fortunes as the lack of manpower. The always-fragile
Southern economy was at a critical point. Clothes, shoes, food,
and horses were scarce for the armies as well as the general
populace; and where these commodities were available, a lack
of transport restricted their distribution. The railroad system
was on the verge of collapse, and a shortage of fodder for animals curtailed use of horses and oxen to pull wagons. Lee even
considered disbanding several artillery battalions since horses
were so difficult to find and sustain. Despite the commander's

efforts to reduce leave and nonessential assignments, recruitment was not filling the ranks, and casualties were hard to replace. An opponent with Grant's strategic abilities could not have appeared at a more inopportune moment for Southern fortunes.

Still, the veteran Confederate infantry camped about Gordonsville did not fear the coming clash. Other Federal commanders had moved south with huge armies and Lee had always prevailed. Jenkins's South Carolina brigade was camped slightly north of the small village. Their commander, still weak and generally confined to his tent, enjoyed the visits of his friends. Coward, who was camped nearby, came often, and the two talked late into the night. On one such visit, Jenkins told Coward about a recurring dream that bothered him. In this dream he relived his entire life until after the next battle when the dream became blank. "Why have I not forgotten this dream, as I have all the others I've had before?" he wanted to know. "It's as clear and the details are as sharp as though I actually lived it."[25]

Early on the morning of May 4 Confederate scouts on Clark Mountain indicated by signal flags the news that Grant was across the Rapidan.[26] Union infantry began crossing soon after midnight at Germanna, Ely's, and Culpeper Mine Fords. They headed due east into the Wilderness, one Union column advancing on the Germanna Road and a second on the Brock Road. A third column struggled cross-country between them. Grant intended to move rapidly through the Wilderness, turn Lee's right flank, and force the Confederate commander to give ground toward Richmond or fight on the move. However, the long line of supply wagons was delayed at the fords, slowing Grant's time schedule. Lee, always aggressive, determined to strike Grant while he was on the move, on ground of Lee's choosing—the snarled, tangled thickets of the Wilderness. This area had been fought over several times in the past, notably during the Chancellorsville campaign. Uneven ravines, deep cuts, woods, and thickets characterized its terrain. The second growth timber of pine, scrub oak, and cedar was so thick as to be impenetrable in places. Officers could not determine the position of their foes and, at times, their own men.[27] A few roads crossed the area and, during the following days, these would become critical possessions.

Lee's orderlies rode swiftly to the scattered camps and the gray-clad infantry responded. Soon Ewell's II Corps was pounding down the Orange Turnpike with A. P. Hill's III Corps in motion on the parallel Orange Plank Road, both striving to intercept the Federal force. Longstreet was to gather his I Corps and move across to follow Hill.[28] Ewell's men soon contacted Federal troops under Major General Gouverneur K. Warren near the intersection of the turnpike and Germanna Roads. Fighting escalated as the two forces exchanged fire at close range until Major General John Sedgwick's VI Corps arrived to join Warren's right. Jubal Early's division was dispatched to extend Ewell's left, and the exchange spread. Meanwhile, A. P. Hill, with two divisions, collided with Federals of the VI Corps reinforced by Major General Winfield S. Hancock's II Corps. A second vicious firefight developed in the tangled woods with neither side gaining a clear advantage. Artillery batteries rushed forward, but the newly budding greenery restricted their usefulness.[29] As infantry slugged it out at point-blank range, casualties grew. At nightfall the two actions slowly sputtered out, with the armies digging in yards apart.

Longstreet's I Corps attempted to close rapidly to assist Hill's hard-pressed troops. Jenkins followed his marching brigade in an ambulance as they moved toward the fires glowing on the Plank Road. James McDowell, chaplain of the Palmetto Sharpshooters, joined Jenkins for part of the night ride and found him worrying about his family. He spoke of the visit of Mrs. Jenkins and Mrs. McDowell to the army when the brigade was stationed on the Blackwater River, and how much they all enjoyed the time together. Previously, Jenkins had discussed with McDowell his recent depression over family tragedies: his infant son lost to fever, the recent death of his mother, and the current serious illness of his wife. As they talked, Jenkins asked for the reverend's prayers and declared himself and his family in the hands of a merciful God.[30]

As the column pressed forward, the sound of gunfire became louder. Clearly the action was growing. Jenkins sent for his horse, mounted, and began to ride past his marching brigade. Lieutenant Colonel James R. Hagood recalled that as Jenkins cantered past, he was elegantly dressed and superbly mounted, as always.[31] As Jenkins came down the line, he passed the Palmetto Sharpshooters; when they cheered him, he smiled and exclaimed, "Now, my boys, don't get scared before you are hurt."[32] Further down the line of marching men, he overtook Colonel Coward, riding at the head of his 5th South Carolina. Slowing, Jenkins rode abreast of Coward, saying, "Old man, we are in for it today—we are to break the enemy's line where the Brock road cuts the turnpike."[33] The two men shook hands and Jenkins continued forward.

At daybreak, overwhelming Federal forces fiercely assailed Hill's two divisions, under Major General Harry T. Heth and Major General Cadmus Wilcox. After some sturdy resistance the two divisions fell back upon Lieutenant Colonel William T. Poagues' artillery battalion. Twelve guns belched smoke and grapeshot, bouncing with recoil, as they attempted to stem the blue tide.[34] The Federal troops pressed closer, and then, suddenly, Longstreet's men were there. Sorrel thought the I Corps's response to that emergency the finest performance he had witnessed. The corps formed under fire in the forest, permitted Hill's two III Corps divisions to pass through their ranks and advanced forward, moving through Poague's still smoking guns. Kershaw's division cleared one side of the road and Field's the other, Brigadier General John Gregg's Texans in front.[35] As his attack stabilized the front, Longstreet sent A. A. G. Sorrel to reorganize several III Corps brigades that had retreated into heavy woods on his right. Sorrel found four brigades in good order, and with Brigadier General William Mahone's Virginians in the lead, attacked the Union left flank.

Micah Jenkins, riding in front of his brigade, was coming up behind Gregg when Longstreet joined him and requested that he ride forward with him to the Brock Road so they might determine how to commit his brigade between Mahone and Gregg. At that moment Sorrel rode up, and he joined the cavalcade as it advanced to meet a jubilant Kershaw. Jenkins approached Sorrel and enthusiastically threw his arm about the staff officer's shoulder, stating: "Sorrel, it was splendid; we shall smash them now!"[36] An orderly of Longstreet dismounted as the group of riders reached the Plank Road fifty yards ahead of the advancing line of Jenkins's brigade. Picking up a stand of Federal colors he raised the trophy high and waved the flag vigorously. Suddenly, scattered shots rang out from Mahone's skirmishers, advancing through thick woods and appearing on the right. The group of officers halted, and at that instant a heavy volley was poured into them. Years later a Private Turner of the 41st Virginia, Mahone's brigade, told Sorrel that his regiment fired the volley into what they sincerely believed was Union cavalry.[37] Longstreet was shot through the neck and into the right shoulder. Jenkins was struck directly in the forehead.[38] Two staff officers were also mortally wounded as well as several orderlies. Jenkins's leading regiment formed action front to the right and prepared to fire. The heroic Kershaw, miraculously unscathed, dashed between the two lines with sword drawn, shouting to Mahone's men, "We are Friends." No further exchange occurred. The two injured generals both fell heavily from their horses. Longstreet, bleeding profusely, was feared mortally wounded. Jenkins lay quietly; the ball having penetrated his brain. He was obviously beyond assistance. Surgeon John C. Haskell, who attended Jenkins while awaiting the ambulance, recalled him rising up and cheering his men repeatedly, then falling back, apparently unaware that he was wounded.[39]

Asbury Coward, leading the 5th South Carolina up the turnpike, heard a volley fired to his front. Shortly thereafter, Lieutenant Colonel James P. Sims of Jenkins's staff spurred by, stating that Jenkins and Longstreet had been wounded by a volley from Mahone's men.[40] Coward rushed forward and, upon reaching his wounded friend, dismounted and clasped his hand. He recognized that the wound was fatal but attempted to arouse Jenkins by exclaiming, "Jenkins, Mike, do you know me?" Later, he recalled that Jenkins's "hand exerted some pressure on mine—then his whole body convulsed and he lay back quietly."[41] Soon an ambulance arrived, and the long, slow journey to a Confederate field hospital began. Reverend McDowell entered the ambulance to accompany his wounded brigade commander and attempted several times to speak with Jenkins, but he was unconscious and speechless. His left side was paralyzed, but he repeatedly lifted his right hand to his wound.[42] Upon arrival at the hospital, Jenkins was carried into a tent, but despite the efforts of two surgeons, he died about 5:00 p.m. without regaining consciousness.

That afternoon, Colonel Coward was wounded in the arm and sent to the rear for treatment. After having his wound dressed, Coward rode to the tent where Jenkins lay. Coward recalled:

> His staff, including two brother-in-laws had prepared the body neatly....there were no convulsions of agony on his handsome face....all was calm....the pangs of death had left no trace....his lips had the suggestion of a smile.[43]

General Micah Jenkins was laid out in his best uniform, clutching his sword, and covered with a blood-red battle flag. Torches burned throughout the night as officers and soldiers who could find reason to be in the rear came to view the body of their slain leader. On Saturday morning his friends placed his body in its coffin, the glass front-piece removed for fear it would break in transit.[44] Then his brigade staff bore the body to a waiting ambulance as the band of the 6th South Carolina played the hymn "Old Hundred."[45] The staff watched solemnly as the ambulance pulled away to the lament of a dirge. Micah Jenkins had begun his last journey home.

Jenkins's remains were conveyed to the Confederate capital, and on May 9 the president pro-tem of the Confederate Senate recognized the South Carolina delegation, which invited the senators to attend General Jenkins's funeral from Blevin's on Bank Street, Richmond, at 6:00 p.m. that evening.[46] The following morning the coffin was entrained for Columbia, South Carolina. Reverend Palmer, who had ridden north with Jenkins only a few weeks before, accompanied the body from Richmond. The train arrived in Columbia about dawn the next day, and Palmer walked beside the hearse as a small military escort carried Jenkins's body to Arsenal Hill, where he would lie in state, guarded by cadets from the Arsenal Academy.

The notification of Jenkins's death to his wife and family occurred in a desperately poignant manner. The daily train from Chester to Yorkville customarily announced news of the war with blasts of its whistle as it neared its destination. Short, rapid, blasts of the whistle meant good news, possibly a Confederate victory. Long, doleful blasts indicated grim news or long casualty lists. On this occasion the train whistle wailed for the entire trip from Chester and when the train reached Yorkville the entire town was waiting. Mrs. Jenkins and her young sons were present in their carriage when the news of Jenkins's death was announced.[47]

Burial was initially in the Episcopal Cemetery at Summerville, where Micah Jenkins was laid to rest alongside his mother, Elizabeth C. Jenkins, who had been interred there only a month before.[48] The Jenkins family was traditionally buried in the family burial ground on Cedar Hall Plantation, but Union troops now occupied Edisto Island, preventing such ceremonies.[49]

Several years later the Jenkins family moved the general's remains, along with his mother's, to Magnolia Cemetery in Charleston, South Carolina. Jenkins was reburied just west of the great oak tree that symbolized the Confederate section of the cemetery. In 1881 the Association of Graduates of the South Carolina Military Academy, in response to inquiries concerning Jenkins's unmarked grave, undertook a drive to locate funds for a fitting memorial. The response was immediate, and funds flowed in from friends in South Carolina as well as former comrades in North Carolina and Virginia. A 12-foot granite monument with the word JENKINS on its base, crossed guns at its top, and a saber and belt on its shaft was erected. The inscription reads:

MICAH JENKINS
BRIG. GEN. C.S.A.
BORN DEC. 1, 1835
EDISTO ISLAND, S.C.

A GRADUATE OF
THE CITADEL
ACADEMY
WITH FIRST HONORS
KILLED AT THE HEAD
OF HIS BRIGADE, IN
THE BATTLE OF
THE WILDERNESS
MAY 6, 1864
"INTEGER VITAE"

ERECTED TO HIS
MEMORY BY THE
ASSOCIATION OF
CITADEL GRADUATES
AND OTHER COMRADES
AND FRIENDS

Uniform coat worn by Micah Jenkins when shot down by friendly fire in the Wilderness.

Courtesy of South Carolina Relic Room and Museum, Columbia

Grave of Brigadier General Micah Jenkins, Magnolia Cemetery, Charleston, South Carolina. In 1902 Caroline Harper Jenkins was interred alongside her husband.

Photograph by Penny Swisher

Epilogue

Upon the sudden fall of Micah Jenkins, his brigade continued in action under the stellar leadership of Colonel John Bratton of the 6th South Carolina, the senior colonel. The impetuous plan of Confederate advance faltered somewhat with the wounding of the two officers, and although General Lee came forward and personally attempted to reorganize the attack the delay so destroyed the timing that in the words of Brigadier General Law, "We received hard knocks instead of victory."[1]

Letters of tribute and condolence flowed to the Jenkins family from friends, soldiers, and officials of the Confederacy almost more rapidly than Jenkins's remains were carried south. In the style of the day, many were flowery and extremely extravagant in offering praise of the deceased soldier. Other messages, many from brigade members, officers, and soldiers, were simpler and more direct. The seriously wounded Longstreet, who had long been Jenkins's commanding officer, sent a lengthy tribute to the governor of South Carolina. Since he could not yet write as a result of his wounds, his wife signed the message. In it he closed with the following remembrance:

> Jenkins was one of the most estimable characters of the
> army. His tastes and talents were for military service. He
> was intelligent, quick, untiring, attentive, zealous in

charge of his duties, truly faithful to official obligations—
abreast with the foremost in battle and within a noble,
humble Christian. In a moment of highest earthly joy, he
was transported to serenest heavenly joy: to that life which
knows no bugle calls, beat of drums, or clash of steel. May
his beautiful spirit, through the mercy of God, rest in
peace!

Amen![2]

Robert E. Lee, Daniel H. Hill, and dozens of others sent ex-
pressions of sorrow to the distraught widow. Perhaps one of
the most meaningful was a brief statement by Major General
Wade Hampton, cavalry commander of the Army of Northern
Virginia and later governor of South Carolina. No slouch as a
soldier himself, Hampton simply said, "Micah Jenkins was the
finest soldier I ever met."[3]

Jenkins's death was recognized by the passage of a resolution in the General Assembly of South Carolina, then meeting in Columbia in a legislative chamber where a portrait of
the general now hangs. Reflecting the deep sorrow and public
sympathy of its populace, the resolution read:

> Resolved: That in the death of General Jenkins, South
> Carolina mourns the loss of one of her noblest, most Pa-
> triotic, and accomplished citizens, and the army of our
> country, a brave, energetic, and skillful officer.
>
> Resolved: That we hold up his many virtues to his Com-
> rades yet spared, and bid them emulate his example.
>
> Resolved: That this resolution, together with the corre-
> spondence of General Longstreet and Governor
> Bonham...be copied into the journal...and sent to the fam-
> ily of the deceased.[4]

Lengthy obituaries appeared in area newspapers. On
May 12, 1864, the *Charleston Mercury* printed a short biog-
raphy of General Micah Jenkins's career and lamented his
untimely death.[5] The outstanding war correspondent, F. G.

DeFontaine, who had accompanied Jenkins's brigade to East Tennessee, even sharing a tent with the general, wrote of the Christian nature of Jenkins's life as he recalled him "kneeling on his blanket every morning and night, returning thanks to the Almighty and invoking blessings on his command."[6] He further discussed Jenkins's amazing ability to maintain a high level of discipline in his brigade, yet find so few occasions to punish offenders. DeFontaine also wrote a lengthy eulogy for the Charlotte newspaper in which he

General Micah Jenkins
Circa 1864
Life and Character of Micah Jenkins

recapped Jenkins's career and his accomplishments. DeFontaine closed his article by stating:

> South Carolina has never had a nobler representative of her chivalry in the field, and no dearer memories can be embalmed in the mausoleum of the people's hearts than those which have hallowed with glory the name of General Micah Jenkins.[7]

In 1903 Coward remembered and wrote of his long-deceased friend:

> Drawn together from age fifteen...our lives flowed together for thirteen years like the sap to twin buds upon a single stem. And yet we were not alike! We seemed rather to be complements of each other. Now as I view him in a perspective of nearly forty passed years, he towers above all my intimate contemporary acquaintances

as the embodiment of all moral excellence, of all the potential of manly greatness. He was vivacious, impulsive,
and impetuous, but his vivacity was clean and pure, his
impulsiveness and impetuosity guarded by honor. I have
never known a man more prompt to make frank and spon-
taneous amends for any hasty word or act that would un-
justly wound another.[8]

All of this was heady and generous praise, but the most
significant tributes to Micah Jenkins were probably never put
to pen. Those soldiers of modest means, who followed him in
harsh campaigns and threatening battles, spoke of their general, usually to each other. Colonel Gage, who commanded
one of the regiments in Jenkins's brigade, was wounded and
at home when news came of the death. He wrote to Jenkins's
father-in-law, D. F. Jamison, and he related an interesting
occurrence:

> Yesterday, an old woman who had three sons and three
> sons-in-law in the brigade walked eight miles to my house
> to get some flour and see if I had news of Lee's Army. This
> woman had been to Virginia and Tennessee to take provi-
> sions to her men and she exclaimed, "I couldn't help but
> cry when I heard General Jenkins was killed, he was so
> good to my boys; always a kind word a pleasant look, an
> encouragement. They loved him so much, and although
> they knew he would carry them into the thickest of the
> fight, they knew they would always find him alongside
> them.[9]

Robert Flavell Jenkins, one of Micah's sons, was later
employed with the Internal Revenue Service and in his trav-
els around South Carolina encountered many old veterans,
some with empty sleeves or wooden legs. He received so many
comments from these battle-scarred veterans when they heard
his name that he began to record them. Many of the old cam-
paigners remembered that Jenkins treated the humblest

private with the same kindness and courtesy that he treated a ranking officer. Jenkins had always attempted to know the name of every member of the brigade, which had made a lasting impression on the old soldiers. Sam Clinton, a one-legged veteran of York County, told Robert: "We boys had to behave ourselves, for the general knew every one of us by name, and would spot us instantly if we did anything wrong."[10] A frequent comment credited to many of the veterans was that General Jenkins never told his men to "go" but rather encouraged them to "follow me."[11]

In the wake of the general's death, Caroline Harper Jenkins, a widow at age 26, with four sons ranging in age from seven months to seven years of age, was faced with an uncertain and insecure future. Many of Jenkins's assets were in Confederate bonds, which had already been devalued and would soon be worthless. The extensive properties on Edisto Island were still occupied by enemy soldiers, and the fate of these holdings was doubtful. Early in the summer following Jenkins's death, Caroline's father succumbed to an attack of yellow fever while visiting in Charleston.[12] The loss of the close relationship she enjoyed with her father, as well as his support and advice, was another devastating blow to the young widow.

The Jenkins and Jamison families assisted Caroline and her young children during the last terrible year of the war and the dark days of reconstruction. Yet the road to recovery, even survival, was hard, and only Caroline's steel will and determination kept her and her family afloat.

Micah's father, Captain John Jenkins, had been extremely ill before his death in 1854, and John, Micah's brother, had taken charge of the family estates at that time. A full 10 years older than Micah, he had served as father figure to the young man since his cadet days. When the war began, John remained at home and moved the Jenkins families and slaves inland to estates safe from the Union army. He organized the "Rebel

Troop" stationed at Adams Run, which was later incorporated as a part of the 3rd South Carolina Cavalry.[13] John was promoted to major in that regiment, and fought with distinction in the battles of Tulifinny, Honey Hill, White Point, and others, defending the vital railway line between Charleston and Savannah.[14] Due to the efforts of Major Jenkins and others in this command, the Union occupation troops, although enjoying the fruits of the island plantations, were confined to those islands.

After the war John returned to Edisto and with his illustrious uncle, Joseph Evans Jenkins, attempted to reclaim and replant the family plantations. Many of the old homes had suffered extensively during the occupation and all were completely stripped of furnishings and livestock. The extensive library at Lands End had been totally destroyed and Brick House was without even draperies. The Edisto Island churches were pillaged and the pipe organ in the Edisto Presbyterian Church taken to New England. The prayer book and altar Bible, donated by Joseph Jenkins of Brick House, had been stolen from Edisto Episcopal Church, but years later the prayer book was returned to the Jenkins family by a repentant Northerner.[15]

Some plantations were seized and occupied by Freedmen, whom General W. T. Sherman's Special War Order No. 15 settled on Edisto by the thousands.[16] These destitute, homeless, former slaves from all over the South had followed Sherman's army from as far as Atlanta. They divided the plantations into small plots and, assisted by missionaries from Northern churches, attempted to start new lives as freemen. But after the war, President Andrew Johnson declared Sherman's war act invalid and the lands and homes were returned to their former owners.[17]

John Jenkins led his extended family back to their rifled homes and borrowed heavily to pay taxes and replant acres of sea island cotton. Lack of labor, caterpillar invasions, and improper soil preparation prevented the huge profits of the past, but slowly the estates began to recover, and hope for a bright future was reborn. In the 1890s these aspirations were dashed by another invasion, that of the tiny boll weevil, which devastated any future for long-stable, sea-island cotton.

Caroline and her sons grew accustomed to the new style of life on the island estates and in Charleston. Although not completely destitute, their standard of living would never approach the prosperity of pre-war days. But thanks to the assistance of John Jenkins and the dogged persistence of Caroline Jenkins, including her operation of a school for young ladies, she and her sons survived and made some profit from their holdings. Mrs. Jenkins and boys made yearly trips to Charleston, where they resided with friends or family. The Hanahan residence on Anson Street was one of their favorite locations.[18] The four boys were boisterous and lively, and it was reported that the tranquil, quiet nature of that particular block changed drastically during their visit.

True to his promise, Asbury Coward enrolled those of Jenkins's sons who applied in the reopened Kings Mountain Military Academy. Former Confederate General John Gordon, then governor of Georgia, stayed overnight at the academy on one occasion and addressed the cadets. Coward introduced Johnny, then 13, to the general as the youngest son of Micah Jenkins. Gordon patted the young boy's head and stated "Ah...Micah Jenkins....The Baynard of the Confederacy."[19] This incident so impressed Johnny that he determined to seek a military career.

Of Micah Jenkins's four sons, two became army officers. The eldest, Micah, attended the United States Military Academy at West Point. He served on the western frontier in several campaigns against the Indians and also fought with bravery and distinction in the war with Spain.[20] His actions in Cuba resulted in a commendation from the president, his promotion to brevet major, and presentation of a commemorative sword by his native state. The youngest, John Murray, was appointed to West Point in 1883, graduating in 1887. In May of 1893, as a lieutenant in the 5th U.S. Cavalry, he was assigned as military training officer at The Citadel. He served for a number of years at that institution, teaching in the ROTC Hall named for his father and developing the military drill of cadets to a level of national recognition.[21] John saw duty in the Philippines during the Spanish-American War, taught at West Point, and held an active command in France during World War I. He retired from the United States Army with the rank of major general.[22]

Caroline Harper Jenkins resided at No. 8, Aiken Row in Charleston for many years. She was active in the careers of her sons and maintained close contact with each, on occasion residing with one or another. She did not hesitate to offer them her advice on marriage, career, or other significant decisions. On one occasion, she and one of the youngsters became temporarily estranged over his engagement to a girl of whom

Jenkins Hall, R.O.T.C. Building, The Citadel

Photograph by Penny Swisher

Caroline disapproved. On February 9, 1902, Mrs. Caroline
Jamison Jenkins died in Charleston at age 63 and was laid to
rest beside her husband, beneath the tall granite shaft in
Magnolia Cemetery. Carrie Jenkins, obedient to the will of
her husband, remained a widow for 38 years.

Colonel John Bratton, succeeding Jenkins as brigade commander, was a capable, well-liked officer who was soon promoted to brigadier. The young physician received excellent
support from the capable group of regimental commanders:
Colonel Johnson Hagood of the 1st South Carolina, Colonel R.
E. Bowen of the 2nd Rifles, Colonel Andrew Coward of the
5th, Colonel Joseph Walker of the Palmetto Sharpshooters,
and Lieutenant Colonel J. M. Steedman who replaced Bratton
in command of the 6th.[23] This core of dedicated officers remained with the thinning brigade until the surrender of the
Army of Northern Virginia at Appomattox.

The well-trained soldiers of the brigade saw hard action
at Spotsylvania Court House, where the 5th and 1st Regiments
were mentioned in army reports as providing outstanding service in the repulse of enemy assaults.[24] Later, the brigade held
the line established across the broken salient in the fierce contest for the mule shoe. As Grant moved closer to Richmond,
Bratton's brigade was selected to participate in an attempt to
recapture Fort Harrison. This position near Drewry's Bluff
was considered important enough for the Confederates to undertake a rare 1864 offensive action. The attack failed miserably, with very heavy casualties among the Carolinians.[25] The
brigade surrendered at Appomattox with all officers present
save a wounded Colonel Walker who was replaced by Captain
Alfred Foster.

Several of Jenkins's contemporaries who survived the war
were instrumental in reconstruction of economic and political
life in the South. One who did not was Charles Tew, valedicto-
rian of the first Citadel graduating class. Tew had returned to
The Citadel as a teacher and had a marked influence on young

Micah Jenkins. He left The Citadel to initiate development of a military school in North Carolina, but his life took a strange and tragic twist. He was elected colonel of the 2nd North Carolina when war began and was shot down at Sharpsburg while leading Anderson's brigade, but his body was never recovered. It was widely rumored that he survived and was made prisoner. His family searched for him during the remainder of the war and for years afterward. Some fifteen years later, his sword was found and purchased by a friend from a Washington, D.C., pawnshop. No definitive answer to his fate was ever known.[26]

John Bratton did not return to the medical profession after the war; instead he became a successful farmer and entered politics. Soon Bratton was a lieutenant in Wade Hampton's powerful political machine, which dominated South Carolina politics for years once Confederate veterans regained the right to vote.[27]

Colonel Asbury Coward enjoyed a long, illustrious career. Shortly after the war, he reopened Kings Mountain Academy in Yorkville. It was a struggling enterprise, however, for Federal occupation forces severely curtailed military training in South Carolina and cadets were not allowed to drill with rifles. Enrollment was limited since only a few families could afford even a modest tuition. Coward was reluctantly forced to close the school for financial reasons in 1886. Soon thereafter, Coward was selected as South Carolina state superintendent of education, and in 1890 was appointed superintendent of The Citadel, which he ably led for 18 years. He and his wife, the former Eliza Blum, had outlived all but one of their 17 children when Coward died in 1925. He was an honest and loyal man, never taking himself too seriously. He delighted in signing his name "A. Coward." When he retired in 1908 he was awarded a prestigious Carnegie pension for his service to mankind. The University of South Carolina added an honorary doctor of laws degree and President Theodore Roosevelt appointed Coward to the West Point Board of Visitors.[28]

Jenkins's rivalry with Evander Law in East Tennessee produced much controversy that soiled the reputation of both excellent officers. After completion of his western assignment, Law resumed command of his stout Alabama brigade and returned to Virginia with Longstreet's I Corps. His brigade was nearby when Longstreet and Jenkins were shot down in the Wilderness. Law fought his unit well in the Wilderness, at Spotsylvania, and at Cold Harbor, where he was severely wounded and placed on convalescent leave. Law concluded his service by volunteering for a cavalry command under Joseph Johnston in North Carolina, where he surrendered and was paroled. Law settled in Florida where, after an extensive career in education, he died in 1920 at the age of 84.[29] After the war he wrote extensively of his experiences, expressing vehemently his animosity for Longstreet and others. Law did not, however, discuss his rivalry with the then-deceased Micah Jenkins.

As for James Longstreet, when hostilities ceased, his political choices and friendship with several Northern generals served to make him persona non grata throughout the South. He became the brunt of Southern writers, villain of all Confederate misfortune. It was difficult for historians to assess his generalship through the cloud of vindictive opinions flowing from the pens of Jubal Early, Evander Law, and others. Longstreet did not possess the literary ability to defend himself, and no champion was forthcoming. Deservedly or not, after the East Tennessee campaign, his star began to fade until he eventually became the most disliked of all Southern leaders. His lack of tact and personal skills only added to his list of critics. A strange ally of the anti-Longstreet faction was the man himself. Later, his petty and vindictive nature came to the fore in his writings. He attempted to blame his shortcoming on others and made the serious mistake of being critical of several of Lee's decisions. By that time, the status of Lee was so elevated that to criticize him was heretical, and Longstreet paid dearly for that indiscretion.[30]

The nature of Edisto Island remains unchanged, although its inhabitants are quite different. The towering live oaks, pines, and palmettos still dominate the landscape with their ghostly trails of Spanish moss. The tide still rises and falls on the sparkling beaches and in the creeks and marshes. Egrets and other wildlife observe the change of seasons. But most of the old manor homes are in ruins or have disappeared. The fields are no longer covered by bolls of white cotton, but instead nurture tomatoes, cabbages, and other high-yield vegetables crops. No longer does a small, insular group of immensely wealthy planters rule as barons on the sea islands: war and a predatory insect destroyed their base of power and prestige, and they have been replaced by truck farmers, merchants, developers, and tourists. No longer do princes ride out from Edisto Island.

Notes

Prologue

1. Nell S. Graydon, *Tales of Beaufort* (Orangeburg, South Carolina: Sandlapper Publishing, 1963), 45 (hereafter *Beaufort*).

2. Lewis P. Jones, *South Carolina: A Synoptic History for Laymen* (Orangeburg, South Carolina: Sandlapper Publishing, 1987), 12–13 (hereafter Jones). The site of the Spanish Fort is currently being excavated from the fairways of the Marine golf course.

3. For an outstanding presentation of life in the Spanish Colony visit the Marine Corps Museum at Parris Island.

4. Walter J. Fraser, Jr., *Charleston! Charleston!: The History of a Southern City* (Columbia, South Carolina: University of South Carolina Press, 1989), 4.

5. Jones, 20.

6. Material on plantation life and the sea islands. Charleston Museum, Charleston, South Carolina.

7. Ibid.

8. Ibid.

9. Jenkins I. Mikell, *Rumbling of the Chariot Wheels* (Columbia, South Carolina: University of South Carolina Press, 1923), 19–20 (hereafter Mikell).

10. An excellent example on display in the Charleston Museum, Charleston, South Carolina.

11. The Webber Collection includes the records of a large number of bills of sale for Edisto Island plantations. Virtually none were more than 350 acres, with many as small as 180 acres.

12. Jones, 168–69.

13. Clara C. Puckette, *Edisto: A Sea Island Principality* (Cleveland, Ohio: Seaforth Publications, 1978), 11 (hereafter Puckette).

14. Mikell, 14.

Chapter 1
A Soldier Develops

1. Beaufort, 90.

2. Webber Collection, Jenkins Papers: South Carolina Historical Association, Charleston, South Carolina (hereafter Webber Collection).

3. Nell S. Graydon, *Tales of Edisto* (Columbia, South Carolina: R. L. Bryan Co., 1955), 45 (hereafter *Edisto*).

4. John P. Thomas, *Career and Character of General Micah Jenkins, C.S.A.* (Columbia, South Carolina: The State Company, 1906), 27 (hereafter *Career*).

5. *Edisto*, 45.

6. Puckette, 4.

7. Interviews with Mr. and Mrs. Harry Hutson, October 17, 1992. Mr. Hutson, a descendant of the Jenkins family, was four years old when the Brick House burned. He maintains a summer cottage at the plantation and acts as guide when tours are conducted. Mr. Hutson kindly granted the author and his wife a tour of the property.

8. Webber Collection.

9. Joseph Edward Jenkins Collection. Edisto Island Museum, Edisto Island, South Carolina.

10. *Career*, 27.

11. *Edisto*, 45.

12. *Career*, 24.

13. Webber Collection.

14. Mikell, 46.

15. *Career*, 23–24.

16. John Donald Duncan, "Pages from Froissart, The Ante-Bellum Career of Micah Jenkins." Unpublished thesis for Master of Arts degree, Department of History, University of South Carolina, Columbia, South Carolina, 1961, 1C (hereafter Duncan).

17. O. J. Bond, *The Story of the Citadel* (Richmond, Virginia: Garrett and Massie Publishers, 1936), 1 (hereafter Bond).

18. John P. Thomas, *History of the South Carolina Military Academy* (Charleston, South Carolina: Walker, Evans and Gogswell Press, 1893), 5 (hereafter *Academy*).

19. Ibid., 38.

20. Ibid., 40.

21. Bond, 178.

22. *Career*, 25.

23. Duncan, 2.

24. Ibid., 3.

25. *Career*, 12.

26. John Jenkins Papers, Micah Jenkins to John Jenkins, March 22, 1853, South Caroliniana Library, Columbia, South Carolina (hereafter John's Papers).

27. Jenkins Family Papers, Commission of Micah Jenkins, January 7, 1854, South Caroliniana Library, Columbia, South Carolina (hereafter Family Papers).

28. Duncan, 5.

29. John's Papers, Micah Jenkins to John Jenkins, May 19, 1854.

30. Family Papers, Jenkins address.

31. Bond, 225.

32. John's Papers, Micah Jenkins to John Jenkins, November 3, 1854.

Chapter 2
Education Is Surely an Honorable Profession

1. John's Papers, Micah Jenkins to John Jenkins, May 19, 1854.

2. John A. May and Joan R. Faunt, *South Carolina Secedes* (Columbia, South Carolina: University of South Carolina Press, 1960), 166.

3. Family Papers, Edward Jenkins to Micah Jenkins, August 12, 1853.

4. Ibid., June 2, 1853.

5. Ibid., Micah Jenkins to Liz LaRoche, April 18, 1855.

6. Ibid., Micah Jenkins to John Jenkins, November 3, 1855.

7. Duncan, 12.

8. *York Observer*, March 28, 1986.

9. John's Papers, John Jenkins to Micah Jenkins, December 17, 1854.

10. Family Papers, Articles of Agreement, Andrew Coward and Micah Jenkins.

11. *Yorkville Enquirer*, June 4, 1868.

12. *York Observer*, March 28, 1986.

13. Family Papers, Micah Jenkins to Liz LaRoche, April 18, 1855.

14. Duncan, 21.

15. Ibid.

16. E. T. Crowson, "Jenkins, Coward and the Yorkville Boys," *Sandlapper* Magazine December 1974: 33 (hereafter Crowson).

17. Duncan, 24.

18. Ibid., 24.

19. Ibid., 39.

20. John's Papers, Micah Jenkins to John Jenkins, January 22, 1856.

21. Ibid.

22. *Yorkville Enquirer*, April 24, 1856.

23. Family Papers, Appointment, August 29, 1856.

24. John's Papers, Micah Jenkins to John Jenkins, October 4, 1856.

25. Duncan, 52.

26. *Yorkville Enquirer*, December 11, 1856.

27. Ibid., May 28, 1857.

28. Ibid., April 1, 1858.

29. Duncan, 59.

30. *Yorkville Enquirer*, June 23, 1859.

31. Ibid., May 3, 1860.

32. Ibid., June 28, 1860.

Chapter 3
Yorkville's Young Leader

1. *Edisto*, 47–48.

2. Ibid.

3. Duncan, 32.

4. *Edisto*, 47–48.

5. Family Papers, Micah Jenkins to John Jenkins, March 20, 1855.

6. Ibid., Liz LaRoche to Micah Jenkins, April 23, 1855.

7. *Edisto*, 150.

8. Joseph E. Hart, Jr. *The Church of the Good Shepherd, York, South Carolina: A Centennial History: 1855–1955* (York, South Carolina: Yorkville Enquirer Press, 1955), 3.

9. Ibid., 4.

10. Ibid., 8.

11. Family Papers, Liz LaRoche to Micah Jenkins, April 23, 1855.

12. Caroline Jenkins Papers, Micah Jenkins to Carrie Jamison, May 10, 1855, William Perkins Library, Duke University, Durham, North Carolina (hereafter Caroline's Papers).

13. *Career*, 24.

14. Caroline's Papers, Micah Jenkins to Carrie Jamison, July 14, 1855.

15. Family Papers, Liz LaRoche to Micah Jenkins, July 5, 1855.

16. *Yorkville Enquirer,* July 17, 1856.

17. Duncan, 33.

18. *Edisto*, 140.

19. Family Papers, Micah Jenkins to John Jenkins, September 2, 1856.

20. Ibid., July 21, 1857.

21. Duncan, 37.

22. Webber Collection.

23. Duncan, 88.

24. Ibid., 91.

25. Family Papers, Micah Jenkins to John Jenkins, January 7, 1860.

26. *Yorkville Enquirer,* February 16, 1860.

27. Ibid., February 23, 1860.

28. Ibid., October 4, 1860.

29. Ibid., December 20, 1860.

30. Ibid., April 21, 1859.

31. Ibid., June 24, 1860.

32. Duncan, 96.

33. *Yorkville Enquirer,* February 7, 1861.

34. Ibid., September 15, 1861.

35. Ibid., February 7, 1861.

36. Duncan, 101.

37. *Yorkville Enquirer,* January 3, 1861.

38. Ibid., January 17, 1861.

39. Caroline's Papers, Micah Jenkins to Caroline Jenkins, January 18, 1861.

40. *Yorkville Enquirer,* February 28, 1861.

Chapter 4
Manassas to Williamsburg

1. Arthur M. Maniqault, *A Carolinian Goes to War,* Ed. R. Lockwood Tower (Columbia, South Carolina: University of South Carolina Press, 1983), 24.

2. Ibid., 25.

3. Caroline's Papers, Micah Jenkins to Caroline Jenkins, May 12, 1861.

4. Micheal C. Harrington, "Youthful Valor: John Marshall Whilden: Boy Major of the Coast Rangers, *Confederate Veteran*, March-April 1992, 16 (hereafter Harrington).

5. Richard Lewis, *Camp Life of a Confederate Boy* (Charleston, South Carolina: The News and Courier Press, 1883), 9 (hereafter Lewis).

6. J. W. Reid, *History of the Fourth Regiment, South Carolina Volunteers* (Dayton, Ohio: Morningside Press, 1975), 11 (hereafter Reid).

7. Clarence C. Buel and Robert U. Johnson, Eds. *Battles and Leaders of the Civil War*, vol. 1, (Secaucus, New Jersey: Castle Press, 1887), 195. (Hereafter *Battles and Leaders*).

8. Harrington, 17.

9. *The War of the Rebellion: A Compilation of the Official Records of the Union and Confederate Armies* (Washington, D.C, Government Printing Office, 1880–1901), vol. 2, 441 (hereafter *O.R.*).

10. *Battles and Leaders*, vol. 1, 176.

11. Ibid., 177.

12. Harrington, 17.

13. *O.R.*, vol. 2, 537.

14. Douglas S. Freeman, *Lee's Lieutenants* (New York: Charles Scribner's Sons, 1943) vol. 1. 57 (hereafter *Lee's Lieutenants*).

15. John's Jenkins Papers, Micah Jenkins to John Jenkins, July 25, 1861. South Carolina Department of Archives and History, Columbia, South Carolina (hereafter South Carolina Papers).

16. Ibid., Micah Jenkins Report.

17. Ibid.

18. Ibid., Micah Jenkins to John Jenkins. July 25, 1861.

19. Ibid.

20. *Lee's Lieutenants*, vol. 1, 78.

21. Caroline's Papers, Micah Jenkins to Carrie Jenkins, July 28, 1861.

22. Lewis, 24.

23. Caroline's Papers, Micah Jenkins to Carrie Jenkins, September 6, 1861.

24. Reid, 57.

25. Stephen W. Sears, *To the Gates of Richmond: The Peninsular Campaign* (New York: Ticknor and Fields, 1992), 164 (hereafter Sears).

26. *Lee's Lieutenants*, vol. 1, 100.

27. Ibid., 118.

28. Ibid., 130.

29. Ibid., 131.

30. Caroline's Papers, Micah Jenkins to Carrie Jenkins, February 6, 1862.

31. Lewis, 36.

32. William B. Edwards, *Civil War Guns* (Harrisburg, Pennsylvania: Stackpole Publishing Company, 1962), 242.

33. Ibid., 210.

34. W. S. Dunlop, *Lee's Sharpshooters* (Dayton, Ohio: Morningside Press, 1988), iii.

35. Reid, 77.

36. *Lee's Lieutenants*, vol. 1, 158.

37. Ibid., 157.

38. Lewis, 29.

39. *Lee's Lieutenants*, vol. 1, 155.

40. Sears, 68.

41. *Lee's Lieutenants*, vol. 1, 176.

42. *O.R.*, Jenkins Report, vol. 11, pt. 2, 435.

43. *Lee's Lieutenants*, vol. 1, 179.

44. *O.R.*, Jenkins Report, vol. 11, pt. 1, 582.

45. *Lee's Lieutenants*, vol. 1, 179.

46. *Battles and Leaders*, vol. 2, 197.

47. *Southern Historical Society Papers*, vol. 10, 42 (hereafter *S.H.S.P.*)

48. Sears, 75.
49. Ibid.
50. Ibid., 79.
51. Ibid., 81.
52. *Battles and Leaders*, vol. 2, 199.
53. Sears, 82.
54. James Longstreet, *From Manassas to Appomattox* (Philadelphia, Pennsylvania: J. B. Lippincott Inc., 1896), 74 (hereafter Longstreet).

Chapter 5
Fame at Seven Pines

1. *Battles and Leaders*, vol. 2, 276.
2. Sears, 84.
3. Reid, 82–83.
4. *O.R.*, vol. 11, pt. 1, 276.
5. Sears, 86.
6. *O.R.*, vol. 11, pt. 3, 475.
7. Ibid., 504.
8. Ibid., vol. 11, pt. 1, 636.
9. Sears, 93.
10. *Battles and Leaders*, vol. 2, 270.
11. Lewis, 60.
12. Caroline's Papers, Micah Jenkins to Carrie Jenkins, May 22, 1862.
13. Ibid., May 25, 1862.
14. Lewis, 31.
15. Caroline's Papers, Micah Jenkins to Carrie Jenkins, May 25, 1862.
16. Sears, 87.
17. *O.R.*, vol. 11, pt. 1, 25.
18. Sears, 103.
19. Ibid., 106.
20. Ibid., 118.
21. Ibid., 120.
22. *Lee's Lieutenants*, vol. 1, p. 226.
23. Ibid.
24. *O.R.*, vol. 11, pt. 1, 943.
25. Sears, 126.
26. Ibid., 132.
27. Evans, vol. 5, 51.
28. Sears, 133.
29. *Battles and Leaders*, vol. 2, 236.
30. Ibid.
31. In Jenkins's Report in *O.R.* he attributes assistance to the 28th Georgia, but all other records, including the reports of Anderson and the regimental commander, credit the 27th. The mistake was likely Jenkins's.
32. Sears, 133.
33. *Career*, 15.

34. South Carolina Archives Papers, Micah Jenkins Report.
35. Sears, 133.
36. *O.R.*, vol. 11, pt. 1, 944, 947–49.
37. *Battles and Leaders*, vol. 2, 235.
38. Caroline's Papers, Micah Jenkins to Carrie Jenkins, June 2, 1862.
39. Reid, 91.
40. South Carolina Archives Papers, Micah Jenkins Report.
41. Sears, 142.
42. Thomas Jewett Goree Papers, Thomas Goree to Sister, June 17, 1862 (Family History Foundation, Bryan, Texas) (hereafter Goree).
43. Evans, vol. 5, 51.
44. *O.R.*, vol. 5, 1001.
45. Sears, 138.
46. *Battles and Leaders*, vol. 2, 238.
47. Sears, 145.
48. *Battles and Leaders*, vol. 2, 443–45.
49. Sears, 121.
50. *Lee's Lieutenants*, vol. 1, 257.
51. Ibid., 258–59.
52. Clifford Dowdey, *The Seven Days: The Emergence of Robert E. Lee* (New York: Fairfax Press, 1978), 93 (hereafter Dowdey).
53. *Lee's Lieutenants*, vol. 1, 248.
54. Ibid. 249.
55. *O.R.*, vol. 11, pt. 1, 944.
56. *Lee's Lieutenants*, vol. 1, 250.
57. Dowdey, 126–27.

Chapter 6
Seven Bloody Days

1. Thomas L. Connelly, *The Marble Man: Robert E. Lee and His Image in American Society* (Baton Rouge: Louisiana State University Press, 1978), 5 (hereafter *Marble Man*).
2. Ibid., 194.
3. Douglas S. Freeman, *R. E. Lee* (New York: Scribner Co., 1946), vol. 1, 603 (hereafter *R. E. Lee*).
4. *Lee's Lieutenants*, vol. 1, 603.
5. Sears, 154.
6. *Marble Man*, 198.
7. Stephen W. Sears, *George B. McClellan: The Young Napoleon* (New York: Ticknor and Fields, 1988), 80 (hereafter *McClellan*).
8. *Marble Man*, 208.
9. Dowdey, 141.
10. Ibid., 140.
11. *Battles and Leaders*, vol. 2, 317.
12. *Lee's Lieutenants*, vol. 1, 300.
13. Sears, 168.
14. Ibid., 181.

15. Dowdey, 153.
16. Sears, 186.
17. Ibid.
18. Ibid., 188.
19. Ibid., 189.
20. Dowdey, 160.
21. Sears, 189.
22. *Battles and Leaders*, vol. 2, 328.
23. Ibid., 319.
24. Sears, 196.
25. Dowdey, 202.
26. Sears, 201.
27. Ibid., 208.
28. South Carolina Archives Papers, Micah Jenkins to John Jenkins, July 8, 1862.
29. Dowdey, 207.
30. Sears, 210.
31. Ibid., 212.
32. *Battles and Leaders*, vol. 2, 336.
33. Ibid., 337.
34. Sears, 214.
35. Dowdey, 223.
36. Sears, 225.
37. Dowdey, 227.
38. Sears, 227.
39. *Lee's Lieutenants*, vol. 1, 532.
40. South Carolina Archives Papers, Battle Report of Colonel Micah Jenkins.
41. Ibid.
42. *Career*, 16.
43. South Carolina Archives Papers, Battle Report of Colonel Micah Jenkins, 2.
44. *Career*, 16.
45. South Carolina Archives Papers, Battle Report of Colonel Micah Jenkins, 2.
46. *Battles and Leaders*, vol. 2, 344–45.
47. Sears, 245.
48. Caroline's Papers, Micah Jenkins to Carrie Jenkins, July 11, 1862.
49. Sears, 252.
50. Caroline's Papers, Micah Jenkins to Carrie Jenkins, July 8, 1862.
51. Dowdey, 249.
52. Ibid., 25.
53. Sears, 258.
54. Dowdey, 276.
55. Ibid., 277.
56. *Lee's Lieutenants*, vol. 1, 554.
57. Sears, 272.
58. Dowdey, 274.
59. Sears, 275.
60. Ibid., 274.

61. Edward P. Alexander, *Fighting For the Confederacy: The Personal Recollections of General Edward P. Alexander,* Ed. by Gary Gallagher (Chapel Hill, North Carolina: University of North Carolina Press, 1989), 110.
62. Dowdey, 286.
63. *Lee's Lieutenants*, vol. 1, 578.
64. Dowdey, 293.
65. *Lee's Lieutenants*, vol. 1, 585.
66. Ibid., 587.
67. Sears, 289.
68. South Carolina Archives Papers, Battle Report of Micah Jenkins.
69. *Career*, 16.
70. Ibid.
71. Sears, 295.
72. South Carolina Archives Papers, Battle Report of Micah Jenkins.
73. *Career*, 16.
74. Sears, 299.
75. Academy, 126–27.
76. Sears, 307.
77. *Career*, 16.
78. South Carolina Archives Papers, Battle Report of Micah Jenkins.
79. Goree Papers, Thomas J. Goree to His Mother, July 21, 1862, 161–62.
80. Caroline's Papers, Micah Jenkins to Carrie Jenkins, July 3, 1862.
81. *Career*, 17.
82. *Battles and Leaders*, vol. 2, 381.
83. Ibid., 409.
84. Sears, 320.
85. Ibid., 321.
86. *Battles and Leaders*, vol. 2, 392.
87. Ibid., 385.
88. Reid, 100, J.W. Reid to wife, June 29, 1862.
89. Ibid.
90. *Lee's Lieutenants*, vol. 1, 672.

Chapter 7
From Manassas to the Blackwater

1. *S.H.S.P.*, vol. 7, 217.
2. John J. Hennessy, *Return to Bull Run* (New York: Simon and Schuster, 1993), 563 (hereafter Hennessy).
3. Ibid., 17.
4. Ibid., 96.
5. *Lee's Lieutenants*, vol. 2, 101.
6. Ibid., 99.
7. Hennessy, 139.
8. Ibid., 224.
9. *Career*, 12.
10. Hennessy, 365.

11. Ibid., 369.

12. Ibid.

13. George Skoch, "The Bloody Fifth," *Civil War Times Illustrated,* vol. 30, no. 5, November-December 1991: 36–43.

14. William Choise, "Memoirs of My Four Years in the War Between the States," Manassas National Battlefield Park Library, 5th South Carolina.

15. George F. Paine, "How I Left the Bull Run Battlefield," *13th Massachusetts Regimental Circular,* vol. 24, 1911, 30–36.

16. Asbury Coward, *The South Carolinians,* Ed. by Natalie Jenkins Bond and Osmund L. Coward (New York: Vantage Press, 1968), 43 (hereafter Coward).

17. *Battles and Leaders,* vol. 2, 499.

18. Harrington, 14–18.

19. Crowson, 32–36.

20. Micah Jenkins Collection, Telegram to Mrs. Caroline Jenkins, Edisto Island Museum, Edisto Island, South Carolina (hereafter Edisto Collection).

21. Coward, 68.

22. Crowson, 35.

23. Jay Luvaas, and Harold Nelson, eds., *The United States Army War College Guide to the Battles of Fredericksburg and Chancellorsville* (Carlisle, Pennsylvania: South Mountain Press, 1988), 326 (hereafter Luvaas and Nelson).

24. Lewis, 33.

25. Luvaas and Nelson, 33.

26. South Carolina Archives Papers, Battle Report of Micah Jenkins, Fredericksburg.

27. Coward, 72.

28. South Carolina Archives Papers, Battle Report of Micah Jenkins, Fredericksburg, 2.

29. Caroline's Papers, Micah Jenkins to Carrie Jenkins, December 21, 1862.

30. Coward, 75.

31. Lewis, 38.

32. Ibid.

33. Ibid., 40.

34. Caroline's Papers, Micah Jenkins To Carrie Jenkins, March 17, 1863.

35. Crowson, 35.

36. *Lee's Lieutenants,* vol. 2, 467.

37. Ibid., 481.

38. Ibid., 490.

39. Ibid., 491.

40. *O.R.,* vol. 18, 993.

41. *Lee's Lieutenants,* vol. 2, 489.

42. Coward, 78.

43. Ibid., 80.

44. Lewis, 51.

45. Ibid., 53.

46. Ibid., 55.

47. Caroline's Papers. Micah Jenkins to Carrie Jenkins, September 10, 1863.

Chapter 8
A Journey West

1. *Lee's Lieutenants*, vol. 3, 220.
2. *O.R.*, vol. 29, pt. 2, 720.
3. Clifford Dowdey and Louis Manarin, *The Wartime Papers of R. E. Lee* (New York: Bramhall House, 1972), 586 (hereafter Dowdey and Manarin).
4. Caroline's Papers, Micah Jenkins to Carrie Jenkins, September 10, 1863.
5. *O.R.*, vol. 27, pt. 3, 908, 1005.
6. *Career*, 8.
7. Ibid.
8. Dowdey and Manarin, 476.
9. George F. Skoch, "A Test of Rebel Rails," *Civil War Times Illustrated*, vol. 30, no. 8, December 1986, 14 (hereafter Rebel Rails).
10. *O.R.*, vol. 30, pt. 2, 21.
11. Thomas L. Connelly, *Autumn of Glory: The Army of Tennessee, 1862–1865* (Baton Rouge: Louisiana State University Press, 1971), 150 (hereafter *Autumn*).
12. Rebel Rails, 15.
13. Ibid., 16.
14. Glen Tucker, *Chickamauga: Bloody Battle in the West* (Dayton, Ohio: Morningside Press, 1976), 95 (hereafter Tucker).
15. Moxley G. Sorrel, *Recollections of a Confederate Staff Officer* (Jackson, Tennessee: McCowat-Mercer Press, 1958), 180 (hereafter Sorrel).
16. Coward, 84.
17. Lewis, 56.
18. Rebel Rails, 17.
19. Coward, 83.
20. Rebel Rails, 18.
21. Guy R. Swanson, and Timothy D. Johnson, "Conflict in East Tennessee: Generals Law, Jenkins and Longstreet," *Civil War History*, vol. 31, June 1985: 102 (hereafter Swanson and Johnson).
22. Patricia Faust, ed., *Historical Times Illustrated Encyclopedia of the Civil War* (New York: Harper and Rowe, 1917), 203 (hereafter Faust).
23. Sorrel, 177.
24. *Yorkville Enquirer*, December 11, 1856.
25. Ibid., June 28, 1860.
26. *Autumn*, 196.
27. *Lee's Lieutenants*, vol. 3, p. 230.
28. *Autumn*, 207–10.
29. Tucker, 389.
30. *O.R.*, vol. 30, pt. 4, 705.
31. Tucker, 384.
32. *Lee's Lieutenants*, vol. 2, 234.
33. Swanson and Johnson, 103.
34. *Lee's Lieutenants*, vol. 2, 217–26.
35. *O.R.*, vol. 30, pt. 2, 65–66.
36. Hal Bridges, *Lee's Maverick General: Daniel Harvey Hill* (New York: McGraw Hill, 1961), 240.

37. *Autumn*, 241.
38. Sorrel, 191.
39. *Autumn*, 244.
40. Longstreet, 465.
41. William Garrett Piston, *Lee's Tarnished Lieutenant: James Longstreet and His Place in Southern History* (Athens, Georgia: University of Georgia Press, 1987), 78 (hereafter Piston).
42. *Lee's Lieutenants*, vol. 2, 236.
43. *Autumn*, 270.
44. Lewis, 60.

Chapter 9
Lookout Valley

1. *Battles and Leaders*, vol. 3, 683.
2. Ibid., 714.
3. Ibid., 671.
4. Ibid., 682–83.
5. Ibid., 683.
6. *Autumn*, 255.
7. Ibid., 257.
8. *O.R.*, vol. 31, pt. 1, 216.
9. Ibid.
10. Swanson and Johnson, 105.
11. *Battles and Leaders*, vol. 3, 718.
12. Ibid., 720.
13. George F. Skoch, "Miracle of the Rails," *Civil War Times Illustrated,* vol. 31, no. 4, September-October 1992: 22.
14. Ibid., 24.
15. *Autumn*, 259–60.
16. Ibid., 260.
17. South Carolina Archives Papers, Micah Jenkins to John Jenkins, November 18, 1863.
18. Ibid., Report of Colonel M.W. Gary, Commanding Hampton Legion.
19. Ibid., Report of Colonel Joseph Walker, Commanding Palmetto Sharpshooters.
20. *Battles and Leaders*, vol. 3, 720.
21. S.C. Archives Papers, Report of Major Grimes, Commanding 1st South Carolina.
22. Ibid., Report of Colonel A. Coward, Commanding 5th South Carolina.
23. Ibid., Micah Jenkins to John Jenkins, November 18, 1863.
24. Lewis, 66.
25. *Battles and Leaders*, vol. 3, 690.
26. South Carolina Archives Papers, Report of Micah Jenkins.
27. *Autumn*, 255.
28. Caroline's Papers, Micah Jenkins to Moxley Sorrel, October 31, 1863.
29. Ibid., Evander Law to Latrobe, November 2, 1863.
30. Ibid., Statement of Lt. Jamison, January 18, 1864.
31. *S.H.S.P.*, vol. 8, 268.

32. South Carolina Archives Papers, Micah Jenkins to Major Latrobe, January 4, 1864.
33. Swanson and Johnson, 105.
34. Ibid., 106.

Chapter 10
Problems in East Tennessee

1. *Autumn*, 262.
2. Ibid., 263.
3. *Battles and Leaders*, vol. 3, 695.
4. Ibid., 711.
5. *O.R.*, vol. 52, pt. 2, 560.
6. Lewis, 67.
7. Caroline's Papers, Micah Jenkins to Carrie Jenkins, November 7, 1863.
8. Lewis, 66.
9. *Battles and Leaders*, vol. 3, 746.
10. South Carolina Archives Papers, Report of Micah Jenkins, 1.
11. William Marvel, *Burnside* (Chapel Hill, North Carolina: University of North Carolina Press, 1991), 298 (hereafter Marvel).
12. Ibid., 301.
13. Lewis, 69.
14. Marvel, 310.
15. South Carolina Archives Papers, Report of Micah Jenkins, 2.
16. *Battles and Leaders*, vol. 3, 747.
17. South Carolina Archives Papers, Report of Micah Jenkins, East Tennessee Campaign, 5.
18. *Battles and Leaders*, vol. 3, 734.
19. South Carolina Archives Papers, Report of Micah Jenkins, East Tennessee Campaign, 6.
20. *Battles and Leaders*, vol. 3, 735.
21. Michael Haskew, "Icy Assault Routed," *America's Civil War,* vol. 4, no. 1, May 1991, 26 (hereafter Haskew).
22. *Battles and Leaders*, vol. 3, 738.
23. Ibid., 740.
24. *Battles and Leaders*, vol. 3, 748.
25. Haskew, 27.
26. Ibid., 26.
27. *Lee's Lieutenants*, vol. 3, 291–92.
28. Haskew, 24.
29. *Battles and Leaders*, vol. 3, p. 741.
30. Ibid., 748.
31. Haskew, 24.
32. Marvel, 328.
33. Haskew, 28.
34. Marvel, 328.
35. *Battles and Leaders*, vol. 3, 748.
36. Ibid., 758.
37. Ibid., 750.

38. Ibid., 744.

39. Lewis, 73.

40. South Carolina Archives Papers, Report of Micah Jenkins, East Tennessee Campaign, 6.

41. Ibid., 5.

42. *Battles and Leaders*, vol. 3, 749.

43. Lewis, 78.

44. Ibid., 86.

45. Piston, 86.

Chapter 11
Crisis in Command

1. Steven Woodworth, *Jefferson Davis and His Generals: The Failure of Confederate Command in the West* (Lawrence, Kansas: University of Kansas Press, 1990), 216 (hereafter Woodworth).

2. *Battles and Leaders*, vol. 3, 711.

3. Woodworth, 307.

4. Ibid., 306.

5. Ibid., 314.

6. Ibid., 316.

7. Piston, 78.

8. *Lee's Lieutenants*, vol. 1, 281.

9. Piston, 81.

10. Ibid., 77.

11. *Lee's Lieutenants*, vol. 3, 299.

12. Piston, 77.

13. Ibid., 78.

14. Coward, 90.

15. *Career*, 12.

16. Ibid., 4.

17. *O.R.*, vol. 31, pt. 2, 285.

18. Ibid., vol. 31, pt. 2, 497–98.

19. Ibid., 505. General Order No. 46.

20. Sorrel, 182–83.

21. William Oates, *War Between the Union and the Confederacy and its Lost Opportunities* (New York: Neale Publishers, 1905), 338–39.

22. *O.R.*, vol. 31, pt. 1, 471.

23. Ibid., 472.

24. Piston, 80.

25. Ibid.

26. *O.R.*, vol. 31, pt. 1, 473–74.

27. Piston, 80.

28. *O.R.*, vol. 32, pt. 3, 583.

Chapter 12
Into the Wilderness

1. Lewis, 91.

2. Coward, 115.

3. *O.R.*, vol. 33, 1054.

4. Ibid., 1286.

5. Coward, 132.

6. Lewis, 93.

7. *Lee's Lieutenants*, vol. 3, 342.

8. *Academy*, 159.

9. Coward, 139.

10. Family Papers, Rev. B. M. Palmer to Mrs. Micah Jenkins, May 25, 1864.

11. Caroline's Papers, Micah Jenkins to Carrie Jenkins, July 26, 1861.

12. Ibid., May 28, 1862.

13. Ibid., Rev. James McDowell to Mrs. Caroline Jenkins, May 28, 1862.

14. *Career*, 16.

15. Edisto Collection. Power of Attorney of Micah Jenkins, May 5, 1864.

16. *Battles and Leaders*, vol. 4, 97.

17. *O.R.*, vol. 33, 317.

18. *Lee's Lieutenants*, vol. 3, 346.

19. *Battles and Leaders*, vol. 4, 103.

20. William Matter, *If It Takes All Summer: The Battle of Spotsylvania* (Chapel Hill, North Carolina: University of North Carolina Press, 1988), i (Hereafter Matter).

21. Piston, 87.

22. *Battles and Leaders*, vol. 4, 152.

23. R.E. Lee, vol. 4, 270.

24. Ibid., 268.

25. Coward, 133.

26. *Lee's Lieutenants*, vol. 3, 344.

27. *Battles and Leaders*, vol. 4, 154.

28. Ibid.

29. *Lee's Lieutenants*, vol. 3, 350.

30. *Career*, 20, Rev. McDowell to Mrs. Caroline Jenkins, 1864.

31. *Academy*, 162.

32. Lewis, 94.

33. Coward, 134.

34. R.E. Lee, vol. 4, 286–87.

35. *Lee's Lieutenants*, vol. 3, 359.

36. Sorrel, 232.

37. *S.H.S.P.*, vol. 20, 70.

38. *Lee's Lieutenants*, vol. 3, 365.

39. Coward, 139.

40. Ibid., 135.

41. Ibid., 139.

42. *Career*, 8.

43. Coward, 137.

44. Ibid.

45. *Career*, 9, Rev. James McDowell to John P. Thomas, September 16, 1903.

46. *S.H.S.P.*, vol. 51, 46.

47. Louise Pettus, "Micah Jenkins and the 5th South Carolina," *York Observer*, October 30, 1988.
48. *Career*, 10.
49. Webber Collection.

Epilogue

1. *Battles and Leaders*, vol. 4, 126.
2. Capers, vol. 5, 238.
3. *Career*, 26.
4. Ibid., 6–7.
5. *Charleston Mercury*, 12 May 1864.
6. *Career*, 6.
7. *Charlotte Observer*, 16 May 1864.
8. *Career*, 11.
9. Ibid., 8, Gage to Jamison, May 19, 1864.
10. Ibid., 9.
11. Ibid.
12. *Academy*, 166.
13. *Tales of Edisto*, 50.
14. Puckette, 29.
15. Ibid., 30–31.
16. Ibid., 31.
17. Ibid., 37.
18. Webber Collection.
19. Ibid.
20. *Career*, 25.
21. Bond, 138.
22. Webber Collection.
23. *Battles and Leaders*, vol. 4, 126.
24. Matter, 230–31.
25. *Battles and Leaders*, vol. 4, 572.
26. *Academy*, 57.
27. *Lee's Lieutenants*, vol. 3, 774.
28. *York Observer*, March 28, 1986.
29. Faust, 202.
30. *Marble Man*, 82–88.

Bibliography

Manuscripts

Duncan, John Donald. "Pages from Froissart: The Ante-Bellum Career of Micah Jenkins." Unpublished Thesis for Master of Arts, Department of History, University of South Carolina, Columbia, South Carolina, 1961.

Goree, Thomas Jewery. Papers and Letters, Family History Foundation, Bryan, Texas.

Jenkins, Caroline. Collection of Papers, William Perkins Library, Duke University, Durham, North Carolina.

Jenkins Family Papers. South Caroliniana Library, University of South Carolina, Columbia, South Carolina.

Jenkins, John. Collection of Papers, South Caroliniana Library, University of South Carolina, Columbia, South Carolina.

————. Private Papers, South Carolina Department of Archives and History, Columbia, South Carolina.

Jenkins, Micah. Sword, Uniform Coat and Flags on display, South Carolina Confederate Relic Room and Museum, War Memorial Building, 920 Sumter Street, Columbia, S.C.

————. Veterans Record. Series A600296. National Archives and Records Administration, Washington, D.C.

Jenkins, Micah, and Joseph Evans Jenkins. Collection and Papers, Edisto Island Museum, Edisto Island, South Carolina.

Material on plantation life on the sea islands, Charleston Museum, 360 Meeting Street, Charleston, South Carolina.

Webber Collection. Miscellaneous Folders on Jenkins Family, The South Carolina Historical Society, 100 Meeting Street, Charleston, South Carolina.

Books

Alexander, Edward Porter. *Fighting for the Confederacy: The Personal Recollections of General E. Porter Alexander*. Ed. by Gary Gallagher. Chapel Hill, North Carolina: University of North Carolina Press, 1989.

————. *Military Memoirs of a Confederate*. Reprint. Dayton, Ohio: Morningside Press, 1990.

Bond, O. J. *The Story of the Citadel*. Richmond, Virginia: Garrett and Massie Publishing, 1936.

Bridges, Hal. *Lee's Maverick General: Daniel Harvey Hill*. New York: McGraw-Hill Publishers, 1961.

Buel, Clarence C., and Robert U. Johnson, Eds. *Battles and Leaders of the Civil War*. 4 vols. Secaucus, New Jersey: Castle Press, 1887.

Connelly, Thomas L. *Autumn of Glory: The Army of Tennessee, 1862–1865*. Baton Rouge, Louisiana: Louisiana State University Press, 1971.

————. *The Marble Man: Robert E. Lee and His Image in American Society*. Baton Rouge, Louisiana: Louisiana State University Press, 1978.

Coward, Asbury. *The South Carolinians*. Ed. by Natalie Jenkins Bond and Osmund L. Coward, New York: Vantage Press, 1968.

Dowdey, Clifford. *The Seven Days: The Emergence of Robert E. Lee*. New York: Fairfax Press, 1978.

Dowdey, Clifford, and Louis Manarin. *Wartime Papers of Robert E. Lee*. New York: Bramhall House Press, 1972.

Dunlop,W. L. *Lee's Sharpshooters or Forefront of Battle*. Dayton, Ohio: Morningside Press, 1988.

Edwards, William B. *Civil War Guns*. Harrisburg, Pennsylvania: Stackpole Publishing Company, 1962.

Elliott, Joseph Cantey. *Lieutenant General Richard Heron Anderson: Lee's Noble Soldier*. Reprint. Dayton, Ohio: Morningside Press, 1985.

Evans, Clement A. "Capers", vol. 5, *South Carolina Military History*. 12 vols. Atlanta, Georgia: 1899.

Faust, Patricia, ed. *Historical Times Illustrated Encyclopedia of the Civil War*. New York: Harper and Row, 1917.

Fraser, Walter J., Jr. *Charleston! Charleston!: The History of a Southern City*. Columbia, South Carolina: University of South Carolina Press, 1989.

Freeman, Douglas Southall. *Lee's Lieutenants*. 3 vols. New York: Charles Scribner's Sons, 1943.

———. *R. E. Lee*. 4 vols. New York: Charles Scribner's Sons, 1946.

Graydon, Nell S. *Tales of Beaufort*. Orangeburg, South Carolina: Sandlapper Publishing, 1963.

———. *Tales of Edisto*. Columbia, South Carolina: R. L. Bryan Co., 1955.

Hart, Joseph E., Jr. *The Church of the Good Shepherd, York, South Carolina: A Centennial History, 1855–1955*. York, South Carolina: Yorkville Enquirer Press, 1955.

Henderson, George F. R. *Stonewall Jackson and the American Civil War*. Gloucester, Massachusetts: Fawcett Press, 1968.

Hennessy, John J. *Return to Bull Run*. New York: Simon and Schuster Publications, 1993.

Izlar, William Valmore. *History of the Edisto Rifles*. Camden, South Carolina: Kohn Press, 1908.

Jones, Lewis P. *South Carolina: A Synoptic History for Laymen*. Orangeburg, South Carolina: Sandlapper Publishing, 1987.

Lewis, Richard. *Camp Life of a Confederate Boy*. Charleston, South Carolina: The News and Courier Press, 1883.

Longstreet, James. *From Manassas to Appomattox*. Philadelphia, Pennsylvania: J. B. Lippincott Company, 1896.

Luvaas, Jay, and Harold Nelson, Eds. *The U.S. Army War College Guide to the Battles of Chancellorsville and Fredericksburg*. Carlisle, Pennsylvania: South Mountain Press, 1988.

Maniqault, Arthur M. *A Carolinian Goes to War*. Ed. R. Lockwood Tower. Columbia, South Carolina: University of South Carolina Press, 1983.

Marvel, William. *Burnside*. Chapel Hill, North Carolina: University of North Carolina Press, 1991.

Matter, William D. *If It Takes All Summer: The Battle of Spotsylvania*. Chapel Hill, North Carolina: University of North Carolina Press, 1988.

May, John A., and Joan R. Faunt. *South Carolina Secedes*. Columbia, South Carolina: University of South Carolina Press, 1960.

Mikell, Jenkins I. *Rumbling of the Chariot Wheels*. Columbia, South Carolina: University of South Carolina Press, 1923.

Oates, William. *War Between the Union and the Confederacy and its Lost Opportunities*. New York: Neale Publishers, 1905.

Piston, William Garrett. *Lee's Tarnished Lieutenants: James Longstreet and His Place in Southern History*. Athens, Georgia: University of Georgia Press, 1987.

Puckette, Clara C. *Edisto: A Sea Island Principality*. Cleveland, Ohio: Seaforth Publications, 1978.

Reid, J. W. *History of the Fourth Regiment, South Carolina Volunteers*. Reprint. Dayton, Ohio: Morningside Press, 1975.

Robertson, James I. *General A. P. Hill: The Story of a Confederate Warrior*. New York: Random House Press, 1987.

Robertson, William Glenn. *Back Door to Richmond: The Bermuda Hundred Campaign, April-June 1864*. Newark, Delaware: University of Delaware Press, 1987.

Sears, Stephen W. *George B. McClellan: The Young Napoleon*. New York: Ticknor and Fields, 1988.

———. *To the Gates of Richmond: The Peninsular Campaign*. New York: Ticknor and Fields, 1992.

Sorrel, Moxley. *Recollections of a Confederate Staff Officer*. Jackson, Tennessee: McCowat-Mercer Press, 1958.

Thomas, John P. *Career and Character of General Micah Jenkins, C.S.A.* Columbia, South Carolina: The State Company, 1906.

———. *History of the South Carolina Military Academy*. Charleston, South Carolina: Walker, Evans, and Gogswell Press, 1893.

Tucker, Glen. *Chickamauga: Bloody Battle in the West*. Reprint. Dayton, Ohio: Morningside Press, 1976.

The War of the Rebellion: A Compilation of the Official Records of the Union and Confederate Armies. Washington, D.C.: Government Printing Office, 1880–1901.

Woodworth, Steven. *Jefferson Davis and His Generals: The Failure of Confederate Command in the West*. Lawrence, Kansas: University of Kansas Press, 1990.

Articles

Choise, William. "Memoirs of My Four Years in the War Between the States." Manassas National Battlefield Park Library, Manassas, Virginia.

Crowson, E. T. "Jenkins, Coward and The Yorkville Boys," *Sandlapper* Magazine, December 1974, 32–36.

Field, Charles W. "Campaign of 1864 and 1865," *Southern Historical Society Papers*, vol. 14, 542–63.

Fulton, W. F. "Incidents of Second Manassas," *Confederate Veteran*, vol. 31, 1923, 451–52.

Harrington, C. Micheal. "Youthful Valor: John Marshall Whilden, Boy Major of The Coast Rangers." *Confederate Veteran*, March-April 1992, 14–18.

Haskew, Michael E. "Icy Assault Routed." *America's Civil War*, vol. 4, no. 1. May, 1991, 22–28.

Law, E. M. "Lookout Valley." *Southern Historical Society Papers*, vol. 8, 500–506.

———. "The Fight for Richmond in 1862." *Southern Bivouac,* vol. 2, 1886–87, 649–60, 713–23.

———. "The Virginia Campaign of 1862." *Philadelphia Weekly Press*, October 26, 1887.

Mayo, Robert M. "The Second Battle of Manassas." *Southern Historical Society Papers*, vol. 7, 1878, 122–25.

Paine, George F. "How I Left The Bull Run Battlefield." *13th Massachusetts Regimental Circular*, vol. 24. 1911, 30–36.

Pettus, Louise. "Asbury Coward, Soldier-Educator." *York Observor*, March 28, 1986.

———. "Micah Jenkins and the 5th South Carolina." *York Observor*, October 30, 1988.

Skoch, George. "A Test of Rebel Rails." *Civil War Times Illustrated*, vol. 30, no. 8, December 1986, 12–18.

———. "Miracle of the Rails," *Civil War Times Illustrated*, vol. 30, no. 4. September-October 1992, 22–24, 56–58.

———. "The Bloody Fifth." *Civil War Times Illustrated*. vol. 30, no. 5. November-December 1991, 36–43.

Stickley, E. E. "The Stonewall Brigade at Second Manassas." *The Confederate Veteran*, vol. 22, 1914, 231.

Swanson, Guy R., and Timothy D. Johnson. "Conflict in East Tennessee: Generals Law, Jenkins, and Longstreet." *Civil War History*, vol. 31, June 1985, 101–10.

Swisher, James K. "Flank Attack at Chancellorsville." *America's Civil War*, vol. 6, no. 4. September 1993, 30–37.

Worsham, John H. "The Second Battle of Manassas." *Southern Historical Society Papers*, vol. 32, 1904, 77–88.

Newspapers

Charleston Courier.

Charleston Mercury, 12 May 1864.

Charlotte Observor, 16 May 1864.

Lynchburg Virginian.

Richmond Times Dispatch.

Richmond Whig.

York Observor, 28 March 1986; October 1988.

Yorkville Enquirer, 24 April, 17 July, 11 December 1856; 28 May 1857; 1 April 1858; 21 April, 23 April, 23 June, 15 September 1859; 16, 23 February, 3 May, 24, 28 June, 4 October, 20 December 1860; 3, 17, 24 January, 7, 28 February 1861; 4 June 1868.

Other References

Caldwell, J. F. J. *The History of Gregg's Brigade of South Carolinians*. Philadelphia, Pennsylvania: King and Baird, 1866.

Chesnut, Mary B. *Mary B. Chesnut's Civil War Diary*. New Haven, Connecticut: Yale University Press, 1981.

Davis, Burke. *Jeb Stuart: The Last Cavalier*. New York: Rinehart and Company, 1957.

———. *They Called Him Stonewall*. New York: Rinehart and Company, 1954.

Dickert, D. Augustus. *History of Kershaw's Brigade*. Newberry, South Carolina: E. H. Aull Company, 1899.

Douglas, Henry Kyle. *I Rode with Stonewall,* Chapel Hill, North Carolina: University of North Carolina Press, 1940.

Dowdey, Clifford. *Death of a Nation*, New York: Alfred A. Knopf Publisher, 1958.

Gordon, John. *Reminiscences of the Civil War*. New York: Scribner's, 1903.

Hood, John B. *Advance and Retreat: Personal Experiences in the United States and Confederate Armies*. New Orleans, Louisiana: Private Printer, 1880.

Jones, Terry L. *Lee's Tigers*. Baton Rouge, Louisiana: Louisiana State University Press, 1987.

Long, A. L. *Memoirs of Robert E. Lee*. Secaucus, New Jersey: The Blue and Gray Press, 1983.

McDonough, James L., and James P. Jones. *War so Terrible: Sherman and Atlanta*. New York: W. W. Norton Co., 1987.

Morgan, W. H. *Personal Reminiscences of the War of 1861–1865*. Lynchburg, Virginia, J. P. Bell Publishing Co., 1911.

Robertson, James I. *The Stonewall Brigade*. Baton Rouge, Louisiana: Louisiana State University Press, 1963.

Sears, Stephen W. *Landscape Turned Red: The Battle of Antietam*. New York: Ticknor and Fields, 1983.

Smith, Gustavus W. *The Battle of Seven Pines*. New York: C. G. Crawford Co., 1891.

Taylor, Walter H. *Four Years With General Lee*. New York: Bonanza Books, 1972.

Thomas, Emory M. *Bold Dragon, The Life of J.E.B. Stuart*. New York: Harper and Row, 1986.

Vandiver, Frank. E. *Jubal's Raid: Early's Attack on Washington, 1864*. New York: McGraw-Hill, 1960.

———. *Mighty Stonewall*. New York: McGraw-Hill, 1960.

Webb, Alexander S. *The Peninsular: McClellan's Campaign of 1862*, New York: Scribner's, 1881.

Wise, Jennings C. *The Long Arm of Lee*. Lynchburg, Virginia: J. P. Bell Publishing, 1915.

Index

First names are given when known.

241